ANCIENT
ALIENS
AND
SECRET
SOCIETIES

MIKE BARA

Adventures Unlimited Press

Ancient Aliens and Secret Societies

by Mike Bara

ISBN 13: 978-1-939149-40-4

Published by:
Adventures Unlimited Press
One Adventure Place
Kempton, Illinois 60946 USA
auphq@frontiernet.net

www.AdventuresUnlimitedPress.com

ANCIENT
ALIENS
AND
SECRET
SOCIETIES

Adventures Unlimited Press

Acknowledgements

I would first like to acknowledge Randall Carlson, whose research made major contributions to the opening portions of this book. I'd also like to thank Sherri Gaston for always taking care of me, Denise Zak for always defending me to "them," Jimmy Church and George Noory for "getting it," my managers Amy Shpall and George Pilgrim, and all the folks at all the wonderful conferences I get to speak at. May we all prosper together.

Other Books by Mike Bara:

Ancient Aliens on the Moon
Ancient Aliens on Mars
Ancient Aliens on Mars II
The Choice
Dark Mission
(with Richard Hoagland)

TABLE OF CONTENTS

Dedication

This book is dedicated to builders of the Monuments of Mars, who tried to repair what they had damaged by guiding us into the future. May your vision become reality.

See Mike Bara at:

MikeBara.Blogspot.com

ANCIENT
ALIENS
AND
SECRET
SOCIETIES

Introduction

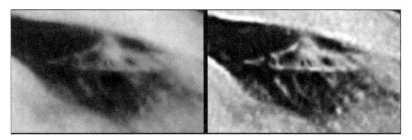

Two views of the "Flying Saucer in a Bunker" from
Ancient Aliens on the Moon.

In my last three books, *Ancient Aliens on the Moon, Ancient Aliens on Mars* and *Ancient Aliens on Mars II*, we have examined the presence of ancient extraterrestrial artifacts on other planets. We have uncovered many mysteries, from the Daedalus Ziggurat to the "Flying Saucer in a Bunker" on the Moon; we have unmasked the truth about the Face on Mars (that it's artificial) dug up the Monolith on Phobos and exposed the awe inspiring reality of "Parrott City" on Mars. But in the course of those books and that journey we have always been left with one nagging and seemingly unanswerable question: What did NASA know and when did they know it?

This book, *Ancient Aliens and Secret Societies*, will attempt to answer that question by asking at least three more questions. First, is there evidence to suggest that some of these ruins we have identified on other planets come from a true Ancient Alien civilization? Is there evidence in Earth's ancient histories, myths and legends to support the Ancient Alien theory that "gods" from on high came down to Earth thousands of years ago and interacted with human beings? Second, did some of this ancient knowledge of Man's hidden destiny fall under the control of a select few self-appointed "anointed ones," who then kept the knowledge for themselves and undermined the original intent of the grantors of Mankind's future history? And third, did this ancient knowledge somehow find its way into NASA in the early 1960s, driving the secret goals, ambitions and desires of the Apollo program and dictating what NASA did and did not show the world of what they discovered?

As we travel these pages I believe the answers to all of these questions will become self-evident and clear. Yes, human beings have had interactions with extraterrestrial beings (as opposed to "Aliens") who helped us crawl out of the dust of the last ice age more than 12,000 years ago. Yes, once these "gods" left for whatever reason, this secret history of the human race was usurped by a self-appointed elite who were supposed to be the caretakers— not the beneficiaries— of the knowledge they had obtained. And yes, NASA knew all about this ancient truth, humanity's true origins and destiny, before they ever launched the first rickety and clumsy rockets into space to confirm it.

It is my personal belief that the universe works on a simple concept that is commonly known in modern times as a legal Trust. In a Trust, there are three parties. The first is the Grantor, the person (or entity) who gifts (grants) an item of value to another person or entity. That item of value can be currency, material goods, an idea, or even just some documents that have an inherent value. The second leg of a trust is the Trustee. The Trustees are charged with seeing that the original intent of the Grantor is carried out in accordance with his wishes. They are not intended to benefit from this role in any way, beyond what may be cited by the Grantor in the original formation of the Trust. The final role in the Trust is the Beneficiary, the person, persons or entities that are meant to receive the gifts specified by the Grantor(s). So I look at the questions this book will review in the context of a legal Trust.

I believe, and I hope this book will show, that the three roles in this Trust are defined as follows: The Grantors are our Ancient Alien ancestors, who granted the sacred knowledge of our extraterrestrial origins to the intended Beneficiaries, being the entire human race. The Trustees of the sacred information were intended to be the secret societies—the priests, mystics and teachers of this ancient knowledge. But somewhere along the line they lost their way. They thought their special knowledge made them special, above all other men, and they kept the secrets they were supposed to tell for themselves, forgetting that they were only the caretakers of them, not the Beneficiaries. What I intend to do with this book is to reconstruct how this tragic usurpation of the "gods'" original intent happened, the consequences it created, and the corrections that must be made to restore the gift that our Ancient Alien brothers intended us to have.

The reason for this is simple. It's time. Time to correct the wrongs that have taken place, and time to set humanity back on the path we were intended to walk. One that these secretive groups have kept us from for far too long.

This will be a long, long journey. We may as well start at the beginning...

Chapter 1
Out of the Ashes

It has long been known that legends of a great flood, in
which almost all men perished, are widely diffused over the world.
—James George Frazer,
Folk-Lore in the Old Testament, Vol. 1.[1]

Virtually all ancient cultures agree on one thing, whether they were ever in contact with each other or not: Thousands of years ago, there was a worldwide global catastrophe, specifically a Great Flood of the Earth.

So many of these widely separated civilizations tell the same story, with details ranging from the flood or deluge itself, to a boat or ark being constructed, to animals and humans being saved, to the sending out of a bird to determine when dry land had reemerged from the waters of the deluge, to the landing on a mountaintop, that it is well-nigh impossible to discount them as coincidence. Modern geologists insist that there is no evidence of such an event, which is a highly debatable conclusion as we will learn. But separate from that, the simple *existence* of similar stories from all over the globe, from civilizations separated by vast extents of time and geographic distance, argues that something is quite wrong with our current understanding of our ancient past. At the least, these widely separated and widely viewed as "primitive" civilizations must have had contact with each other, despite the experts' claims to the contrary. Otherwise we are faced with an even more untenable proposition: that each of these ancient civilizations drew their creation/flood myths from the same root source. It also follows that this root source must have been a vast, widespread and highly advanced antediluvian civilization. In other words, *Atlantis*.

Setting aside for the moment the question of whether the Biblical deluge actually occurred, a quick study of the myths themselves almost forces one to consider the Atlantis scenario first and foremost. The details of these stories are so exact in their concurrence that it makes the idea of a single root source a virtual lead pipe cinch. We can begin by simply noting on a few graphs and tables the identical details from civilizations separated by eons of time and thousands of miles.

D = Destruction by Water
G = (God) Divine Cause
W = Warning Given
H = Humans Spared
A = Animals Spared
V = Preserved in a Vessel

D			H	A	V	01 Australia- Kurnai
D	.	W	H	A	V	02 Babylon- Berossus' account
D	G	W	H	A	V	03 Babylon- Gilgamesh epic
D	G	W	H	.	V	04 Bolivia- Chiriguano
D	.	.	H	A	V	05 Borneo- Sea Dayak
D	.	.	H	A	V	06 Burma- Singpho
D	G	.	H	A	V	07 Canada- Cree
D	G	W	H	A	V	08 Canada- Montagnais
D	G	.	H	A	V	09 China- Lolo
D	.	W	H	A	V	10 Cuba- original natives
D	G	W	H	A	V	11 East Africa- Masai
D	G	W	H	.	V	12 Egypt- *Book of the Dead*
D	G	.	H	.	V	13 Fiji- Walavu-levu tradition
D	G	W	H	A	.	14 French Polynesia- Raiatea
D	.	.	H	A	V	15 Greece- Lucian's account
D	G	.	H	A	V	16 Guyana- Macushi

D	G	.	H	.	V	17 Iceland- Eddas
D	G	.	H	.	V	18 India- Andaman Islands
D	.	W	H	A	V	19 India- Bhil
D	G	W	H	.	V	20 India-Kamar
D	.	W	H	A	.	21 Iran- Zend-Avesta
D	G	.	H	.	V	22 Italy- Ovid's poetry
D	G	.	H	.	V	23 Malay Peninsula- Jekun
D	.	W	H	.	V	24 Mexico- Codex Chimalpopoca
D	.	W	H	A	V	25 Mexico- Huichol
D	G	.	H	.	V	26 New Zealand- Maori
D	.	W	H	A	.	27 Peru- Indians of Huarochiri
D	.	W	H	.	V	28 X. Russia- Vogul
D	.	W	H	A	V	29 U.S.A. (Alaska)- Kolusches
D	G	.	H	A	V	30 U.S.A. (Alaska)- Tlingit
D	.	W	H	A	V	31 U.S.A. (Arizona)- Papago
D	G	.	H	A	V	32 U.S.A. (Hawaii)- legend of Nu-u
D	.	.	H	A	V	33 Vanuatu- Melanesians
D	.	.	H	A	V	34 Vietnam- Bahnar
D	.	.	H	A	V	35 Wales- Dwyfan/Dwyfan legend
35	**18**	**17**	**35**	**24**	**32**	**Total Occurrences out of 35**

Adapted from NW Creation Network.[2] Used with permission.

The table above illustrates the point quite clearly. Out of 35 listed major flood myths (there are many other examples) from civilizations spanning vast distances and time and across all six continents, we see the same story told over and over again. All 35, from the ancient *Egyptian Book of the Dead* to the more modern American Indian tales of the Tlingit tribe of Alaska, agree that the world was destroyed by water. All 35 also agree that at least some humans were deliberately spared by a deity or deities, and 32 of these flood stories claim this was done by the construction of a vessel, in essence the Ark of Noah. To a lesser extent, the stories also agree that animal life was also spared, that a warning was given, and that the Flood itself was caused by the deities, usually because of their displeasure with Man's conduct. That's a pretty amazing degree of consistency.

A comparison of the language used in the various stories is also illuminating. The Egyptian *Book of the Dead* contains several passages which seem to refer to the displeasure of the gods and the Deluge:

> The great god Ra once assembled the other gods and said, 'Behold, the men which have been begotten by myself, they utter words against me: tell me what you would do in such a case. Behold I have waited and have not slain them before listening to their words.'
>
> The gods replied, 'Let thy face permit it, and let those men who devise wicked things be smitten and let none among them survive.' So the goddess named Hathor went forth among them and slew the men upon the earth: and behold Sechet for many nights trod with his feet in their blood even to the city of Hierapolis. The anger of Ra is appeased.'[3]
>
> *And later:* 'And further I (the god Tum) am going to deface all I have done; this earth will become an ocean through an inundation, as it was at the beginning.'[4]

In the Indian/Vedic/Hindu scriptures, the Noah character takes on the name "Manu," but the details are similar. According to the *Matsya Purana*, Manu, who lived long ago, saved a small fish from the jaws of a large fish while washing himself. The fish told Manu, "If you care for me until I am full grown I will save you from terrible things to come." Manu asked what kind of terrible things. The fish told Manu that a great flood would soon come and destroy everything on the Earth. The fish instructed Manu to build a large ship (an ark) since the flood was going to happen very soon, and to save all types of animals and "the seeds" of many others. As the rains started Manu tied a rope from the ship to the fish, which had grown very large, and the fish guided the ship as the waters rose. Eventually, as the deluge continued, the entire Earth was covered by water. When the waters began subsiding the fish led Manu's ship to a mountaintop.[5]

In the Aztec tradition, the story is very similar. A man named Tapi, who was very pious, lived long ago. The Creator told Tapi to build a boat, and that he should take his wife and a pair of every animal that was alive into this boat. Like the Biblical Noah, he was shunned and told he was crazy by the local people. Then the rain started and the flood came, and men and animals tried to climb the mountains to escape but died when even the mountains were submerged. Finally the rain ended and Tapi decided that the water had receded when he let a dove loose that did not return, just as in the Biblical version.

The United States also has many ancient tales that concur with the idea of a Biblical flood, although scholars try to claim—with little to no evidence—that their creation myths were "contaminated" by European settlers much later. The Ojibwe Indians, who have lived in Minnesota since approximately 1400AD, have one example of such an account:

> There came a time when the harmonious way of life did not continue. Men and women disrespected each other, families quarreled and soon villages began arguing back and forth. This saddened Gitchie Manitou [the Creator] greatly, but he waited. Finally, when it seemed there was no hope left, the Creator decided to purify Mother Earth through the use of water. The water came, flooding the Earth, catching all of creation off guard. Only a few of each living thing survived.

Then it tells how the Noah character, Waynaboozhoo, survived by floating on a log in the water with various animals.

The Delaware Indians, some 1,100 miles separated from the Ojibwe, tell a similar tale:

In the pristine age, the world lived at peace; but an evil spirit came and caused a great flood. The Earth was submerged. A few persons had taken refuge on the back of a turtle, so old that his shell had collected moss. A loon flew over their heads and was entreated to dive beneath the water and bring up land. It found only a bottomless sea. Then the bird flew far away, came back with a small portion of Earth in its bill, and guided the tortoise to a place where there was a spot of dry land.

The Inca Empire, whose roots stretch all the way back to the Caral-Supe civilization and the founding of Machu Picchu a millennium after the emergence of human civilization in Sumer, have a nearly identical story which they insist came from their ancient ancestors:

During the period of time called the Pachachama, people became very evil. They got so busy coming up with and performing evil deeds they neglected the gods. Only those in the high Andes remained uncorrupted. Two brothers who lived in the highlands noticed their llamas acting strangely. They asked the llamas why and were told that the stars had told the llamas that a great flood was coming. This flood would destroy all the life on earth. The brothers took their families and flocks into a cave on the high mountains. It started to rain and continued for four months. As the water rose the mountain grew, keeping its top above the water. Eventually the rain stopped and the waters receded. The mountain returned to its original height. The shepherds repopulated the Earth. The llamas remembered the flood and that is why they prefer to live in the highland areas.[6]

The Hopi tribe of the southwestern United States tells an even more complex and interesting history of the Great Flood. Many of the Hopi oral traditions were first written down in the

18

Frank Waters on Hopi lands in the 1960s.

early 1960s by Frank Waters in his book *The Book of the Hopi*. In that book, the Hopi explain that this world is what they call the "Fourth World of Man" and will be the last one before a final cataclysm pushes the human race into a perfectly balanced "Fifth World." According to the Hopi, the previous three worlds were destroyed by various global catastrophes. At a speech at the U.N. in 1992, a Hopi elder named Thomas Banyacya explained the previous three worlds and what had happened to them:

> The creator (Great Spirit) made the first world in perfect balance where humans spoke one language, but humans turned away from moral and spiritual principles. They misused their spiritual powers for selfish purposes. They did not follow nature's rules. Eventually the world was destroyed by sinking of land and separation of land by what you would call major earthquakes. Many died and only a small handful survived.
>
> Then this handful of peaceful people came into the second world. They repeated their mistakes and the world was destroyed by a freezing which you call the great Ice Age.
>
> The few survivors entered the third world. That world lasted a long time and as in previous worlds, the people spoke one language. The people invented many machines and conveniences of high technology, some of which have not yet been seen in this age. They even

19

had spiritual powers that they used for good. [But] they gradually turned away from natural laws and pursued only material things and finally only gambled while they ridiculed spiritual principles. No one stopped them from this course and the world was destroyed by the great flood that many nations still recall in their ancient history or in their religions.

The Elders said again only small groups escaped and came to this fourth world where we now live.

So, in essence what these stories say is that the first civilization was destroyed in an Atlantis-like sinking of the continents, the second world was destroyed by an ice age (probably preceded by a polar axis shift) and the highly advanced third world was destroyed by—you guessed it—a Great Flood. What is not commonly discussed is that these stories are also littered with references to survivors following "stars" in the sky to new safe havens from which to rebuild the world, and the presence of the Ant or "insect" people who guided them. These "stars" sound for all the world

The "Ant People" of Hopi lore.

like current descriptions of UFOs, and the "Ant People" tend to bear more than a casual resemblance to the grey aliens of modern day abduction stories.

But the similarities between these various flood myths is nothing compared to the nearly identical narratives of the Hebrew and Sumerian creation stories. The Sumerian story is told on a single tablet called the *Eridu Genesis*, dated to around 1600 BC and found near Nippur in what is today modern day Iraq. In this version, which is expanded in the *Epic of Gilgamesh* and has been alternately translated by Zechariah Sitchin in his "12th Planet" books, the Sumerian "gods," Anu, Enki, Enlil and Ninmah, who have created man, become aware of a coming global cataclysm that will sweep the world with a great flood. These "gods" are members of an extraterrestrial race called the Anunnaki who "created" human bodies by crossing their DNA with that of the local (probably Neanderthal) inhabitants ("We shall make Man in our own image").

After these "gods" have a council on the issue, they agree that Man has become disrespectful if not dangerous and decide not to warn or attempt to save the humans in any way. However, one of the gods—Enki—loves mankind and decides to warn one of his favorite humans, Utnapishtim, to build a boat (ark) and populate it with animals, people and the "seeds of the Earth," a fairly obvious reference to not only plant and vegetable seeds but also possibly animal DNA samples. Utnapishtim builds the ark, which is named *The Preserver of Life*, and loads it with people and animals, as instructed. However, the other gods become aware of Enki's defiance of their decree, and cast him down to Earth to die with Utnapishtim and the humans. However, under Enki's guidance the ark survives, and the stories of the birds and the final resting place on a mountaintop are repeated. The similarity between the Sumerian and Biblical versions are so close that few scholars today argue that one is not based upon the other. The following table illustrates the key matching story points:

BABYLONIAN	BIBLE
Take the seed of all creatures aboard the ship	Gen. 6:19 And of every living thing of all flesh you shall bring.
I boarded the ship and closed the door.	Gen. 7:1 Come into the Ark Gen. 7:16 The Lord shut him in.
I sent out a dove . . . The dove went, then came back, no resting-place appeared for it, so it returned.	Gen. 8:8 He sent out a dove...But the dove found no resting-place . . . and she returned.
Then I sent out a raven...it was the waters receding, it ate, it flew about to and fro, it did not return.	Gen. 8:7 He sent out a raven, which kept going to and fro until the waters had dried up from the Earth.
I made a libation on the peak of the mountain.	Gen. 8:20 Then Noah built an altar to the Lord (on the mountain) and offered burnt offerings.

Adapted from NW Creation Network. Used with permission.[7]

The differences between the two tales are equally interesting, and may in fact point more or less to the "Atlantean" scenario. In the Biblical version, a seemingly omniscient "God" decides that man has become evil, and must be cleansed from the Earth for his transgressions. This infallible God then *changes his mind* and decides to save a handful of "good" humans and instructs Noah to build the ark and put all the animals "two by two" into it in order to save them as well. Realistically, this version of events seems unlikely. If a single God was all-seeing and his judgment infallible, why would he decide he had made a mistake in his initial judgment of Man and choose to save a handful of these wicked creatures after all? The passages in Genesis 6 make God's initial intent clear:

> 5 Then the LORD saw that the wickedness of man was great on the earth, and that every intent of the thoughts of his heart was only evil continually.
>
> 6 The LORD was sorry that He had made man on the earth, and He was grieved in His heart.
>
> 7 The LORD said, "I will blot out man whom I have created from the face of the land, from man to animals to creeping things and to birds of the sky; for I am sorry that I have made them.

In the next verse, God then changes his mind and decides that Noah, his family and the animals are worth saving after all. Which raises the question. Does an all-knowing, all-seeing God really change his mind on such issues?

Probably not.

In this context, the Sumerian version of the Deluge tale makes far more sense, with a conflict between a committee of lower (some would say extraterrestrial) "gods" deciding man's fate and a single dissenter (Enki) intervening to save Mankind at the last minute. It gets even more obvious that the Biblical version is a re-dressed remake of the Sumerian yarn when you consider the actual meaning of the word "Lord" in the bible. As I wrote about this in my second book, *The Choice*:

> The name of God appears in the Bible some 4,473 times in 3,893 different verses. But the vast majority of these references are to a specific entity named "Yahweh," also known as Jehova, or YHWH. Anyone who has read Zechariah Sitchin's 12th Planet series will know that Yahweh is most likely not a God of any kind, but rather a visitor from some other place and time. But, there is also a second reference to God in the bible. It takes the form of the masculine plural word Elohim, which is used singularly

only 30 times—all in the first chapter of Genesis—and it has a different meaning. It refers to a single, all knowing, all loving God force that exists everywhere. Yahweh Elohim, the "Lord God," only starts to appear in Genesis 2.4 and that reference seems to be to a master over the Earth or sub-servant of the one true God, Elohim. Thus, the Lord God is not a god at all, but rather a representative of God here on Earth.

So when the Genesis verses refer to the Lord, they are really referring to a corporeal being called the *Yahweh Elohim,* or the Lord God. This being is probably the leader of the Anunnaki overseer(s) of the Earth in the ancient past, either Anu or Enlil. In some of Sitchin's translations, he claims that the Sumerian version makes it clear that Enlil bears a great deal of animus toward Man, but that Enki is much more favorable to them. When the council rules against Enki, he defies them and helps Noah/Utnapishtim to escape the Flood. To me, this makes a great deal more sense than an omnipotent God that is of two minds.

In any event, it simply cannot be coincidence or cultural contamination that so many ancient cultures have memories and oral traditions describing the same worldwide cataclysmic event. Either they all *experienced* the same set of events, or somebody *told* them all about the event. Either way, our history is not what we have been led to believe.

Which brings us, finally, to the question of whether the Flood really happened at all.

Modern geologists and mainstream scientific materialists will argue that it didn't. They insist that there is nothing in the geologic record to support the idea of massive, catastrophic global flood in the recent geologic past or for that matter, *ever* in the history of planet Earth. However, there are a growing number of independent geologists (read, not funded by governments or major universities) who take issue with that assumption.

The Earth at glacial maximum during the last ice age.

There have been at least five major ice ages in Earth's past (the Huronian, Cryogenian, Andean-Saharan, Karoo Ice Age and the Quaternary glaciation) lasting for hundreds of millions of years of Earth's geologic history. At times, ice has extended as far south as the equator. The ice ages have been offset by interglacial periods of widespread warming. At the peak of the last Pleistocene ice age about 20,000 years ago, the Earth was about 10 degrees Fahrenheit colder on average than it is today (about 59°F). Our current Holocene epoch is an interglacial period where ice sheets retreat, global temperatures rise, and the Earth in general becomes a balmy and rather pleasant place to live. These interglacial periods make it easier to grow food and cultivate the Earth, and are therefore ideal periods in which human civilizations can rise and advance.

Modern humans first emerged about 160,000 years ago at a minimum, although subsequent fossil discoveries are likely to push that date even further into the past. Recent tests on the mitochondrial DNA of the human genome suggest that modern man may go back as far as 250,000 years into the past.[8] What we

25

don't really know for sure is just why ice ages come and go, and more specifically, what ended the last ice age and allowed modern humans to advance to the point we have today.

Randall Carlson, the lead researcher of a group that runs the Cosmographic Research web site,[9] has developed a theory which includes a great deal of geologic evidence supporting the idea of great floods, especially in North America and Siberian Russia. His site also provides evidence that these floods were caused by a massive impact, probably from a comet of immense size, into the north polar cap around 12,500-13,000 years ago. This cometary impact not only instantly liquefied billions of tons of frozen water ice at the North Pole, it may have also played a hand in shifting the orbit of the Earth, the axial tilt of the planet, and pushed the Earth out of the last ice age. As a side note, I have always suspected/believed that the "ideal" orbit of the planet Earth was 360 days, and that this is the source of our use of 360 degrees to define a circle. I have long thought that some kind of major impact pushed the Earth into a different orbit, adding five and a quarter (give or take) "extra" days to the orbit and giving us our current path around the sun. The impact theorized by Carlson may be the source of this shift.

Author and researcher Graham Hancock, among others, has always been a leading proponent of the idea that some cataclysmic event destroyed much of what he views as a highly advanced antediluvian human civilization around 12,500 years ago. In his view, this event drove mankind virtually back into the Stone Age, and resulted in the few survivors with advanced technology travelling the globe to help wandering bands of humans rebuild. Others have attributed these advanced beings to aliens, but the question still remains open.

What we do know for sure is that this time period was very close to the end of what is known as the Pleistocene epoch of geological history. The Pleistocene lasted from about 2.5 million years Before Present to around 11,700 years Before the Present. The Pleistocene epoch was characterized by the waxing and waning of massive amounts of glacial ice over the surface of the

Earth, and as such is generally considered to be the epoch of ice ages. The Pleistocene came to an end, or at least an interruption, at the onset of the current geological epoch, known as the Holocene, which is much warmer and is characterized by the (more or less) permanent retreat of glacial ice from northern climes. Carlson assumes that a major impact in the North Polar region melted the ice caps in a instant, caused catastrophic flooding throughout the northern hemisphere, and may be the source of many of the flood stories.

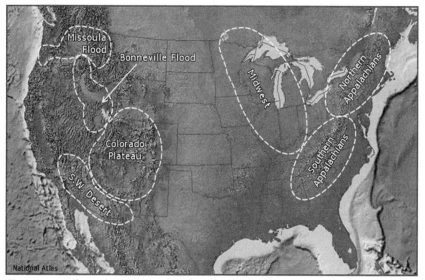

Event map of North America showing areas of catastrophic flooding dating to around 12,500 BC. (Randall Carlson)

Carlson has also recently found evidence for a similar catastrophic flood from the same period in northern Siberia, another strong indicator that some kind of rapid melting event took place around 12,500 years ago. He lays out his arguments in this way:

> The answer to your question regarding the melting of the ice caps is a qualified yes, I do think the most reasonable explanation is that there was some form of cosmic impact. I have pondered and researched this question for several

decades and I can say that there is no easy answer to the events of 12,500 to 13,000 years ago. It is not just the giant floods, there is also the sudden extinction of the Pleistocene megafauna, extreme temperature changes of up to 10 degrees in only a few years, the apparent disappearance of the North American Clovis culture, massive biotic shifts on a global scale and so on. At present no convincing explanation exists for any of these phenomena, at least in my opinion, so I come to an extraterrestrial cause as much by default, even though up until a few years ago there was not much in the way of hard evidence for such an event, it was more a circumstantial case. Now, however, the hard evidence is emerging in the form of soot, nanodiamonds, magnetic grains and spherules, and platinum group metals, all associated with a distinctive stratigraphic layer that comes at the boundary of the so called Bolling-Allerod/ Younger Dryas climate shift ca 12,900 years before present. It is this horizon that separates the extinct Pleistocene fauna from the extant Holocene fauna and the Clovis culture from the subsequent cultural group, the Folsom. It was also the trigger for the climatic changes that ultimately brought the planet out of the ice age, but not before a 1200 to 1300 year phase of extreme cold set in. There was a second spasm of warming at about 11,600 years ago that delivered the coup de gras to the ice age, after which the Earth's climate quickly warmed to its current interglacial state.

Carlson also takes note of the efforts of the gradualists to discount the theory:

It appears that there is a determined effort underway to discredit the Younger Dryas Impact Hypothesis (as it has come to be called). I have examined the criticisms of the opponents of the theory and I believe they raise some valuable questions but ultimately do not make a convincing case. Their attacks have compelled the impact proponents to really do their homework and as it now stands the evidence for some form of cosmic impact ca 12,900 years ago is considerable.

To be clear on some of the details. The Pleistocene epoch lasted from about 2.6 million years ago to about 11,600 years ago, according to the most recent chronologies. Throughout the course of the entire Pleistocene there may have been several dozen glacial-interglacial cycles. The most recent glacial cycle is usually called the Wisconsin and is considered to have started about 104,000 to 105,000 years ago. The Late Wisconsin phase of the ice age began about 26 thousand years ago. It was this final cyclic phase which was catastrophically terminated between 11 and 13 thousand years ago.

There were basically three great ice sheets that formed in the northern Hemisphere during the Late Wisconsin phase. They were the Laurentide, which formed around the region of Hudson Bay and grew outwards in a more or less radial pattern from there. It was the most massive of the three. The Cordilleran ice sheet formed over the Canadian Rockies and Coast Mountains and expanded until it reached the Pacific Ocean on the west and confronted the expanding Laurentide Ice sheet east of the Rocky Mountain foothills in Alberta. It was the least massive of the three, containing only perhaps a million cubic miles of glacial ice. The Fennoscandian ice sheet covered northwest Europe and was intermediate in size between the other two. Altogether the volume of the three ice sheets was in the ballpark of six to seven million cubic miles, greater than the combined ice sheets of Antarctica and Greenland today. It was the sudden, severe and catastrophic melting of these great ice masses that, I believe, spawned many of the flood myths that still come down to us today. Geological evidence now proves that the melting of all three massive ice sheets was extreme, but no explanation exists as to the cause of this extraordinary melting. Interestingly, there is some evidence to suggest that the North Polar Region, now occupied by the Arctic Ocean, was basically ice free during this time, which is really strange. The ice sheets of the Late Wisconsin were not technically speaking, polar. Again, there are still many questions about the events of 12-13 thousand years ago. There was a series of extremely complex, and I might say, improbable, changes that occurred at that time. But they happened and the critics of the impact hypothesis, who sound like they can't bury this heresy quick enough, are going to be left with a glaring deficiency of plausible explanations for the giant floods, the sudden extinction of half the world's megafauna, the sudden and severe climate and environmental changes, the cultural upheavals, or the rich tradition of world mythology which, I suspect you would agree, holds a lot more historical truth than has been admitted by conventional scholars of antiquity.[10]

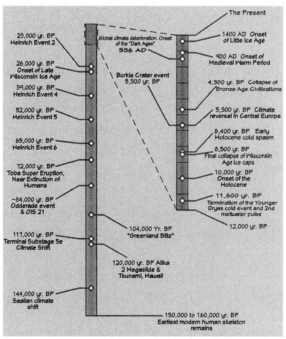

Event map of North America showing areas of catastrophic flooding dating to around 12,500 BC. (Randall Carlson)

What Carlson's work establishes, in my mind at least, is a strong probability that there were catastrophic floods in the northern hemisphere 12,500 years ago. These floods were probably caused by a comet impact near the North Pole, and resulted in devastating changes to the Earth's climate. But his work is also at odds with the Biblical accounts, which describe "40 days and 40 nights" of *rain* as the cause of the deluge, not fire from the sky followed by catastrophic water flows.

Of course, the writers of the Bible (or for that matter the Sumerian epic) most probably lived pretty far south of the North Pole, in what is today the Middle East. So the comet impact may have had a different effect there than it did in North America and Siberia. But if the Biblical account is then true, what could have caused the rain?

Depiction of the Water Vapor Canopy above the Earth.

There is one theory, put forth mostly by the Creationist movement, which fits the Biblical descriptions of the Flood nicely. It's called the Water Vapor Canopy theory.

The theory is simply that the Earth, in prediluvian times, was covered in a suspended layer of water vapor above what we know today as the atmosphere. Some of the water may have been in the form of ice, but most of it would have been liquid droplets. If this primordial water vapor canopy in fact existed, there would have been several effects, including higher atmospheric pressures at higher altitudes (you could breathe comfortably at the top of Mount Everest, for instance) and a much healthier, balmy climate that would exist pretty much all over the world. As Biblical scholars have noted, there is a description of it in the Bible:

> And God said, Let there be a firmament (the expanse of the sky) in the midst of the waters; and let it separate the waters (below) from the waters (above). And God made the firmament (the expanse) and separated the waters which were under the expanse from the waters which were above the expanse. And it was so. (Genesis 1:6-7; Amplified)

In this case, the interpretation seems to be that the "waters below" are the oceans, the "firmament" is the atmosphere, and the "waters above" constitute the water vapor canopy. Another passage seems to support the concept, describing a vapor layer that watered the ground with dew and "rose" to the skies:

> When no plant of the field was yet in the Earth, and no herb of the field had yet sprung up. The Lord God had not (yet) caused it to rain upon the Earth, and there was no man to till the ground. But there went up a mist (a fog-vapor) from the land, and watered the whole surface of the ground. (Genesis 2:5-6; Amplified).

There are other passages which imply that the stars could not be seen in the time before the Flood, and that blue skies and rainbows were never seen until after it:

> I set my bow (rainbow) in the cloud, and it shall be
> for a token or sign of a covenant or solemn pledge between
> Me and the Earth, and it shall be that when I bring clouds
> over the Earth, and the bow (rainbow) is seen in the cloud,
> I will (earnestly) remember my covenant or solemn pledge,
> which is between Me and you and every living creature
> of all flesh, and the waters shall no more become a flood
> to destroy and make all flesh corrupt... (Genesis 9:13-15;
> Amplified).

If in fact such a water vapor canopy existed, these are exactly
the conditions that would have to have existed on Earth. It would
be a lush, warm, moist paradise under which Man could have
lived and flourished. It would have been darker, in all probability,
which may explain why modern man needs sunglasses in the
modern daylight. Perhaps his eyes were meant for an environment
where such eye protection was unnecessary? It would also be an
atmospheric environment where rainbows would never be seen,
because the water vapor canopy would keep direct sunlight from
reaching the water droplets in the lower atmosphere, as it does
today. It would also explain one other mystery of the Bible: why
did so many of the Patriarchs of the Bible live so long?

According to the scriptures, Adam himself—the first and
genetically purest of men—lived to be 930 years old. After
Adam, for 10 generations, the average age at death of the Biblical
patriarchs was 857.5 years, a seemingly impossible life span.
Most of this is dismissed as superstitious nonsense by Biblical
critics, but if the water canopy theory were real, it might very
well be possible. Such a water vapor canopy would effectively
block a great deal of harmful solar and ultraviolet radiation. These
cosmic rays and solar radiation bombard our cells today, causing
cell damage, RNA and DNA degradation, and is at least a major
contributor to the phenomenon we call "aging." Protected from
this damaging radiation, human beings might conceivably live

much longer than we do today. As the following table shows, the life spans of Biblical characters began to shorten considerably after the Flood, until they reached a relatively "normal" span of 70 years for King David of Israel.

The First 23 Patriarchs

Generation	Name	Age at Son's Birth	Age at Death	Born (After Adam)	Died (After Adam)	Born (Before Christ)	Died (Before Christ)
1	Adam	130	930	0	930	4000	3070
2	Seth	105	912	130	1042	3870	2958
3	Enosh	90	905	235	1140	3765	2860
4	Cainan	70	910	325	1235	3675	2765
5	Mahalaleel	65	895	395	1290	3605	2710
6	Jared	162	962	460	1422	3540	2578
7	Enoch	65	365	622	987	3378	3013
8	Methuselah	187	969	687	1656	3313	2344
9	Lamech	182	777	874	1651	3126	2349
10	Noah	502	950	1056	2006	2944	1994
11	Shem	100	600	1558	2158	2442	1842
	Flood			1656		2344	
12	Arphaxad	35	438	1658	2096	2342	1904
13	Salah	30	433	1693	2126	2307	1874
14	Eber	34	464	1723	2187	2277	1813
15	Peleg	30	239	1757	1996	2243	2004
16	Reu	32	239	1787	2026	2213	1974
17	Serug	30	230	1819	2049	2181	1951
18	Nahor	29	148	1849	1997	2151	2003
19	Terah	70	205	1878	2083	2122	1917
20	Abram	100	175	1948	2123	2052	1877
21	Isaac	60	180	2048	2228	1952	1772
22	Jacob		147	2108	2255	1892	1745
23	Joseph		110				

Adapted from http://www.arksearch.com/nabefore.htm

All of this is pretty interesting, and it's all consistent to a degree. Why, for instance, would an ancient text like the Bible claim that there were no rainbows before the Flood if it wasn't true? What would be the point of even making such a claim if it wasn't derived from an actual living memory?

And what would happen if a celestial object, like a comet, struck this water canopy at thousands of miles per hour, perhaps at an oblique angle, and proceeded to strike the Earth in the North Polar Region? First, you'd have catastrophic flooding in the northern regions, exactly as Carlson describes. Second, most of the water vapor canopy above the flight path of the comet would be super-heated and evaporate into space as gas. Suspended water droplets below the comet's path would be vaporized as steam and might also escape into space. But a substantial amount of the water would be shaken loose by the turbulence of the shockwave and fall to Earth as rain.

Lots and lots of rain.

But as Carlson points out, you don't actually need a water vapor canopy to account for the Biblical "forty days and forty nights" of rain. If, as he has well established, the catastrophic floods in North America and Siberia were caused by a cometary impact, such an impact might also account for the Biblical descriptions of rain. A high speed impact into an ice sheet or the Arctic Ocean would inject enormous (Biblical) amounts of water vapor into the upper atmosphere. All that water vapor, if it didn't escape the Earth's gravitational pull, could then do only one thing: Ffall to the Earth, as rain.

As Carlson himself puts it:

> I do believe a comet, or for that matter an asteroid, impacting into an ice sheet, just as into an ocean, would inject enormous amounts of water vapor into the atmosphere. If the impact was large enough to loft several trillion tons of water vapor into the stratosphere it certainly would seem like prolonged torrential rainfall on an extreme scale would be one consequence.

As it turns out, there is strong evidence of just such an impact at exactly the right time to account for the Biblical flood. Recent papers have laid out the case for what is known as the Younger Dryas Impact event, dated to 12,800 years ago. What geologists are calling the Younger Dryas Boundary Field spreads across an enormous footprint spanning four continents, including North America and Europe. One of the papers, *"Nanodiamond-Rich Layer across Three Continents Consistent with Major Cosmic Impact at 12,800 Cal BP"*[11] tracks the path of this incredible object from the Middle East, across Europe and the Atlantic ocean and then to North America by examining sites which show evidence of massive impacts. The 32 sites (in 11 different countries) all show the presence of nanodiamonds (diamonds too small to be seen with the human eye) in soil samples dated back to the Younger Dryas temporal boundary. Nanodiamonds, which form during high-energy impacts like cometary or asteroid strikes, are a telltale sign of such events. The 32 samples sites also have other signatures of a comet strike like cosmic impact spherules, high-temperature melt-glass, fullerenes, grape-like clusters of soot, charcoal, carbon spherules, glasslike carbon, helium-3, iridium, osmium, platinum, nickel, and cobalt. In order for some of these objects to form, they would have had to be heated to over *2,200 degrees Celsius,* a

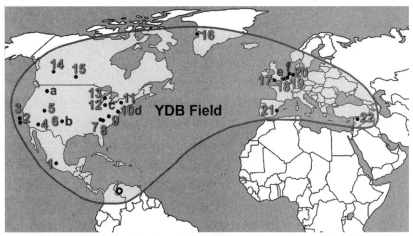

Graphic from Kinzie, Firestone, Kennett et al, "Nanodiamond-Rich Layer across Three Continents Consistent with Major Cosmic Impact at 12,800 Cal BP," *The Journal of Geology*, 2014, volume 122, p. 475–506.

temperature only possible as a result of cosmic impact. What this all adds up to is de facto *proof* of a series of major, catastrophic impact events in the Younger Dryas (and Biblical flood) time period of 12,800 years ago.

In looking at the graphic provided in the paper, it is patently obvious that an immense celestial object—either a comet or asteroid—broke up as it neared Earth and splattered the planet with fragments like a shotgun blast. Moving east to west as the various pieces entered the atmosphere, the Earth was bombarded with mega explosive events from Turkey in the east to California in the west, and from at least Greenland in the north to Venezuela in the south. Obviously, the researchers couldn't take samples from the oceans, but it is fairly obvious that such impacts also took place in the Atlantic and Pacific oceans, providing the vast amounts of stratospheric water vapor to account for the "40 days and 40 nights" of Biblical rain. There is also evidence that some of these objects measured two kilometers in diameter, and struck the northern ice caps just as Carlson has surmised.

Carlson has also raised the otherwise inexplicable existence of vast, dried up salt lakes in places like Utah and Nevada as a line of evidence supporting this possibility:

> One of the things I have been researching is the geomorphic evidence for such "pluvial" events in the geological record. This takes the form of investigating playa lake basins. These are dried up beds of lakes that once existed for a short period of time and then evaporated leaving "evaporates" or concentrated mineral sediments that accumulated on the lake bottom. A famous example of this kind of feature is the Bonneville Salt Flats, remnant of ancient Lake Bonneville, of which the Great Salt Lake is but a diminutive left over puddle. There are dozens and dozens of similar examples. In fact, all over the now arid southwest of the U.S. are to be found the leftovers of large bodies of water that existed temporarily and then disappeared. Some of these such as Lake Bonneville, which

was really more like an inland sea, rose up to its maximum level very rapidly and then overflowed catastrophically, in this case through a mountain pass at the north end of the lake which caused the lake level to drop over three hundred feet in a matter of several months and in the process largely cutting the Snake River Canyon as it exists today. Intense, prolonged rainfall seems, by default, to be the only explanation for such an event. Another example is ancient Lake Manly which occupied the basin of Death Valley. The encrusted salt deposits on the floor of Death Valley are the mineralized remains of the sediment that once was entrained in the body of water. There are relict shorelines that can still be seen today nearly a thousand feet above the valley floor. Since Death Valley has no outlet to the ocean the water of extinct Lake Manly had to have slowly evaporated and in the process the mineral content of the water became more and more concentrated.

He also pointed out the presence of massive boulders, obviously transported by water, that exist today in hundreds of creek valleys the world over. The volume of water currently flowing through these creeks and rivers could not possibly have transported such massive boulders to their present locations. Other than massive floods and/or rainfall, how did they get there?

Carlson also cites the James River flood in Virginia in August of 1969 as a similar, although smaller scale, "pluvial event." The flood occurred when Hurricane Camille made its way inland from the Gulf and then stalled over the state, dumping over 30 inches of rainfall in the headwaters of the James River in less than 24 hours. It was discovered in the aftermath that boulders up to six feet in diameter had been entrained in the sediment load of many of the creeks flowing from James River. It was said that in some places the rainfall was so intense that birds actually drowned in the trees. Some of the hydrologists looking at the creek valleys that carried away the waters of this deluge estimated that in the scale of flood events this ranked as "a ten thousand year flood," or in other

Giant flood-transported boulders in the Cumberland River valley in Kentucky.

words, a flood on a scale that occurred perhaps once every 10 millennia. The only difference might be that the 1969 flood mainly affected several counties in Virginia. The floods of old apparently affected whole continents. Carlson then concludes:

> So the question becomes what could trigger such a rainfall of such a vast scale? I can think of one agency that would be the most obvious, likely candidate for providing the trigger and that would be a cosmic impact into water, either ocean or ice could do the job.

On this, I wholeheartedly agree with Carlson: The only feasible source for the amount of energy that could rapidly melt six million plus cubic miles of ice in a short time and inject vast amounts of water into the upper atmosphere is a major impact event or series of events. Such an impact would neatly fit the ancient myths of the various ancient cultures I've cited (and many more) and is also consistent with the Biblical account of weeks and weeks of rain as the source of the great flood. This catastrophe

39

ended a brief period of warming that had commenced prior to the impacts and triggered the Younger Dryas cooling period, which lasted over 1,300 years and extinguished or nearly extinguished all kinds of life on the planet. About 11,500 years ago, the interglacial warming resumed, and the Earth began to climb out of the ashes of the cataclysm.

The Bible of course goes on to describe the end of Noah's journey: the search for dry land, the flights of the birds sent out to find it, and then the eventual discovery of dry land. As to the location of this "dry land" the Bible states explicitly that Noah's Ark came to rest on or around Mount Ararat in modern day Turkey. Genesis 8:4 states: *"And in the seventh month, on the seventeenth day of the month, the ark came to rest on the mountains of Ararat."*

If that were true, and if the Biblical (and other) accounts of arks and deluges were true, then there should be some evidence of that on or around Mount Ararat, shouldn't there?

Yes. Indeed there should be.

(Endnotes)

1   *Folk-Lore in the Old Testament*, Vol. 1 (London: Macmillan Publishing Co., 1919), p. 105.
2   http://www.nwcreation.net/noahlegends.html
3   Urquhart, John, "The Testimony of Tradition to the Flood" in Bible League Quarterly, no.152, 1937, p.119.
4   Skinner, John, *A Critical and Exegetical Commentary on Genesis*, Clark, Edinburgh, 1951.
5   http://www.nwcreation.net/noahlegends.html
6   *Thematic Guide to World Mythology*, by Laura Stookey, pp.57.
7   http://www.nwcreation.net/noahlegends.html
8   "Fossil reanalysis pushes back origin of Homo sapiens," *Scientific American*, February 17, 2005.
9   http://www.cosmographicresearch.org/
10 Personal communication, 10-28-2014
11 *The Journal of Geology*, 2014, volume 122, p. 475–506.

Chapter 2
From the Sky Down

The "Ararat Anomaly" on Mount Ararat in Turkey.

While the water vapor canopy theory certainly has its critics among the anti-Christian left and the science trolls, most of the criticisms are based on variables which are unknowable, such as the density and composition of the canopy itself and/or the atmospheric pressure and composition in the prediluvian world. But the other aspects of the Biblical myths, the story of the Deluge, the Ark and how it came to rest "on the mountains of Ararat," are, as we have just read, sufficiently testable to be considered scientific theories. As the geological evidence mounts for the Younger Dryas Impact scenario and the deluge it would have caused, the Biblical tales take on a much more hard-edged reality. But the fact remains that the only proof anyone will fully accept regarding the Flood myths will be if someone actually finds the Ark itself. For centuries, explorers and Christian scholars have been trying to do just that.

Over the years, several expeditions have been mounted to search for the wreckage of the Ark of Noah, despite reluctance from the Turkish government to allow such explorations. Their reasons have been only marginally convincing, as the Turks have argued that the area around Mount Ararat is a sensitive military restricted zone, given that it borders both Iran and the former Soviet Union. But the fact remains that there appears to be little in the way of military activity or even remote sensing stations in the area, primarily because the isolated and rugged terrain make major military maneuvers in the area well-nigh impossible. But long before there was a Soviet Union, attempts were made to find the wreckage of the Ark and solve the mystery once and for all.

The great explorer Marco Polo (1254–1324) voyaged to the region in the 13th century, and he is actually known to be the person who named the tallest peak in the area "Mount Ararat." It had a different name prior to that among the local population, although Polo did not make note of it in his book *The Travels of Marco Polo*. He did however write about the expedition, and in the book he noted that the local tradition held that Ark rested there: "In the heart of the Armenian mountain range, the mountain's peak is shaped like a cube (or cup), on which Noah's ark is said to have rested, whence it is called the Mountain of Noah's Ark." Other than noting that the peak was always covered in some kind of ice or snow, making an attempt to climb it nearly impossible, there is no indication that Polo found anything of significance.

But there was later confirmation in the 19th century that local legends held that the Ark was indeed somewhere atop the mountain. Dr. Friedrich Parrot made an ascent of the mountain and although he saw no sign of the Ark, he wrote in his 1829 book *Journey to Ararat* that "all the Armenians are firmly persuaded that Noah's Ark remains to this very day on the top of Ararat, and that, in order to preserve it, no human being is allowed to approach it."[1]

In 1876, James Bryce, a British viscount, historian, statesman, diplomat, explorer and Professor of Civil Law at Oxford, found a slab of hand-hewn timber at the 13,000 foot level on an expedition to Ararat. Bryce claimed to have found a piece "four feet long and five inches thick" which he described as being "evidently cut by some tool." He also claimed it was so far above the tree line that it "could not possibly be a natural fragment of one." His sample has never been tested, at least not publically, and its present day whereabouts are unknown.

The first half of the 20th century saw several new stories of sightings of the Ark emerge, the most intriguing of which was

BRYCE FOUND A PIECE OF TOOLED GOPHERWOOD AT 13,000 FEET

Sept. 13 - 1876

"Mounting steadily on the other side, I saw at a height of over 13,000 feet, lying on the loose blocks, a piece of wood about four feet long and five inches thick, evidently cut by some tool, and so far above the limit of trees that it could not possibly be a natural fragment of one. Darting on it with a glee that astonished the Cossack and the Kurd, I held it up to them, made them look at it, and repeated several times the word "Noah." The Cossack grinned, but he was such a cheery, genial fellow that I think he would have grinned at whatever I said, and I cannot be sure that he took my meaning, and recognized the piece as a fragment of the true Ark. . . Whether it was really gopher wood, of which material the Ark was built, I will not undertake to say, but am willing to submit to the inspection of the curious the bit which I cut off with my ice-axe and brought away. Anyhow, it will be hard to prove that it is not gopher wood. And if there are any remains of the Ark on Ararat at all - a point as to which the natives are perfectly clear - here rather than at the top is the place where one might expect to find them, since in the course of ages they would get carried down by the onward movement of the snow-beds along the declevities. This wood, therefore, suits all requirements of the case. In fact, the argument is for the case of the relic, exceptionally strong: the Crusaders found the Holy Lance at Antioch, and the Archbishop who recognized the Holy Coat at Treves, not to speak of many others, proceeded upon lighter evidence. I am, however, bound to admit that another explanation of the presence of this piece of timber on the rocks at this very height did occur to me. But as no man is bound to discredit his own relic, and such is certainly not the practice of the Armenian Church, I will not disturb my reader's minds or yield to the rationalizing tendencies of the age by suggesting it."

Quoted from

Transcaucasia and Ararat, 1896, pp 280-281.

by James Bryce

Carveth Wells, well-known travalogue writer, explorer, and broadcaster, told us that this data from Bryce was all of the information he had on the existance of Noah's Ark to induce him to make his attempt to find it in 1931. He failed because the Russian Government refused to let him cross the Turkish border. (However, it was winter when he arrived there, as his photographs of Mt. Ararat shows, and he could not have reached it.)

Bryce's firsthand account of his discovery on Mt. Ararat.

probably the account of George Hagopian. Most of the Hagopian story comes from Charles Berlitz' 1987 book *The Lost Ship of Noah*, but much of the account had been published previously in other sources. Berlitz was able to actually interview Hagopian in 1970, shortly before his death, and have him recount his story in first person.

According to Hagopian, he saw the Ark on two occasions as a young boy around 1900-1908 and even climbed to the top of it. Hagopian, an Armenian, said that a four-year drought had hit the area around Mt. Ararat and that he and his uncle ventured up the mountain to find sources of water for their sheep, which were dying because of the intensely dry conditions. It took eight days to climb the mountain and reach the grazing areas. As they ventured up the mountain, they passed the Ahora Gorge and the ruins of the Monastery of St. Jacob along the way. According to legend, Saint Jacob tried many times to climb Mount Ararat to find Noah's Ark, which was buried under thick layers of ice at Parrot Glacier upon the top of the mountain. He would climb the mountain, fall asleep and wake up downhill from where he had been. After repeated

A drawing made at George Hagopian's instruction of his encounter with the Ark of Noah.

failed attempts, one day God said him in a dream, "Do not try to find the Ark anymore. I will give you a piece of a wood of what the Ark was hewn." When he woke up, to his amazement he found the wood lying nearby. He decided to build the monastery at the location where he found the wood.[2]

Hagopian, who was eight years old at the time of his experience, said that as the mountain passes grew more treacherous, his uncle hoisted him upon his shoulders and carried him the rest of the way. Eventually they came to a ridge upon which rested a great, rectangular wooden structure partially covered by snow and ice. It also had a wooden staircase descending from the roof, which his uncle boosted him up to so he could climb on the roof.

Hagopian's encounter is described by Berlitz thusly:

> It had flat openings like windows along the top and a hole in the roof. Hagopian had first thought it was a house made of stone but when his uncle showed him the outline of planks and told him it was made of wood he realized it was the Ark, just like other people had described it to him. His uncle boosted him up from a rock pile to reach the Ark roof telling him not to be afraid, 'because it is a holy ship…' (and) 'the animals and people are not here now. They have all gone away.'
>
> Hagopian says he climbed on the roof and knelt down and kissed the surface of the roof which was flat and easy to stand on. While they stood alongside the Ark his uncle shot into the side of it but the bullets bounced off as if it were made of stone. He then tried to cut off a piece of the wood with a sharp knife and was equally unsuccessful. On this first visit to the Ark they spent two hours there looking at it and eating some of their provisions. When Hagopian returned to his village eager to tell the other boys about his adventure they replied, rather anticlimactically, 'Yes, we saw that Ark too.'

Although Hagopian died in 1972, he swore until his dying

day that he could lead an expedition back to the Ark if a similar drought (and glacial melt) ever occurred again. In the subsequent years however, the area in which he and his uncle had supposedly found the Ark has been mostly covered in ice and snow.

There is, however, some reason to take his account seriously. First, depending on which report you believe, it is clear that Hagopian passed either a polygraph (lie detector) test and/or a voice stress analysis which indicated he was telling the truth. There is also the story of Ed Davis, who claimed that in 1943 he climbed Mt. Ararat along the same path as Hagopian and found the Ark broken into two pieces. While Davis' claim remains unsubstantiated, he did pass a lie detector test himself at the time. It also seems likely that if Davis was fibbing, he would have recounted seeing the Ark in in exactly the same condition as Haopian allegedly found it. Why create a discontinuity by differing from Hagopian's version so extensively?

Ed Davis' rendering of the Ark as he saw it in 1943.

But the strongest support for Hagopian's claim may have come from a sighting of an Air Force fighter pilot of what may have been Hagopian's Ark.

In 1959, then Lieutenant Gregor Schwinghammer was flying a patrol around Mt. Ararat in an F-100 fighter plane belonging to the 428th Tactical Observation Squadron. According to Berlitz, the American pilots had been told about the Ark by a Turkish liaison pilot assigned to them "and on several occasions had been guided past Mount Ararat on routine observation flights." One day Schwinghammer was on a patrol and spotted what he described as a "boat like" object on Mount Ararat. "He stated that the Turkish liaison officer had accompanied him and another pilot in a counterclockwise swing around Mount Ararat in the course of which they saw 'an enormous boxcar or rectangular barge visible in a gully high on the mountain.' Captain Schwinghammer specified that it seemed to be banked, indicating that it was not stationary but movable and somehow had become caught there as it slid down the mountain. He remembered that he had later heard at the base club that some pictures had been taken of this object."

Berlitz had Schwinghammer commission a sketch of the object he sighted, making sure he knew nothing of the story of George Hagopian. When the drawings of Hagpian and Schwinghammer were compared, they were a remarkable match. The Ark was in the same position on the mountain and both pictures showed a rectangular boat or barge on a ledge.

The Arks.

47

Schwinghammer was then made aware of Hagopian's story. According to Berlitz, when he saw Hagopian's drawing he said, "That looks just like what I saw. The object had the same angle on the mountain and the position was the same. The only difference is that I did not notice any 'windows' along the top." This is understandable because of the aircraft's speed and altitude and also because the object was partially covered by snow." Berlitz also conducted an interview with Schwinghammer that was very illuminating:

Question: What did the other pilots think about what you and they had seen?

"We used to talk about it in the bar after flying. Some of the pilots thought it was the Ark and others didn't know what to think. I was not convinced about that but I knew that I had seen a large rectangular building like a barge or a ship high up on the mountain."

How far away from the object were you when you saw it?

"We were coming down from 5000 feet. I think we were at more like 3000 feet when we sighted it. I remember that we were doing 380 knots. The Turkish liaison pilot said to us, 'That's where Noah's Ark is supposed to be. Look! You can see it now!' I estimate that I saw it at a 45° angle. It appeared to be hanging at 45° or 30° degrees down the mountain."

Did you take any photographs of it?

"No. We were in too much of a hurry. We had two hours of fuel; it took us forty-five minutes to get there in the F-100. We had time enough to make just one pass around the mountain and return. We had to be very careful. The Russians had a radar installation right on the border. A C-130 had recently been shot down. The pilot was a guy named Dick Skiddip."

From your memory, where was the object on the mountain?

"You can tell approximately from the map. The point where I place the Ark we saw was about 4000 feet from the top on the southeast slope, perhaps four o'clock from due north. I think most of the time it is covered with ice and snow and that we just saw it at a time when part of it was protruding from the snow. I know that I saw a rectangular structure that looked like a ship. It was at a period in time or history and we were there at that time. Other pilots in the squadron remember having taken part in flights over Ararat or having heard that other pilots had seen a shiplike object on the mountain."

Unbeknownst to either Berlitz or Schwinghammer at the time of the interview, the US government was already well aware of the "Ark" he may have spotted on Mt. Ararat as far back as 1949, some 10 years before his sighting. In fact, the intelligence community had already given it a nickname: the "Ararat Anomaly."

1949 US Air Force reconnaissance photo of the "Ararat Anomaly."

The anomaly was first spotted in a low level (14,000 feet) aerial reconnaissance photo taken on June 17, 1949. The photo remained classified for over 45 years before it and several subsequent photos of the area were released under a freedom of information act request in 1995. It appears to show a block-like, possibly artificial object that may have been broken into two pieces (just as Ed Davis had described) and been subsequently covered over by fresh ice and snow.

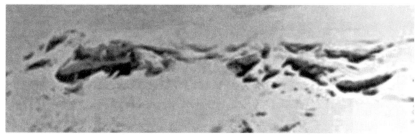

Close up of the "Ararat Anomaly" debris field.

Dubbed the "Ararat Anomaly" by the C.I.A., the object bore more than a passing resemblance to the Ark as described by Ed Davis. Cloven into two pieces by glacial ice in the 40-some years between his sighting and George Hagopian's, the image showed what looked like support struts or inter-deck vertical beams in the shadows. The object was found at about the 15,000 foot level and was subsequently photographed by various defense agencies in 1956, 1973, 1976, 1990 and 1992 using both aerial overflights and satellite imagery. In 2006, a satellite image was released showing the area covered by fresh ice and snow (see above), but the object underneath appeared to have a distinctly rectangular shape which is quite unnatural in appearance. Subsequent 3D reconstruction of the satellite data supported this conclusion.[3] One satellite image was later subjected to a "panchromatic texture uniqueness analysis." This is a form of fractal analysis which attempted to determine if the Ararat Anomaly was different from the surrounding natural terrain, but the results were inconclusive.[4]

In 2014, footage surfaced on YouTube of an object alleged to be the Ararat Anomaly filmed from a helicopter.[5] The footage was purported to be that of helicopter pilot George Greene, who

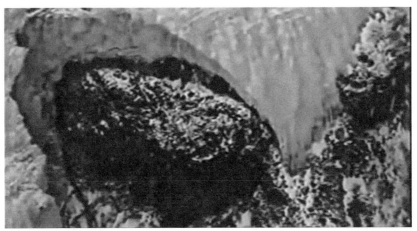

Screen cap from YouTube video of an "ice cave" near the peak of Mt. Ararat.

claimed to have observed the Ark on Ararat in 1953. He said it was lying on the side of a vertical rock cliff at the 13,000 to 14,000 foot level and he claimed to have "photographed" it from the air in his helicopter. Greene was found drowned in a swimming pool in British Guiana in 1962, and his photographs (or films, if he took any) have not been seen since. At least one Ark investigator claimed that what Greene had found was actually "a huge chunk of basalt," but the footage (if it is real) would seem to stretch that claim to the limit.

In reality, the footage is from a helicopter flyover of the peak of Ararat by Chuck Aaron and Bob Garbe in 1989.[6] It exactly matches a 1989 drawing and photographs made from their descriptions of what some researchers call an "ice cave" at the 14,000 foot level.

Truthfully, the "ice cave," which has never been explored, certainly could be artificial, but it does not appear to be in the same location as the Ararat Anomaly, which has the same dimensions (roughly) as the Ark. The ice cave, however, does seem to have a series of equally-spaced "icicles" which look remarkably like support struts. However, until the site in explored in more detail, it will remain a mystery along with the Ararat Anomaly.

But, while both sites seem worthy of further exploration, neither is as promising as what is now known as the "Durupinar

51

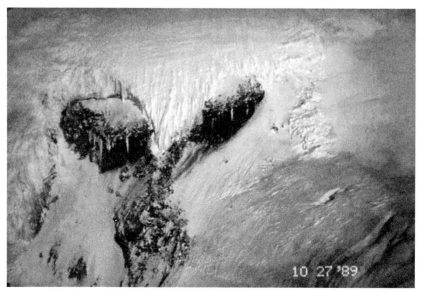

The Aaron/Garbe "Ice Cave" image.

site."

Found at an altitude of 6,449 feet above sea level in the mountains around Mt. Ararat, the so-called Durupinar site is in many ways the better candidate to be Noah's Ark than the Ararat Anomaly ever was. Given that Mt. Ararat was not named as such until the 1300s by Marco Polo and that the Bible says only that the Ark "came to rest on the mountains of Ararat," not necessarily *the* mountain itself, the surrounding area should have been given further scrutiny far sooner. Some geologists also argue that what we know today as Mt. Ararat was a far smaller peak in antediluvian times, and that most of its volcanic growth has been post flood— in the period after the Younger Dryas comet impact of 12,800 years ago. The Durupinar site is also on a mountain the locals call Mt. Judi, which according to some later ancient records is the place the Ark came to rest.

The site was first discovered by a Kurdish shepherd named Reshit Sarihan in May of 1948, after heavy rains and three significant earthquakes exposed the formation from the surrounding mud. Subsequent warm weather melted the adjacent snow and ice, further exposing the formation. According to an

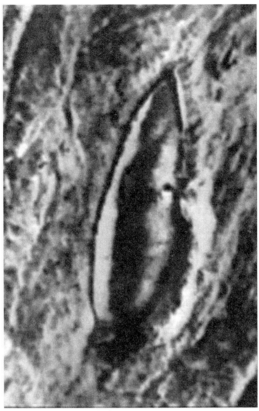

1960s-era aerial reconnaissance photograph of the Durupinar site.

Associated Press article at the time:[7]

Reshit had passed through the area many times, but this time, he spotted what he called 'the prow of a ship' jutting out from the melting ice. Reshit said it was the prow of a ship protruding into a canyon down which tons of melting ice and snow had been gushing for more than two months. The prow was almost entirely revealed, but the rest of the object still was covered. The contour of the earth, Reshit said, indicated the invisible part of the object was shaped like a ship. The prow, he added, was about the size of a house. Reshit climbed down to it and with his dagger tried to break off a piece of the bow. It was so hard it would not break. It was blackened with age. Reshit insisted it was not a simple rock formation. 'I know a ship when I see one,' he said. 'This is a ship.'

At the time, other villagers in the area also visited the site, and also declared that it was in their opinion a ship. The site was first noted by western authorities in 1959, when a Turkish Army captain named Llhan Durupinar[1] was reviewing NATO Geodetic Survey photographs of the area and noticed a boat-shaped formation.

Durupinar then informed the Turkish government of his observation and the photos were sent to the United States and shown to Dr. Arthur J. Brandenburger, a world famous expert in photo interpretation (his satellite photo interpretations were crucial in the Cuban Missile Crisis). His conclusions were decisive: "I have no doubt at all that this object is a ship. In my entire career I have never seen an object like this on a stereo photo. Even the approximate length of the object fits (the given length of the Ark)."[8] Based on Brandenburger's analysis, an expedition to the site was formed, sponsored by an unnamed American benefactor. A group from the "Archeological Research Foundation," which included

Members of the Archeological Research Foundation expedition at the Durupinar site in 1960. The photo appeared in the September 5, 1960 issue of *LIFE* magazine. The boat formation is in the background.

evangelist George Vandeman, Durupınar, author Rene Noorbergen and Dr. Brandenberger, surveyed the site in September, 1960.

The research team spent a few days at the site, digging and surveying inside the formation, but conducted no real in-depth scientific tests. In the end, they found nothing they considered of consequence. Expecting to find petrified wood beams on the exterior, they instead found only what they judged to be ordinary rocks and declared the site to be an "odd geological formation," and "a freak of nature and not man-made." Noorbergen declared in the LIFE magazine article that "there were no visible archaeological remains."[9]

The site was subsequently ignored for nearly 20 years until an independent researcher named Ron Wyatt decided to conduct a more complete investigation. Forming the first of some 24 expeditions to the Durupinar site in 1977, Wyatt has long championed it as the best possibility to be the remains of the actual Ark. Wyatt attempted to convince NASA astronaut Jim Irwin, a long time Ark hunter and the eighth man to walk on the surface of the Moon, to visit the site but he never did and later declared, "I've done all I possibly can, but the Ark continues to elude us." In 1985 Wyatt was able to put together an expedition where he was accompanied by former United States Merchant Marine sailor and Ark researcher David Fasold and geophysicist Dr. John Baumgardner. As soon as Fasold saw the Durupinar formation, he stated it was a shipwreck, not a natural formation.

Fasold brought along (then) state-of-the-art ground penetrating radar instruments and other equipment, and found that the Durupinar formation had vertical (keel) and horizontal "beams" running the length and width of it, exactly as a ship would. In addition to finding this regular internal structure, they also measured the site and found that it was almost the exact dimensions of the Ark given in the Bible: 515 feet, or 300 Egyptian cubits.

I will be blunt here. My background is in aerospace structural engineering and consulting and I will state flatly that if Fasold's mapping of the horizontal supports and keel beams is correct, then

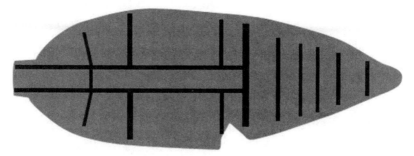

Map of the buried "keel beam" structures under the Durupinar formation.

there can be no doubt the Durupinar site is artificial, or that it is a ship. The style, spacing, form, fit and function of the beams in the diagram are unmistakably the product of human engineering. Whether it is the Ark or not is another question, but I will not be dissuaded on this point.

Wyatt and Fasold also found large stones with holes punched in them nearby, and it was argued that these were drogue stones which would have been dragged by the Ark in order to stabilize it, and eventually anchor it to the bottom once a resting place was found. After further investigation, Fasold concluded that, based on tests of the drogue stones, they were of local origin and not from the Holy Land. This result led Fasold to repudiate his earlier work for a time, but he was eventually convinced by later expeditions that the drogue stones found at the Durupinar site were local recreations of actual drogue stones that had been found at the site by the natives but which had fossilized or eroded away. His best friend June Dawes noted after his death that reports of him denying the significance of the Durupinar site were overblown, and said, "He [Fasold] kept repeating that no matter what the experts said, there was too much going for the [Durupınar] site for it to be dismissed. He remained convinced it was the fossilized remains of Noah's Ark."[10]

After Fasold's death, Wyatt continued to mount expeditions to the site and conduct more extensive tests. One of the things that he found was four equally-spaced vertical "ribs" near the stern on the starboard side of the formation, and a single vertical "post"

David Fasold with one of the alleged "drogue stones" near the
Durupinar site.

protruding from the mud opposite (and in line with) them. The
port side "rib" is also curved, as it would be if it was a structural
rib frame on a ship. There are also hints of more port side ribs next
to the main one but they are buried deeper in the mud and appear
only as stumps. They will require excavation to determine their
actual shape and horizontal spacing.

Simply put, regularly-spaced vertical "posts" like these do
not occur in nature. The most likely explanation for their presence
on the Durupinar formation is that they are exactly what Wyatt
thinks they are: fossilized wooden rib posts. If they are remnants of
the Ark (and what other ship could end up at 6,500 feet elevation?)
they would have, in the course of the intervening 12,800 years
since the Younger Dryas impact event, long since taken on the
characteristics of the local rock. Organic matter like the wood

Fossilized equally-spaced "rib posts" on the Durupinar Ark formation.

the Ark is made of would have petrified, and only a careful archeological excavation of the site will reveal its true shape.

Wyatt has also found other clues which hint that the Durupinar formation may be the Ark, or at the very least a very ancient ship which somehow ended up on the top of a mountain. Core samples taken on the starboard side found samples of petrified animal dung, an antler and what was identified as the hair of a cat. What this means, obviously, is that if the Durupinar site is a ship, this "ship" contained animals of various types. Wyatt also used metal detectors to find samples of what he believes are metal rivets embedded in wooden planks. These claims have been disputed (as they always are), but Wyatt had the "rivets" tested by metallurgical labs and it was discovered that not only did they contain iron, but also substantial quantities of aluminum *and* titanium, meaning that the metal was actually an aluminum/titanium/iron *alloy*. Such a mixture of elements cannot be achieved by nature, but only by a sophisticated knowledge of metallurgy and forging. Rivets and washers found at the site made of this particular alloy would have light weight, great strength and high resistance to the corrosive effects of water. In other words, they'd be perfect for the Ark. Given that titanium wasn't "discovered" in the modern world until 1791, this implies that either the Durupinar formation is a "boat" of very recent origin or the ancients who built the Ark had a very advanced knowledge of metalworking. Since we know by the highly eroded condition of the formation that it is at least several thousands of years old (not merely a few hundred) we are left with the only logical conclusion being that the builders of this "Ark" knew what they were doing. The Bible (specifically Genesis 4:22) describes a character named "Tubal-Cain" as something of a master metalworker if not an alchemist and sorcerer, and from those brief descriptions it seems possible that antediluvian metalworkers might be able to forge such advanced alloys, particularly if they were members of an advanced group of high priests (more on that later).

Eventually, Wyatt listed some 15 points which he felt argued that the Durupinar site was indeed the actual wreck of Noah's Ark. They included:

1. It is in the shape of a boat, with a pointed bow and rounded stern.

2. Exact length as noted in Biblical description, 515 feet or 300 Egyptian cubits. (Egyptian not Hebrew cubit would have been known to Moses, who studied in Egypt then wrote Genesis.)

3. It rests on a mountain in Eastern Turkey, matching the Biblical account, *"The ark rested.... upon the mountains of Ararat"* Genesis 8:4. (Ararat being the name of the ancient country Urartu which covered this region.)

4. Contains petrified wood, as proven by lab analysis.

5. Contains high-tech metal alloy fittings, as proven by separate lab analyses paid for by Ron Wyatt, then performed later by Galbraith Laboratories.[11] Aluminum metal and titanium metal were found in the fittings which are man-made metals.

6. Vertical rib timbers on its sides, comprising the skeletal superstructure of a boat. Regular patterns of horizontal and vertical deck support beams are also seen on the deck of the Ark.

7. Occupied ancient village at the Ark site at 6,500-foot elevation matching Flavius Josephus' statement, "Its remains are shown there by the inhabitants to this day."

8. Dr. Bill Shea, archaeologist, found an ancient pottery shard within 20 yards of the Ark which has a carving on it that depicts a bird, a fish, and a man with a hammer wearing a headdress that has the name "Noah" on it. In ancient times these items were created

59

by the locals in the village to sell to visitors of the Ark. The Ark was a tourist attraction in ancient times and today.

9. Recognized by Turkish Government as Noah's Ark National Park and a National Treasure. Official notice of its discovery appeared in the largest Turkish newspaper in 1987.

10. Visitor center built by the government to accommodate tourists further confirms the importance of the site.

11. Huge anchor stones were found near the Ark and in the village Kazan, 15 miles away, which hung off the rear of the ark to steady its ride.

12. The Ark rests upon Cesnakidag (or Cudi Dagi) Mountain, which is translated as "Doomsday" Mountain.

13. Dr. Salih Bayraktutan of Ataturk University stated, "It is a man-made structure, and for sure it's Noah's Ark." This same article also states, "The site is immediately below the mountain of Al Judi, named in the Qur'an as the resting place of the Ark." Houd Sura 11:44

14. Radar scans show a regular pattern of timbers inside the Ark formation, revealing keels, keelsons, gunnels, bulkheads, animal chambers, ramp system, a door in right front, two large barrels in the front 14' x 24', and an open center area for air flow to all three levels.

Whether the Durupinar site or the Ararat Anomaly are proven someday to be the final resting place of Noah's Ark, one thing is certain: human civilization in ancient times seems to have emerged "from the sky down," rather than from the plains upward. As more and more ancient ruins are uncovered and the search for artifacts like the Ark continue, we continue to find mystery after mystery at high altitude. From the ancient ruins at Machu Picchu to the lines on the plains of Nazca to the "H blocks" of Puma Puku, we find evidence from all over the world that human civilization in the Holocene (post ice age) began at high altitude. While the valley civilizations of upper and lower Egypt and Sumer are given the most attention due to the number of artifacts and monuments that survive, archaeologists are finding more and more evidence that the high mountain "terrace" civilizations came first. If in fact there were a catastrophic flood—whatever its cause—then this is exactly what we would expect to see: human civilizations emerging first in the high mountains and later on the low plains.

Perhaps the most intriguing argument for this idea can be made from the recent discovery of the ancient site of Göbekli Tepe in Turkey.

The ruins of Göbekli Tepe in southwestern Turkey.

Discovered at 2,500 feet above sea level, even mainstream archaeologists admit that the site dates to at least the 10th millennium BC, putting it right in the ball park for being one of the first human settlements after the Younger Dryas impact event. The temple was first noted by an American expedition in 1964, but wasn't really "worked" until German archaeologists began digging in 1994. Klaus Schmidt of Heidelberg University led the dig until his death in 2014. The site is megalithic, with enormous stone pillars of precise construction and alignment implying that it was something far more sophisticated than a primitive gathering place for post ice age cavemen.

Arguments have raged over whether Göbekli Tepe calls for a paradigm shift in our thinking about the ancient world, but the fact remains that the technology required to create it and other nearby cities and towns is far in advance of what primitive hunter-gatherer cavemen could have achieved. The site is considered religious in nature, but it's unclear what the residents of the area were worshipping. The only hint is that massive statues of giant humans have been found among the ruins, implying that perhaps *they* were the subject of the locals' reverence. A *Newsweek* article by Patrick Symmes in the March 1, 2010 issue quotes Johns Hopkins archeologist Glenn Schwartz as saying, "In the Bible it talks about how God created man in his image. Göbekli Tepe is the first time you can see humans with that idea, that they resemble gods." What is even stranger is that no one has ever found a contemporaneous human habitat that remotely resembles Göbekli Tepe's grandeur or technological sophistication. "The problem with this discovery," as Schwartz put it in the *Newsweek* article, "is that it is unique." No other monumental sites from the era have been found.

One thing the archaeologists do agree on is that around 10,000 years ago, the inhabitants of Göbekli Tepe suddenly abandoned it and moved to the plains below. Their explanation of this is that for reasons unknown, the inhabitants simply moved into the valleys below and then apparently deliberately buried the entire Göbekli Tepe complex. In reality, this makes no sense. If the valleys below were hospitable, why didn't the inhabitants simply build Göbekli Tepe there instead of (somehow) dragging 10-ton plus precisely cut megalithic stones thousands of feet up the mountain, only to eventually bury the whole thing?

Logically they wouldn't. Quite obviously, the lower valleys simply weren't accessible at the time the site was constructed. This implies that something, probably massive amounts of water left over from the Great Flood, prevented them from living in the valleys. When the water receded, the makers of the Temple moved down the mountain and covered Göbekli Tepe to preserve it for the future.

When you add it all up—the Biblical stories, the possible locations of the Ark, the proximity of Göbekli Tepe to the Durupinar site, the sophistication of the megalithic architecture there—it seems to imply that not only did civilization start (or restart) at high altitude, but it may have been guided by someone with advanced knowledge of science, astronomy, agriculture and architecture. Göbekli Tepe itself may even be a monument to these advanced beings and the role they played in leading humanity out of the ashes of the Younger Dryas impact event and its horrific aftermath. The question is, who were they?

The Bible, for one source, makes it clear. They were called The Watchers.

(Endnotes)

1   *Journey to Ararat,* Dr. Edward Parrot, 1829. London. p.162

2   http://en.wikipedia.org/wiki/Saint_Hakob_of_Akori_monastery

3   http://www.satimagingcorp.com/gallery/gallery-3d/quick-time-mt-ararat-low/

4   https://drive.google.com/file/d/0BwlNU8avxOwROURxT2hiTW9Z-RzQ/edit

5   https://www.youtube.com/watch?v=n3SJDKbKQX8

6   http://www.setterfield.org/Ark/The_Ark.html

7   Edwin B. Greenwald, "Turk Reports 'Ship' Atop Mt. Ararat," Associated Press article, 13 November 1948.

8   *The Ark File*, p118

9   Noorbergen, Rene (2004). *The Ark File,* TEACH Services, Inc. p. 128. ISBN 978-1572582668. Retrieved 4 June 2014

10   Dawes, June (2000). *Noah's Ark: Adrift in Dark Waters*. Belrose, NSW: Noahide. ISBN 0-646-40228-5.

11   http://www.viewzone2.com/lab-report-rivet.jpg

Chapter 3
Ancient Aliens?

The Watchers, a race of giant angelic beings, does battle with an army of humans as depicted in the 2013 film *Noah*.

When men began to increase on earth and daughters were born to them, the divine beings saw how beautiful the daughters of men were and took wives from among those that pleased them. The LORD said, 'My breath shall not abide in man forever, since he too is flesh; let the days allowed him be one hundred and twenty years.' It was then, and later too, that the Nephilim appeared on earth – when the divine beings cohabited with the daughters of men, who bore them offspring. They were the heroes of old, the men of renown.

—Genesis 6:1-4

Just as with the flood myth itself there are many stories from ancient cultures all over the world about a race of beings, sometimes appearing as giants, who either helped their "Noah" escape the flood or helped the survivors of the flood rebuild human civilization after it. These "men of renown" may very well have been the true architects of Göbekli Tepe, or the Osirion in Abydos, Egypt, or any number of other megalithic structures of ancient times. Even the *Book of the Hopi* mentions a strange race of "ant people" or "insect people," not unlike today's modern "grays" of abduction lore, that not only helped the Hopi to survive the flood but also led them back to a place where they could begin to rebuild civilization—one better in accordance with "God's Laws" than the previous one.

But the most curious and interesting of these beings to me are The Watchers of the Bible. Little was known of them until the recent discoveries of new Biblical era texts. The story of The Watchers can be pieced together from both canonical (Biblical) sources and from apocryphal (non-sanctioned) sources like The Book of Enoch. Enoch, according to the Bible, was Noah's great-grandfather and is the only human in the Old Testament who was "taken to heaven" by God, and never faced a corporeal death on Earth.

The Book of Enoch was discovered (or rediscovered) in 1773 by Scottish traveler James Bruce, who found three copies on his journey to Abyssinia (Ethiopia). The book is also referenced by Sir Walter Raleigh (1552-1618) who mentioned that it contained references to "the course of the stars, their names and motions" in his 1616 book *History of the World*. The first English translation of The Book of Enoch came in 1821.

The Biblical references to The Watchers are brief but significant. In Daniel 4:13 the king Nebuchadnezzar describes a dream in which he sees an angelic presence descend from heaven and pass a harsh judgment on him. "I was looking in the visions in my mind as I lay on my bed, and behold, an angelic Watcher, a holy one, descended from heaven." The Watcher then informs Nebuchadnezzar that this judgment is by his authority granted under God: "This sentence is by the decree of the angelic Watchers And the decision is a command of the holy ones, In order that the living may know That the Most High is ruler over the realm of mankind, And bestows it on whom He wishes And sets over it the lowliest of men."

The last reference to The Watchers is in Daniel 4:23, where Daniel tries to interpret the dream in a way that flatters the king: "In that the king saw an angelic Watcher, a holy one, descending from heaven…" These passages curiously refer to The Watchers as emissaries of God who seem to have the autonomy to act in God's name. But there is no doubt that they are angelic, holy beings in and of themselves.

As far as I know, these are the only specific references to The Watchers within the Holy Bible. However, the apocryphal books, like the Book of Enoch the Book of Jubilees and others, flesh out the story considerably. The picture they paint is of an initially non-corporeal race of beings that are very high up in the hierarchy of heaven, ranking only below the Seraphim, the Cherubim and the Opannim. These four classes of "Higher Angels" that are closest to God are tasked with many different responsibilities toward God's creations, especially man. These responsibilities include interceding for humans (1 Enoch 15:2), mediating between God and man (Testimony of Daniel 6:2), guiding men in the righteous way of life and reporting to God on what they see (Jubilees 4:6), revealing God's secrets (1 Enoch 60:11), preparing Man for the judgment of the righteous and wicked (1 Enoch 103:2-3) and teaching men knowledge and crafts (1 Enoch 7:1; 8:1). Exactly why an omnipotent, all-seeing God would need assistants to watch over the Earth is never really explained, but that is not necessarily unusual for the Bible.

For reasons not entirely clear, at some point 200 Watchers actually descend (fall) to Earth in physical form. There are references in some of the apocryphal books about a war in heaven led by a Watcher named Satanail (Satan, obviously) which results in the damnation of The Watchers and their imprisonment or detention in various "lower Heavens" or even under the ground. In this scenario, the 200 Watchers are sent to Earth as some kind of punishment. Personally, I find this unlikely, since other works say that The Watchers are sent to Earth to take care of and guide Man, and it also makes no sense to me that God would send rebels or evildoers to watch over his prized possession, mankind.

Whatever the case, The Watchers who are sent to Earth take on a physical form, perhaps for the first time, and set about their task of guiding Man according to God's wishes. Jubilees 4:15 describes this: "The angels of the Lord who were called Watchers descended to earth to teach mankind and to do what is just and upright upon the earth." At some point however, this task becomes too difficult for the Watchers, who appear to be cut off from God and find themselves isolated and unappreciated. At that point, there is a shift in The Watchers' thinking which leads to calamity.

For whatever reason—perhaps it's the inherent sensual corruption of taking physical form—The Watchers begin to turn from their task of guiding mankind in God's ways to giving in to their own selfish lusts. They begin to desire the daughters of men, and this leads them to break God's holy decree that they not defile themselves in this way. In 1 Enoch 6:1-7, the story is told this way:

> In those days, when the children of man had multiplied, it happened that there were born unto them handsome and beautiful daughters. And the angels, the children of heaven, saw them and desired them; and they said to one another, 'Come, let us choose wives for ourselves from among the daughters of man and beget us children.' And Semyaz, being their leader, said unto them, 'I fear that perhaps you will not consent that this deed should be done, and I alone will become (responsible) for this great sin.' But they all responded to him, 'Let us all swear an oath and bind everyone among us by a curse (oath) not to abandon this suggestion but to do the deed.' Then they all swore together and bound one another by (the curse). And they were altogether two hundred.

So here we have a specific personage in the leader of The Watchers named Semyaz, talking the other Watchers into breaking their vows to God and taking the daughters of men for themselves. He also demands that if one of them does it they all must, so that if their sin is discovered by God they will all face his wrath, not just the ringleaders. Once this blood oath (or curse) was agreed, they proceeded to choose human wives for themselves. But things did not go so well.

Says 1 Enoch 7:1-5:

> They took wives unto themselves, and everyone (respectively) chose one woman for himself, and they began to go unto them. And they taught them magical medicine, incantations, the cutting of roots, and taught them (about) plants. And the women became pregnant and gave birth to great giants whose heights were three hundred cubits. These (giants) consumed the produce of all the people until the people detested feeding them. So the giants turned against (the people) in order to eat them.

Although the Bible nor any other source ever specifically mentions the appearance of The Watchers, it's a safe bet that they were humanoid (they'd have to be, in order to mate with human females) and they were probably much taller than today's modern man. The simple fact that human females begat them offspring that were "giants" suggests that they themselves were somewhat gigantic in stature. These offspring were also known by a specific name, the *Nephilim*, which is often cross-translated simply to "giants." Others, like Sumerian cuneiform scholar Zecharia Sitchin, who we shall discuss presently, connect the word to the term *fallen*, or even *fallen angel*. Sitchin argues the word means "Giants/Angels, who from Heaven to Earth came down." However, as Masonic scholars Christopher Knight and Robert Lomas state in their book *Uriel's Machine*, *Nephilim* also translates from Arabic as "Orion."[1] So I would argue that the Nephilim are more precisely described as "Giants (from Orion) who from Heaven to Earth came down." Note that for later reference.

At any rate, things apparently went south pretty fast at that point. The Nephilim turned out to be fairly serious jerks who saw themselves as superior to man, and as the Bible says, built a world of cities and temples and pretty much consumed everything around them. Roman historian Flavius Josephus wrote of The Watchers and the Nephilim in his work *Antiquities of the Jews* in 93 AD and describes them as follows: "*For many angels of God accompanied with women, and begat sons that proved unjust, and despisers of all that was good, on account of the confidence they had in their own strength.*"

The first Book of Enoch went into even more detail:

> But now the giants who are born from the (union of) the spirits (Sons of God, The Watchers) and the flesh (Daughters of Men) shall be called evil spirits upon the earth, because their dwelling shall be upon the earth and inside the earth. Evil spirits have come out of their bodies. Because from the day that they were created from the holy ones they became the Watchers; their first origin is the spiritual foundation. They will become evil upon the earth and shall be called evil spirits. The dwelling of the spiritual beings of heaven is heaven; but the dwelling of the spirits of the earth, which are born upon the earth, is in the earth. The spirits of the giants oppress each other, they will corrupt, fall, be excited, and fall upon the earth, and cause sorrow. And these spirits shall rise up against the children of the people and against the women, because they have proceeded forth (from them). —1 Enoch 15

What this passage seems to be saying is that the Nephilim, because they have the spark of heaven in them from their fathers, The Watchers, will take over the role of The Watchers and oversee man's development. But it also warns that because they are half human, they will never be truly of the spirit, which is heavenly and not of the Earth, so they will inevitably war against each other and cause great sorrow, even to the point of eventually turning on those they are meant to serve, guide and protect—man. In essence what the Nephilim are is God-Men, demigods or perhaps God-Boys, who have incredible knowledge and power but weak and corruptible spirits. The Book of Enoch makes clear that this is a combination that will inevitably lead to disaster:

> Here shall stand in many different appearances the spirits of the angels which have united themselves with women. They have defiled the people and will lead them into error so that they will offer sacrifices to the demons as unto gods, until the great Day of Judgment in which they shall be judged till they are finished. —1 Enoch 19:1

At the same time, it seems The Watchers broke even more laws by teaching human women what sure sounds like witchcraft (magical medicine, incantations, the cutting of roots, and… plants) and the men about how make weapons of war and the arts and sciences. These were evidently not things that man was meant to know.

The results were disastrous. The Nephilim began to build cities, weapons, armies of humans and make war among themselves. They laid waste to Earth in the course of this and used up the resources to the point that they began to eat humans as a food source. It is also possible, given their vile nature, that the Nephilim, the "men of renown" of the Bible, turned to eating human flesh simply for their own amusement. The humans were so despondent at this conduct that they "called out to God" for a remedy. According to Jubilees 5:6, God was none too happy with The Watchers for creating this whole mess, and stripped them of their powers. "Against his angels whom he had sent to the earth he was angry enough to uproot them from all their (positions of) authority." God then sent four Archangels, Michael, Gabriel, Uriel and Raphael, to straighten the mess out. Uriel then warns Noah that God is going to send a great flood to cleanse the Earth of the wicked Nephilim, and tells him to build the Ark. Raphael captures some of the leaders of the Watcher rebellion and imprisons them in the earth where they are to reside until the Day of Judgment. Yet according to the Book of Jubilees, 10 percent of the Nephilim actually are pardoned from the imprisonment, and are the root source of all evil present today on the Earth.[2]

All of this of course sounds pretty wild and contradictory. If God is all-knowing and all-seeing, how is it that he didn't realize what The Watchers were up to here on Earth until the Archangels told him? That and many other factors don't quite add up, except perhaps in a very different context, which we will examine next. Interestingly, we get a hint of what that explanation might be from an Egyptian source in the first century AD.

Philo of Alexandria (20 BC-50 AD) wrote a commentary on Genesis 6 called *Concerning the Giants*. In it, he emphasized that the passages regarding The Watchers were not mythical, but described actual events and living beings:

> And when the angels of God saw the daughters of men that they were beautiful, they took unto themselves wives of all of them whom they Chose. Those beings, whom other philosophers call demons, Moses usually calls angels; and they are souls hovering in the air. And let no one suppose, that what is here stated is a fable, for it is necessarily true that the universe must be filled with living things in all its parts.[3]

What Philo seemed to be implying—almost 2,000 years ago—is that these beings not only could have existed but *must* have existed, because the universe is filled with living creatures of a shape and form which is beyond our comprehension. In other words, they came from somewhere else.

They were aliens.

Fascinatingly, a Sumerian cuneiform scholar would come to the same conclusion using a completely different set of evidence nearly 2,000 years later. His name was Zecharia Sitchin.

Zecharia Sitchin (1920-2010) was born in Azerbaijan (Soviet Socialist Republic) and raised in British-controlled Mandatory Palestine. Sitchin attended and graduated from the University of London, where he majored in and received a degree in economics. Returning to what had now become Israel, his education allowed

Zecharia Sitchin with a reproduction of the cylinder seal designated VA 243.

him to acquire a deep knowledge of modern and ancient Hebrew as well as Semitic and European languages, the Old Testament, and the history and archeology of the Near East. He was an editor and journalist in Israel for several years before moving to New York City in 1952, where he was an executive for a shipping company. Around this same period, he began to teach himself Sumerian cuneiform and made many overseas journeys to archaeological sites. He was one of the few scholars in the world who could actually read and interpret ancient Sumerian cuneiform texts.

His interest in ancient languages and archaeology began at an early age, when as a schoolchild he was taught about the Bible and learned the story of the Nephilim as told in Genesis 6. The story of the "giants" who were sons of the Gods and had taken human females as wives fascinated him. When he asked his teachers about it, he was quickly rebuffed, which only added to his curiosity. "The word Nephilim is commonly, or used to be, translated giants... Those were the days when there were giants upon the earth. I questioned this interpretation as a child at school, and I was reprimanded for it because the teacher said 'You don't question the Bible.'"

He was so intrigued that he taught himself Hebrew in order to read the original text of the Torah. When he read that, he was in for a surprise. The word Nephilim did not mean simply "giants" as his teachers had told him:

> But I did not question the Bible; I questioned an interpretation that seemed inaccurate, because the word, Nephilim (or Nefilim), the name by which those extraordinary beings, 'the sons of the gods' were known, means literally, "Those who have come down to earth from the heavens."

Sitchin himself became obsessed with these giants and how they came to be on Earth, and felt there was a great mystery to be unraveled. But it all started with the simple debate with his teachers over the meaning of that single word, "Nephilim."

> "So, what did it mean? This led me to biblical studies and then to mythology and archeology and all the other subjects, including the study of ancient languages, which became my education and avocation. So, my research and my decision to write about it started with a question: Who were the Nephilim?

Through the course of his studies, he found that all of the other ancient texts, including the Bible and Egyptian *Book of the Dead*, seemed to point further back in time, to ancient Sumer. But what he found surprised him; many of the common word interpretations were wrong, and what these texts truly revealed was absolutely astonishing:

> All the ancient scriptures, the Bible, the Greek myths, the Egyptian myth and texts, the pyramid texts, everything, led to the Sumerians, whose civilization was the first known one—six thousand years ago. I focused on Sumer, the source of these legends and myths and texts and

information. I learned to read the cuneiform Sumerian texts and came upon their persistent and repeated statements that those beings, whom the Sumerians called Anunnaki, came to earth from a planet called Nibiru. The planet was designated by the sign of the cross and Nibiru meant 'planet of crossing.'[4]

At that point, he shifted his emphasis to exactly what the "planet of crossing" was and what had gone on there:

The question thus shifted in my research from who were the Nefilim and the Anunnaki, to what planet is Nibiru? Forced to become proficient in astronomy, I had to learn enough about it to deal with the subject. I found out that the scholars were divided. Some said it (Nibiru) was Mars, which of course was described and known to the ancient people, and others said, no, it was Jupiter. Those who said it was Jupiter and not Mars, had very convincing arguments why it could not be Mars. And those who said it was Mars and not Jupiter had very convincing arguments also.

Being able to go directly to those ancient sources, clay tablets and cuneiform scripts, it seemed to me that neither was right, because the description of Nibiru and its position when it nears the Sun indicated that it could not be Mars, and it could not be Jupiter. And then one night I woke up with the answer: Of course, it is one more planet that comes periodically between Mars and Jupiter; it is sometimes nearer to Mars and sometimes nearer to Jupiter, but it isn't Mars or Jupiter.

This led Sitchin to reason that what the ancient Sumerian epics were telling him was a true story of beings named the Anunnaki who came to Earth from another planet—an as yet undetected (or unacknowledged) member of the solar system which the Sumerians called "Nibiru." He also came to realize that the Sumerians were not making any of this up. They were simply recounting what the Anunnaki themselves had related to them:

> Once I realized that this was the answer, that there is one more planet, everything else fell into place. The meaning of the Mesopotamian Epic of Creation on which the first chapters of Genesis are based and all details about the Anunnaki, who they were, who their leaders were, how they traveled from their planet to Earth, and how they splashed down in the Persian Gulf and about their first settlement, their leaders and so on and so on everything became clear! The Sumerians had immense knowledge. They knew about Uranus and Neptune and described them, and they knew about Pluto. They were proficient in mathematics and, in many respects, their knowledge surpassed modern times. They said, 'All that we know was told to us by the Anunnaki.'

Sitchin's research led him to conclude that the ancient Sumerians knew about planets in the solar system that were not visible without telescopes, and based on a cylinder seal designated

Cylinder seal VA 243, which shows the god Enki and a diagram of the solar system in the background.

VA 243, that they numbered them from the farthest away (Pluto) to the innermost. The Sumerians believed that the solar system consisted of 11 planets (including the Moon) and that the Anunnaki lived on the 12th planet, Nibiru. All this knowledge came from the Anunnaki.

Sitchin felt compelled to tell the world of what he had found, and he put all of his re-interpretations of the Sumerian epics into his first book, *The 12th Planet*, in 1976. It was an immediate sensation similar to Erich von Däniken's *Chariots of the Gods*, and has sold millions of copies the world over and been translated into dozens of languages. It of course quickly came under attack for various assertions made in its pages, ranging from the dates he gave for certain events to the mechanics of Nibiru's orbit, which astronomers claimed was impossible. But Sitchin felt *The 12th Planet* stood up well against these assaults:

> The first book's innovation, its impact, was the realization that the ancient peoples, beginning with the Sumerians, knew of and described and spoke of one more planet in our solar system. It was not a discovery like that of Pluto in the 1930s (of which the Sumerians knew six thousand years ago). Pluto was a very interesting astronomical discovery; textbooks had to be revised. But to the average person, the man on the street, it really made no difference. Nibiru, on the other hand was a different story. If Niburu exists, (and this is the planet that astronomers nowadays call Planet X) then the Anunnaki exist.

And it therefore logically follows that the Anunnaki are then still out there somewhere, perhaps destined for a return to Earth someday.

Sitchin's take on the Epic of creation was very unique and obviously controversial. But it told a tale that was eerily reminiscent of the Bible's description of The Watchers and their impact on Earth.

In *The 12th Planet*, Sitchin's sequence of events tells a

Close-up of VA 243, showing the Sun and 11 "planets," including Nibiru.

fascinating tale of extraterrestrial intervention in human history. According to his story, the Sumerians say that billions of years ago, the Anunnaki home world, Nibiru, passed through the outer solar system wreaking havoc. According to Sitchin, the Babylonian *Enuma Elish* creation myth, derived from the earlier Sumerian, tells the tale of the early (and violent) history of our solar system. In the story, a rogue planet, Nibiru, which the Babylonians renamed "Marduk," entered the outer solar system and collided

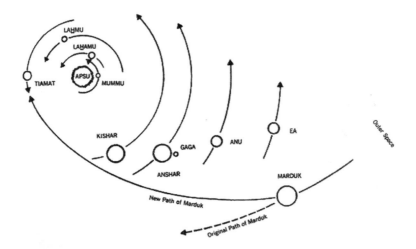

Sitchin's diagram of the path of Marduk/Nibiru, altered by an encounter with Uranus billions of years ago.

with Uranus, tipping it on its side and flinging Pluto away into its current exotic orbit. This altered the path of Nibiru and sent it into the inner solar system on a collision course with Tiamat, a water rich "super earth" sized planet which was the primordial Earth.

As Nibiru passed very near Tiamat, a moon or chunk of trailing debris hit Tiamat, shattering it into at least two smaller pieces. One of these pieces may have become Earth's moon, the other Earth itself, and the rest of the debris drifted beyond the orbit of Mars to become the asteroid belt. Sitchin later declared the Earth's Moon was a preexisting body the Sumerians called Kingu, which acquired a great deal of water in its early encounter with Tiamat. In the *Enuma Elish*, the passages make this clear, along with an indication that this was long before life on Earth had arisen (or was placed here): "And chaos, Tiamat, the mother of them both, Their waters were mingled together. And no field was formed, no marsh was to be seen; When of the gods none had been called into being."

Of course, most astronomers immediately rejected all aspects of Sitchin's interpretation of the Sumerian cosmologies. But there have since been a few straightforward observations which support it.

First, in the 10 July, 2008 issue of the scientific journal *Nature*,

Diagram of the impact which shattered Tiamat, which became the modern Earth.

a new paper found evidence that the early Moon was packed with water, nearly all of which has now escaped to space.[5] It also suggested that water and "volatiles" were lost due to a superheated impact with a Mars-sized object, pretty much exactly as Sitchin has suggested. It is somewhat difficult for me to logically dismiss this as mere coincidence. But the idea of this incredible impact being a real historical event is even easier to accept when one simply does one thing—look at the Earth itself.

Earth, with and without its oceans.

We are taught that the Earth is spherical, like every other body in the solar system of any significant size. Even my favorite science nerd, Neil deGrasse Tyson, fell into this observational trap when he savagely attacked critics of global warming by calling them "science deniers" and "Flat Earthers." "You don't talk about the spherical Earth with NASA, and then say let's give equal time to the Flat Earthers…," he said on CNN. But the reality is the notion of the Earth being spherical is an illusion created by the presence of Earth's oceans. It is anything but spherical. There is no conventional explanation for this. Every other major or minor body in the solar system is spherical. The Earth is not. If something dried up all its "volatiles" and water, it would not look anything like what we would call a planet. At best, it would be half a planet. In fact, it looks like nothing so much as a deformed corn nut.

80

The true shape of Earth, without its oceans.

The most obvious reason for this is something along the lines of the scenario that the Babylonians lay out in the *Enuma Elish*. Something big; really, really big, smashed into the Earth a long time ago and shattered it (*"And chaos, Tiamat…"*). What was left was probably quickly cooled by the intermingling of their waters (*"Their waters were mingled together…")* with the result that Earth was not in a molten state long enough to assume a solid spherical form.

There really is no other explanation for the shape of the Earth beyond what Sitchin claims the Sumerians (and later Babylonians) describe. Certainly conventional science makes no effort to explain this incredible anomaly, probably because there isn't an explanation beyond Sitchin's that would hold up to any sort of critical analysis. What we are left with is an enduring mystery that has only one plausible explanation—the Sumerians' version of the birth of the solar system is correct, as is Sitchin's interpretation of their records. But that becomes very dangerous ground, because if you accept that Sitchin's interpretation of the *Enuma Elish* is correct, the odds rise greatly that the rest of his translations and interpretations are true too.

And that makes a whole bunch of people very, very uncomfortable.

Now, I myself have a problem with some of the details of Sitchin's work, but not the basic facts. Clearly, something dramatic happened to tip Uranus on its side. Clearly, the Earth is a shattered remnant of a once larger world, and just as clearly, it is only half a planet. The bigger issue is, how did the ancient Sumerians *know* all this? The obvious answer is they didn't, unless somebody told them the story.

Like, the Anunnaki…

Sitchin went on to interpret hundreds of other books, cuneiform tablets and cylinder seals over the course of his life's work. The story that emerged was stunning in its accuracy and detail, and certainly destabilizing to many established hierarchies, not the least of which was the Christian Church and institutionalized academia. They of course are his biggest critics. But when we compare the Sumerian tales of the Anunnaki to the Hebrew tales of The Watchers, it soon becomes evident they are discussing the same events.

In Sitchin's version, after Nibiru's collision with the primordial Tiamat, it was knocked into an elongated, egg-shaped orbit that took it far beyond the orbit of Neptune and then back into the inner solar system every 3,600 years (a "shar" in the Sumerian language). Sometime after these catastrophic events, Nibiru became inhabited by a humanoid race of giants on the order of eight- to ten-feet tall which the Sumerians called the Anunnaki. The Earth went through various phases of life, finally culminating in the presence of Homo erectus and Neanderthal man circa 300,000 years ago. About that time, during one of Nibiru's passages through the inner solar system, the Anunnaki arrived on Earth in vehicles that, as described, sound a lot like chemical rockets. They established bases in Mesopotamia in what is now modern day Iraq to mine gold, which they apparently needed for some unknown purpose. The initial teams of Anunnaki were small, perhaps as few as the 200 Watchers the Bible talks about, and the labor was unpleasant. Some workers were sent to southern Africa to work the mines where gold was more plentiful.

According to the texts, the Anunnaki, for whom a 3,600-year "shar" was but one year, tired of the toil and staged a rebellion against their master, an Anunnaki king named Anu, about 200,000 years ago. In response, Anu agreed to fashion a worker from the local genetic stock to alleviate the workers' complaints ("We shall make Man in Our own image"). The Anunnaki's chief scientist, a female named Ninmah, was commissioned by the high god Enki (Lord of the Earth) to create this race of workers. After several disastrous attempts, Ninmah (later Isis in the Egyptian pantheon) succeeded and showsedoff her creation, the "Adamu," to the other Gods.

Ninmah presenting the Adamu to the Anunnaki.

The Adamu is a cross between either Homo erectus and/or Neanderthal man and the Anunnaki themselves. According to the myths, Enki loves man but his brother, another high god named Enlil, despises them.

At any rate, things go on pretty well for a while until Anu, and the other high gods return to Nibiru and leave the workers to their own devices. Anu "divides the Anunnaki and assigns them to their proper stations, three hundred in heaven, three hundred on the earth," again much like the Biblical Watchers. Against the laws of Anu, the leftover workers, like The Watchers, see that the daughters of men are desirable and take them for wives, producing demigod-like offspring.

Upon Anu's return some 3,600 years later, he finds the Earth to be a lawless mess and a conference is convened. The Anunnaki are aware of a possible threat to the Earth, and Enlil, who hates man, argues that they should not intervene and allow the humans and the abominations (the Nephilim) to be exterminated in the disaster to come. Sitchin believes that the alignment of the magnetic poles of the Earth and Nibiru would cause the Earth to topple over on its axis, causing the catastrophic Great Flood, but as we've established, a comet impact in the poles could achieve the same result. In any event, a vote is taken and despite Enki's impassioned pleas, it is decided to let the Flood wipe the Earth clean of the mess that has been made. Enki promises to abide by the decision of the council, which consists of himself, Anu, Enlil and Ninmah.

But Enki disobeys and decides to warn the humans through his favorite human slave, Utnapishtim (later Atrahasis), who is the Sumerian version of Noah. To get around his agreement not to warn man, Enki simply speaks out loud within the hearing range of Utnapishtim, but not in the same room, about what is to come. He explains how to build the Ark, which animals to put on board and that its existence must be kept secret. Very late in the game, Enlil discovers the existence of the Ark and the council sentences Enki to banishment on Earth. He rides out the Flood aboard the Ark and afterwards helps Utnapishtim, and his family reestablish civilization.

At some point after this, it's not clear when, the permanent Anunnaki settlements on Earth are abandoned and most of the Anunnaki return to Nibiru. However, some of the workers who rebelled preferred to remain on Earth as gods and kings rather than return to Nibiru as simple workers ("It is better to rule in Hell than to serve in heaven."). These workers are probably the "10 percent" of the Nephilim that survived the Flood referenced in the Book of Jubilees.

It isn't difficult to decipher what happened after that. These worker castes set themselves up as kings and built armies, made war amongst themselves and slowly died out over the next few

Artist's depiction of David battling Goliath.

thousand years. Their offspring became more and more like modern man as they diluted their bloodlines by interbreeding, until David slew the last of the Anunnaki god kings, Goliath, in the valley of Elah and established the kingdom of man on Earth.

Sitchin of course has been heavily criticized by both academics and religious leaders for his interpretations of the Sumerian texts. However, most of these criticisms are unfounded or poorly reasoned.

First, they argue that Nibiru would be too cold to host a humanoid race, giants or not, because it would spend 99% of its orbit beyond the current orbit of Pluto. However, this overlooks a viable alternative interpretation of the Nibiru myth by author Andy Lloyd, which he calls the Dark Star theory. The Dark Star theory simply assumes that Nibiru is not a planet but an orbiting moon of a smoldering brown dwarf "failed" star, which is itself orbiting our sun at a great distance. If this was the case, Nibiru could certainly draw enough light and heat from the brown dwarf to make it habitable. It also might explain why modern man has to wear sunglasses outdoors, given that our eyes seem to be poorly adapted to this planet. Maybe we have Anunnaki eyes…

Diagram of the orbit of Sedna (NASA).

Astronomers also argue that Nibiru's long, elliptical orbit could not possibly remain stable, given current perturbation theory. But in 2003, NASA-funded astronomers discovered a body they named 90377 Sedna, which had a far longer and even more elliptical orbit than Nibiru's proposed orbit. Journeying from the outer solar system around the sun every 11,400 years, more than three times longer than Nibiru's proposed orbit, Sedna blew away all the preconceived notions of orbital mechanics.

Before his death, Sitchin also pointed out that modern man's (Homo sapiens sapiens) genetic ancestry had been traced back to 200,000 years ago, the exact date he gave for the Anunnaki rebellion and the creation of man. He further pointed out that the International Human Genome Sequencing Consortium had discovered some 223 genes in the human sequence which do not have the required predecessors on the genomic evolutionary tree. In other words, they are not a product of a normal "vertical" evolutionary sequence from one species to another. They were somehow inserted into the human genome, as if someone had simply cut and spliced the human genetic code the way an old school film editor might cut and splice a reel of Super 8 Kodak film. These genes were found to have been inserted into the human DNA strand recently, although no one knows exactly when.

My guess is about 200,000 years ago.

"It is a jump that does not follow current evolutionary theories," said Steven Scherer, director of mapping of the Human Genome Sequencing Center, Baylor College of Mechanics. At first these 223 genes were dismissed as "junk DNA," but after finding that the genes controlled a number of higher brain functions, the scientists involved quickly switched gears and

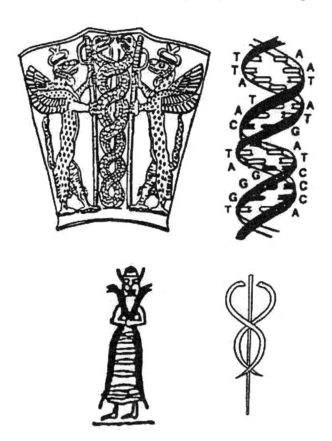

Depictions of Enki showing the DNA double helix.

87

attacked the offending genes by suggesting that they were the product of "horizontal insertion" from bacteria, rather than a vertical insertion from an intelligent source. However, at least one expert, Robert Waterson, co-director of Washington University's Genome Sequencing Center, stated that it was unclear whether humans got the DNA from bacteria or bacteria got the DNA from humans. "It is not clear whether the transfer was from bacteria to human or from human to bacteria," he was quoted as saying in the journal *Science*. Either way, the reality is that there is chunk of our DNA that has mysterious, to say the least, origins. The "horizontal insertion from bacteria" claim is simply a desperate and unfounded attempt to find an explanation for the 223 genes' inexplicable presence in the human genetic sequence.

Other critics have attacked Sitchin more directly, arguing that his interpretations of the Sumerian texts are simply wrong. Foremost among these is Michael Heiser, a committed Christian who has made debunking Sitchin something of his life's work. Heiser and other critics are fond of pointing out that Sitchin's interpretations of certain words and phrases are "incorrect" according to the most commonly accepted academic understandings of them. Virtually all of their criticisms are based on this perspective. However, logically these attacks are actually meaningless. Sitchin taught himself Sumerian at a time when only a few people in the world knew how to read cuneiform texts. Today, people like Heiser have become more numerous and they have learned the language from academic sources such as 2006's *Sumerian Lexicon*, all of which postdate Sitchin's publication of *The 12ᵗʰ Planet*.[6] Obviously, mainstream academia and religious zealots would be the most threatened by Sitchin's interpretations, and they subsequently would have the most to lose if he turned out to be correct. The fact that Heiser disagrees with Sitchin's interpretation carries no more weight than if Kim Jong Un disagreed with them. The *Sumerian Lexicon* is no more authoritative a source than Sitchin himself. In fact, one reviewer declared it to be "a book compiled by a dilettante who understands the basics of neither lexicography nor Sumerology."[7] Heiser's own biography states that "He has also studied… Sumerian independently," meaning that he has no formal education in the language, but—just like Sitchin—is self-taught.

In other words, Sitchin's critics, Heiser included, have no real academic basis in fact for their claims that his interpretations are "wrong." What little academic basis there is for their differing interpretations of certain words come from a highly questionable source (the *Sumerian Lexicon*) which appears to have been rushed into publication after Sitchin's perspective began to gain traction with the general public. The fact that Heiser and some of Sitchin's other critics may hold degrees in other specialties is irrelevant, since Sitchin's interpretations themselves show that there is no consensus on the meaning of the Sumerian texts. What we are left with then is a straightforward case of "he said/he said," with one self-taught Sumerian scholar against another. The only difference is, as we have just read, a number of Sicthin's assertion have been successfully tested (or at least supported), and Heiser's have not. Heiser comes off as nothing but a Christian fundamentalist with an axe to grind. His interpretations of the words and phrases carry no more scientific weight than Sitchin's do.

What all these different tales add up to for me is a story that has remained consistent over time, with only minor alterations. The similarities between the Biblical Watchers and the Sumerian Anunnaki are too great for one not to have been sourced from the other. Further, they also seem to share many traits in common with later Egyptian gods that may actually trace their ancestries back much further. The four archangels, Michael, Uriel, Gabriel and Raphael seem to correspond to the Anunnaki Anu, Ninmah, Enki and Enlil, and likewise to the Egyptian Osiris, Isis, Horus and Set.

The only question that remains for me is, what are these ancient stories and possibly extraterrestrial "gods" trying to tell us?

(Endnotes)

1 *Uriel's Machine*, Fair Winds Press; 3rd edition (August 1, 2001), ISBN-13: 978-1931412742

2 Jubilees 10:8-9

3 Philo, *On the Giants* II: 6-9

4 http://www.sitchin.com/adam.htm

5 Nature, 10 July, 2008, pp170 "THE EARLY MOON WAS RICH IN WATER."

6 Halloran, John A. (2006). *Sumerian Lexicon: A Dictionary Guide to the Ancient Sumerian Language*. The David Brown Book Company. ISBN 0-9786429-0-2.

7 http://www.academia.edu/626344/Review_of_J._A._Halloran_Sumerian_Lexicon_supplemented_with_a_reply_to_Hallorans_response_

Chapter 4
The Dawn of the Secret Societies

Egyptian gods Osiris, Isis, Horus and Set as depicted in ancient temple reliefs.

At some point after the Great Flood 12,800 years ago, human civilization began to rebuild itself. Megalithic sites like Göbekli Tepe in Turkey, Machu Picchu and Nazca in Peru, Stonehenge in Britain, Angkor Wat in Cambodia and Yonaguni off the coast of Japan are evidence of these early attempts at restoring some semblance of organized human culture. Virtually all of these ancient sites and civilizations describe some sort of assistance from beings, like the Anunnaki or The Watchers, who came from on high and assisted humanity in this renewal of a "time before"—a "first time"—when human civilization had achieved great things and reached great heights.

Divers inspect the Yonaguni structure.

Today, for the most part, these high civilizations are in ruins. Some, like Yonaguni, are even submerged in over 30 meters of water from the rising seas as the last ice age glaciers melted. Yonaguni, in fact, is very controversial because there is an ongoing dispute between geologists and archaeologists as to its artificiality. First discovered by divers in 1986, there was little dispute that it was an artificial structure in the beginning. It was extensively documented by Dr. Masaaki Kimura, a Japanese geologist of some renown in his own country. Based on 12 different and specific lines of evidence, Dr. Kimura concluded that the Yonaguni megalith was man-made, and dated back to at least 10,000 years ago. These 12 points, as compiled by author Graham Hancock,[1] are as follows:

1. "Traces of marks that show that human beings worked the stone. There are holes made by wedge-like tools called kusabi in many locations."

2. "Around the outside of the loop road [a stone-paved pathway connecting principal areas of the main monument] there is a row of neatly-stacked rocks as a stone wall, each rock about twice the size of a person, in a straight line."

3. "There are traces carved along the roadway that humans conducted some form of repairs."

4. "The structure is continuous from under the water to land,

and evidence of the use of fire is present."

5. "Stone tools are among the artefacts found underwater and on land."

6. "Stone tablets with carving that appears to be letters or symbols, such as what we know as the plus mark '+' and a 'V' shape were retrieved from under water."

7. "From the waters nearby, stone tools have been retrieved. Two are for known purposes that we can recognize, the majority are not."

8. "At the bottom of the sea, a relief carving of an animal figure was discovered on a huge stone."[2]

9. On the higher surfaces of the structure there are several areas which slope quite steeply down towards the south. Kimura points out that deep symmetrical trenches appear on the northern elevations of these areas which could not have been formed by any known natural process.

10. A series of steps rises at regular intervals up the south face of the monument from the pathway at its base, 27 meters underwater, towards its summit less than six meters below the waves. A similar stairway is found on the monument's northern face.

11. Blocks that must necessarily have been removed (whether by natural or by human agency) in order to form the monument's impressive terraces are not found lying in the places where they would have fallen if only gravity and natural forces were operating; instead they seem to have been artificially cleared away to one side and in some cases are absent from the site entirely.

12. The effects of this unnatural and selective clean-up operation are particularly evident on the rock-cut 'pathway' [Kimura calls it the 'loop road'] that winds around the western and southern faces of the base of the monument. It passes directly beneath the main terraces yet is completely clear of the mass of rubble that would have had to be removed (whether by natural or by human agency) in order for the terraces to form at all.[3]

Other geologists disagreed with Dr. Kimura's assessment. German science writer Dr. Wolf Wichmann visited the site briefly in 1999 and declared "I didn't find anything that was man-made."[4] Dr. Robert Schoch of Boston University, who will factor in to our later discussions, at first felt the structure was natural but later shifted his opinion:

> I believe that the structure can be explained as the result of natural processes. The geology of the fine mudstones and sandstones of the Yonaguni area, combined with wave and current actions and the lower sea-levels of the area during earlier millennia, were responsible for the formation of the Yonaguni Monument about 9000 to 10,000 years ago.[5]

However, after meeting extensively with Dr. Kimura and diving the site again, Schoch softened his position:

> After meeting with Professor Kimura, I cannot totally discount the possibility that the Yonaguni Monument was at least partially worked and modified by the hands of humans. Professor Kimura pointed out several key features that I did not see on my first brief trip. If I should have the opportunity to revisit the Yonaguni Monument, these are key areas that I would wish to explore.[6]

Schoch also conceded a key point that Hancock had made in his book *Heaven's Mirror*, in which he asserted that around 10,000 years ago, the Yonaguni Monument would not only have been above water, but would have stood exactly on the ancient Tropic of Cancer:

> The ancients, I suspect, knew where the tropic was, and they knew that its position moved slowly. Since Yonaguni is close to the most northerly position the tropic reaches in its lengthy cycle, the island may have been the site of an astronomically aligned shrine.[7]

Two views of the Yonaguni "face" from the History Channel.

The whole controversy was seemingly settled in the early 2000s when the History Channel sent a documentary team to the site and discovered two different "face" sculptures at the same depth as the Yonaguni Monument nearby. One of them bore markings that were unmistakably Mesoamerican, giving rise to an even deeper mystery as to how such a sculpture could have found its way all the way across the Pacific in ancient times. To this day, no answer to that has been forthcoming, but many still cling to the idea that the Yonaguni Monument is a natural formation.

But by far the most intriguing and best preserved artifacts from this ancient period come not from Japan, Peru or even Sumer. They come from the great megalithic monuments of ancient Egypt.

Almost as soon as the waters of the Flood receded, the earliest signs of human civilization began to emerge in an area now known as the Levant. Encompassing parts of modern day Turkey, Mesopotamia (Iraq) and stretching into Upper and Lower Egypt, one can see a steady progression from the "Mountains of Ararat" down into the Tigris/Euphrates valley and west to the Nile delta.

Lake Van in Turkey is a completely landlocked salt water lake at 5,380 feet above sea level very near Mt. Ararat. Geologists who dispute the Great Flood and the ancient tales of an Ark coming to rest in this area will have a hard time explaining how saline-rich seawater got to such an altitude without the benefit of the Great Flood. In any event, the earliest signs of terraced agricultural civilizations are also in this area, with the megalithic temples of Göbekli Tepe following quickly.

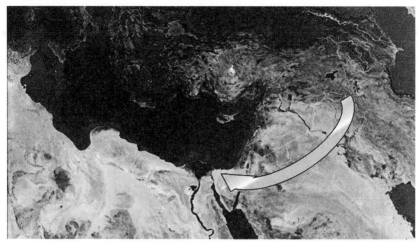

The path of rising human civilization, from the base of Mt. Ararat to the Nile delta and Upper and Lower Egypt circa 12,000 BC to 3100 BC.

From there, we see signs of the "cradle of civilization" coming down out of the higher altitudes and restarting civilization in ancient Sumer (6500-3100 BC) and the rise of what is called "Dynastic Egypt" in about 3100 BC. There is a clear "from the sky down" pattern to this, beginning in the foothills of Ararat and moving down to what is now roughly sea level in the Nile valley. Likewise there is an apparent east to west "pincer movement" of development, with each succeeding civilization being more advanced than the last as we move from the terraced agricultural sites in turkey to Göbekli Tepe, to the Mesopotamian Tigris/ Euphrates civilizations of Ubaid, Sumer, Akkad, Assyria and Babylonia and finally to the most advanced of all, Dynastic Egypt. Each of these successive empires seems to get smarter and more prolific in their writings, recordkeeping, feats of engineering and monumental architecture.

Of all this, there is but one surviving record that tells the story from beginning to end. Called *The Lost Book of Enki* by Sitchin, it consists of 12 stone tablets discovered in the library of Nippur ("Enlil's City") in south central Iraq. These tablets are claimed to be the direct testimony of Enlil's brother and rival, Enki, and if taken at face value, cover the entire record of the Anunnaki's presence here on Earth from both before the Flood and after. While the tablets have been disputed and Sitchin's account regarded as "historical fiction," I can tell you for a fact that is not true. Sitchin knew full well that the information contained in *The Lost Book of Enki* was anything but fiction. The tale it tells is alternately sad, compelling, desperate and triumphant, and it bears summarizing here because it specifically tells just how and why these ancient aliens created secret societies.

As Enki tells it, how the Anunnaki came to inhabit Nibiru is a mystery. The story confirms that Nibiru orbits the Sun in a very elongated path, spending a great deal of time far outside the commonly accepted boundaries of the solar system. When it is near the Sun, Nibiru becomes very hot, but when it is in deep space, it becomes very cold. Enki describes Nibiru as a nascent world with a very thick atmosphere, fueled and renewed by a constant stream of volcanic eruptions. This thick vapor canopy helps the planet retain heat when it is far from the sun, and deflects away harmful cosmic rays and excessive heat when it passes through the inner solar system. In this way the atmosphere protects the planet and moderates the climate, gives rise to lakes, streams, and lush vegetation, and allows "all manner of life in the waters and on the land to sprout." Eventually, by whatever means, the Anunnaki arise on Nibiru and begin to till the land, raise "four-legged creatures" for shepherding, form clans and tribes, found cities and build armies. The planet is divided into two large factions, the north and the south, and at some point the north makes war against the clans and tribes of the south. The war is long and fierce, with much destruction on both sides, and even includes great "Weapons of Terror"—the Anunnaki term for nuclear bombs.

The destruction was vast and widespread, and for "several cycles" (remember, a "year/shar/cycle" on Nibiru is 3,600 Earth years) "desolation reigned in the land [and] all life was diminished." In the face of this, a truce was declared and a peace treaty negotiated. It was agreed that a new planetary government would be formed with a single king as the absolute ruler of Nibiru. Each side presented a candidate, and after a drawing of lots the king was selected from the north: "The first king after peace was made, a warrior of the north he was, a mighty commander." In order to unify the two sides, the new king was married to a royal lady of the south, who would rule by his side as queen: "Husband and wife let them be, as one flesh to become. The royal throne into one flesh combined, an unbroken line of kingship established!" The new king quickly built a new city he named "Agade," the Anunnaki word for unity. He then set about the task of restoring order, prosperity and peace to the lands of Nibiru, and by Enki's account he was extremely successful and the people prospered.

Because there were more women than men left after the wars, it was decided that each Anunnaki, including the king, should take more than one wife but that the "First Wife" should be the legal spouse. This created a problem in succession in the event that the first son was born to one of the lesser wives (concubines). It was decided that the first male child of the "First Wife" would be the legal heir, superseding a first born male son by a secondary wife.

By the rule of the fifth king of Nibiru, Anshar, things began to deteriorate. "In the reign of Anshar, the fields diminished their yields, fruits and grains lost abundance. From circuit to circuit, nearing the Sun heat grew stronger; in the faraway abode, coolness was more biting." Anshar called Nibiru's intellectual elite, the savants, to an emergency meeting in Agade. The savants studied the problem and declared that it had happened before in Nibiru's history and was an inevitable consequence of Nibiru's exotic orbit. This gave rise to the Anunnaki's spiritual distinction between what they called *fate* and *destiny. Fate* was the ultimate consequence of conscious freedom of choice, while *destiny* was a chain of events put into motion by God. The savants further discovered that the volcanos were no longer "belching" as they had before, and the atmosphere was thinning because of it. This led to crop failures and pestilences, and the people of Nibiru suffered more and more.

Anshar gave way to his son Enshar, a young king of tremendous scientific knowledge and wisdom. In an effort to solve the growing environmental problems Nibiru faced, he began to explore the outer solar system with "celestial chariots." They discovered that the five outer planets they explored, Pluto,

Neptune, Uranus, Saturn and Jupiter, contained little that could help them with their troubles. The inner worlds of the solar system, Mercury, Venus, Earth and Mars, were beyond the reach of the Nibiruan space probes because of the asteroid belt between them and the outer planets. Called the "Hammered Bracelet" by Enki, it, for all intents and purposes, made the inner solar system off limits. "Beyond, like a boundary, the Hammered Bracelet the Sun encircled; As a guardian of the heavens' forbidden region with havoc it protected. Other children of the Sun, four in number, from intrusion the bracelet shielded."

As Nibiru's atmosphere continued to deteriorate, attempts were made to reinforce it but some felt a better strategy might be to somehow force the volcanos to increase their belching, and thus reinforce the atmosphere that way. But none of the savants could figure out a way to make that work. As the land dried up even more, Enshar gave way to his son by a concubine, and Du-Uru became the seventh ruler of Nibiru. As things grew even worse, to the point that fertility was now diminishing, Du-Uru's wife Dauru found a baby boy at the palace gate and Du-Uru adopted him as his legal heir, naming him Lahma. With the atmosphere and life on Nibiru at a critical stage, Lahma was given two choices to deal with the problem. The first solution was to use "Weapons of Terror"—nuclear bombs—to blast the volcanos and awaken their belching to rebuild the atmosphere. The other was to obtain large quantities of a rare metal—gold—and suspend it in the atmosphere to rebuild the shield. There was very little gold on Nibiru or the outer worlds, but it existed in great quantities in the Hammered Bracelet.

But Lahma was a weak and indecisive leader, and the situation became so chaotic that he sought council only from his wife. This led to great dissatisfaction in the royal court, to the point that some openly spoke of rebellion:

> In the land strife was abundant; food and water were not abundant. In the land unity was gone; accusations were abundant. In the royal court the princes were astir; at the

king accusations were directed: 'Foolishly, unreasoning, greater calamities instead of cure he brought forth!'

This finally reached a boiling point and rebellion broke out, led by a prince named Alalu:

From the olden storehouses, weapons were retrieved; of rebellion there was much speaking. A prince in the royal palace was the first to take up arms. By words of promise, the other princes he agitated; Alalu was his name. Let Lahma be the king no more! he shouted. Let decision supplant hesitation! Come, let us unnerve the king in his dwelling; let him the throne abandon! The princes to his words gave heed; [to] the gate of the palace they rushed.

Alalu and his supporters trapped Lahma in his throne room, but when they broke through Lahma went to the tower of his palace; Alalu chased him and threw him from it, killing Lahma. Alalu then went to the throne room and declared himself King: "Without right or council, a king he himself pronounced." The people were unsure of this new king, and there was much consternation in the hierarchy of Nibiru. The High Council of the planet summoned Alalu and demanded that he prove his royal lineage. After much discussion of bloodlines and consultation of records, Alalu declared that he was of the line of an unrecognized concubine of a former ruler. At the meeting to render a decision, a young prince named Anu stepped forward and declared that as a direct descendant of a much purer line, he had the better claim to the throne. The council wavered, and then brought Alalu in to inform him of the new claim. Alalu, who could have started a civil war with a single word, saw that Anu had a great deal of support in the High Council and offered a compromise; he, Alalu, would retain kingship but Anu would be made his heir and crown prince. Anu agreed and was to be wed to one of Alalu's daughters to seal the pact.

Alalu then moved swiftly to construct a fleet of "celestial

boats" to go to the Hammered Bracelet and retrieve gold. But "By the Hammered Bracelets the boats were crushed; none of them returned." Alalu then ordered that the volcanos be nuked, and they were, and there was a great deal of expectation that this would solve Nibiru's worsening climate problems. It did not. The people began to turn on Alalu.

> In the land rejoicing receded; rains were withheld, winds blew harder, The belching by volcanoes did not increase, the breach in the atmosphere did not heal. In the heavens Nibiru its circuits kept coursing; from circuit to circuit heat and cold grew harder to suffer. The people of Nibiru ceased to revere their king; instead of relief; misery he caused!

Anu saw his chance. He openly challenged Alalu to hand-to-hand combat, the winner to be declared king. After a fierce battle, Anu defeated Alalu and assumed the throne. Fearing the same fate Lahma had suffered at his own hands, Alalu went to the spaceport and stole a spacecraft armed with nuclear weapons. The destination he set?
Earth.

> Unbeknownst to others, to the place of the celestial chariots he hurriedly went. Into a missile-throwing chariot Alalu climbed; by a secret from the Beginning he chose his destination. To snow-hued Earth Alalu set his course...

Alalu knew that at the least, he'd be exiled from Nibiru and at the worst, he'd be killed as he had killed Lahma to usurp the throne, so he fled in his spaceship (called an Eagle) with but one course in mind—Earth. During his time as king he had studied the many old records of Nibiru's formation and become convinced that Earth, the former Tiamat according to the ancient records, might contain vast stores of gold, just as the asteroids had. Knowing it was his only chance to regain the throne, Alalu, full of doubts and fears, set his course for Earth and overcame many perils along the way. Encountering the fearsome "Hammered Bracelet," the asteroid belt, he blasted a safe path through it with his ship's nuclear missiles. Falling toward Earth and finding it in the throes of the last ice age, he had to decide between attempting a splashdown in the water or a landing in the temperate belt. Deciding on land, he piloted the ship as best he could to a rough crash landing on Earth, somewhere in the Tigris/Euphates valley. Alalu exited his damaged Eagle and an Anunnaki set foot on the soil of Earth for the first time.

The date is some 400,000 years ago.

Testing the air and water, Alalu now ventures out and explores the planet, finding a lush world of sweet fruits and plentiful life. It is noted in the texts that he finds the sun so bright he has to wear sunglasses. "The brightness outside was blinding; the rays of the Sun were overpowering! Into the chariot he returned, a mask for the eyes he donned."

In the waters of this new world, christened Earth, he finds what he came for—gold. Ecstatic, Alalu returns to his Eagle and sends a signal home to Nibiru: "On another world I am, the gold of salvation I have found; the fate of Nibiru is in my hands; to my conditions you must give heed!"

Upon hearing this news back on Nibiru, Anu is astounded. He is shocked not only that Alalu has found gold, but that he has even survived the arduous journey. The king and his counselors are so stunned that they actually believe he is faking the transmission, but the sages and savants confirm the signal has come from beyond the Hammered Bracelet.

Anu goes to the house of the celestial chariots and sends a signal to Alalu, expressing gratitude that he lives and reassuring him of his hallowed place:

> Anu the king, to you his greetings sends; of your well-being to learn he is pleased; For your departing from Nibiru there was no reason, enmity is not in Anu's heart; If gold for salvation you have indeed discovered, let Nibiru be saved!

Alalu is determined to press his advantage into another power grab and he quickly answers Anu with more demands:

> If your savior I am to be, your lives to save, Convene the princes to assembly, my ancestry declare supreme! Let the commanders make me their leader, bow to my command! Let the council pronounce me king, on the throne Anu to replace!

Alalu's demands create a great deal of consternation on Nibiru. They cannot depose Anu without knowing if what Alalu is saying is true, or even which of the inner planets the transmissions are coming from. One of the elder sages tells the council that Alalu is well versed in the old knowledge of the formation of the solar system, and that if he claims to have found gold, he is surely somewhere on Earth. One of Anu's sons, Enlil, who is Anu's heir even though he is the second born son by his lawful spouse, reminds the assembly that Alalu is not to be trusted. All his reign on Nibiru brought them was calamity and chaos, and he lost the throne in righteous combat with Anu. "Calamities were his handiwork, by single combat in wrestling he the throne forfeited." Enlil points out that Alalu is in no position to set conditions, and that many questions remain to be answered. Among them are the issue (1) if there is even enough gold on Earth to rebuild Nibiru's atmosphere, and (2) how will they get the gold through the Hammered Bracelet to Nibiru. Alalu is informed of these deliberations and agrees to send proof of his claims, along with an account of how he made it to Earth. Once this information is received, Alalu demands to be made king once more.

The sages and savants are appalled that Alalu used Weapons of Terror to blast his way through the asteroid belt. They speculate that this could have grave ramifications for Nibiru on its next circuit near the belt, and they also express concern that Alalu is piling up more and more bad karma by his actions. Given that Anu has been made king by both his bloodlines and his victory in single combat over Alalu, they cannot countenance removing him from the throne.

Anu's other son, Enki, a young prince of impressive wisdom and knowledge who is well respected by the sages and advisors, then makes a proposal to the council. As Anu's firstborn son by a concubine, Enki is wedded to Alalu's daughter Damkina. He states that this makes him uniquely qualified to mediate this issue:

> My father by birth is Anu the king, Alalu by marriage my father is. To bring the two clans into unison was my espousal's intention; Let me be the one in this conflict unity to bring! Let me Anu's emissary to Alalu be, let me be the one Alalu's discoveries to uphold!

Enki offers to lead an expedition to Earth to confirm Alalu's discoveries and return the gold to Nibiru. Alalu will be declared king of the Earth and if the gold can be used to rebuild the atmosphere as the savants believe, then Alalu will be given a second chance at single combat with Anu to reclaim the throne of Nibiru. Enlil, Enki's rival, objects, but Anu praises his son's idea and the proposal is transmitted to Alalu, who agrees to it.

A large celestial boat is constructed to carry "50 heroes" to Earth. A "Tablet of Destiny," a combination astrological chart and navigation path to Earth, is created. On the fateful day a huge crowd gathers to see them off.

> At the Place of the Chariots multitudes gathered, to bid farewell to the heroes and their leader (Enki) did they come. The last to embark was Enki; to the gathering he bade farewell. Before his father Anu he knelt down, the king's blessing to receive. So did Anu to his son speak a blessing, bidding him farewell. 'My son, the Firstborn: A far journey you have undertaken, for us all to be endangered; Let your success calamity from Nibiru banish; go and in safety come back!'

Enki then tenderly kisses his wife Damkina goodbye, indicating that he had a true affection for her and she was not just a political spouse. Lastly, his brother and rival Enlil locks arms with Enki and wishes him well: "Be blessed, be successful! to him he said."

The Eagle departs and it is piloted by Nibiru's best pilot Anzu, whose name means "He Who Knows the Heavens." Anzu deftly guides the ship through the worlds of the outer solar system, slingshotting the spacecraft toward the dreaded Hammered Bracelet. As the ship encounters the first asteroids—remnants of the ancient clash between Tiamat and Nibiru—Enki employs an ingenious water cannon system to blast the asteroids out of the ship's path. After a harrowing journey through the asteroid belt, the ship finally emerges in the clear and the 50 heroes see the magnificent sight of the Sun up close for the first time. However, Anzu warns that they have used too much water, and they will not make it to Earth without stopping off and getting more. Enki orders the ship to divert to Mars, which according to the Anunnaki records still has liquid water at this time (400,000 years ago). After landing by a lake and replenishing their supply of water, the ship takes off again and heads for Earth.

As they approach, Earth's beauty is so breathtaking that Anzu and Enki fall silent as they see her for the first time. After using the Moon's gravitational pull to bleed off speed, the Eagle is inserted into Earth orbit and they try to make contact with Alalu. Finally getting a homing beacon, they realize that the ship is too heavy for the marshes where Alalu has set up his camp and will come in too fast for a landing. Enki decides the only possibility is a risky splashdown in the water. Anzu deftly pilots the ship to a rough splashdown, and then the ship floats like a boat as they head toward Alalu's beacon. Traveling up the rivers, the ship is brought to rest in the marshes and the crew exits, their eyes gazing upon Alalu's camp for the first time.

At the edge of the marshes, a sight there was to behold: Gleaming in the sunrays was a chariot from Nibiru;

105

Alalu's celestial boat it was! Impatient, Enki donned his Fish's suit (spacesuit); within his chest his heart was like a drum beating. Coming out of the waters, ashore Enki stepped: On dark-hued Earth he was standing! Ahead he could see Alalu standing, with his hands with vigor waving. Alalu toward him came running; his son by marriage he powerfully embraced. 'Welcome to a different planet!' Alalu to Enki said. In silence did Alalu Enki embrace, with tears of joy his eyes were filled.

Triumphantly, they send word of their successful arrival back to Nibiru.

The Anunnaki quickly set about creating an encampment, which they call Eridu. It takes six days, which pass for them with astonishing quickness, to construct the camp and on the seventh day they rest. Alalu, king of the Earth, declares that from that day forward the seventh day will always be a day of rest on Earth.

Then they set about the task of finding gold. Unfortunately, their efforts in the region of Eridu yield far less gold than they will need to save Nibiru. Enki and Abgal, another of the 50 heroes, assemble an aircraft (sky chamber) from components of the celestial chariot and begin to travel and map the Earth, looking for rich veins of gold:

In the sky chamber with Abgal did Enki upward soar, the Earth and its secrets to learn. Over great mountains they roamed, in the valleys great rivers they saw; Steppes and forests below were stretched, thousands of leagues was their reach. Vast lands separated by oceans they recorded, with the Beam That Scans the soils they penetrated.

Meanwhile on Nibiru, Anu is becoming impatient, and he instructs Enki to make Alalu's spacecraft fit for flight and to return whatever quantity of gold they have, so that they can test it in their atmosphere. Upon inspection, Abgal and Enki discover that there are still seven nuclear missiles aboard Alalu's skiff, and they secretly remove them to the sky chamber and then hide them in a secret place far away from Eridu. Anzu, who has been tasked with repairing Alalu's spacecraft, discovers the missing weapons and confronts Enki about it. Enki tells him that the weapons are forbidden, and cannot be used here on Earth. Anzu insists that he cannot make it through the Hammered Bracelet without either nuclear missiles or water cannon, and that Enki has doomed him to fail in the efforts to transport the gold to Nibiru. Abgal then steps forward and says that *he* can pilot the ship through the asteroid belt without the nuclear weapons. Alalu agrees and orders Anzu to stay behind on Earth. A Tablet of Destiny is transmitted from Nibiru, setting the ideal time for the trip to be made, and on the anointed day, Abgal loads the gold on Alalu's ship and heads for home.

Abgal slingshots the ship around the Moon and Mars to gain speed, and then follows Enki's course to traverse the asteroid belt. Once beyond it, Abgal catches sight of the reddish glow of Nibiru and his heart rises. Guiding the ship to a safe landing in the place of the chariots, he is greeted with a hero's welcome by Anu and the populace as he delivers the gold. The gold is quickly ground to a powder and then distributed into the breach of the atmosphere using beams from some kind of crystal device. At first, the breach holds, but as Nibiru cycles through toward the inner apex of its orbit, the heat from the sun begins to dissipate the gold and the breach reappears. Alarmed, Anu commands Abgal to return to Earth with new equipment and more heroes to obtain more gold. After being greeting with great joy, the second expedition proves even less successful than the first, prompting Enki to search the Earth even more intently. In his travels, he discovers a region of South Africa, which he names the Abzu, that is rich in gold. Beaming the information back to Nibiru, there is hope in the news but doubt as to how to obtain the gold from under the ground. Enki's half-brother, Enlil, speaks against his brother, claiming that they need proof what Enki is telling them is true, and suggesting that he must go to Earth to take charge of the operation. Anu agrees and orders him to travel to Earth.

Upon his arrival, Enlil is greeted warmly by Enki, but coolly by Alalu. Taking scout ships to see for himself, Enlil confirms Enki's finding but realizes they must establish much larger settlements with sophisticated mining equipment. However, Alalu, Enlil and Anzu cannot agree on how to split up the responsibilities, so Enki suggests that they summon Anu to Earth to settle the dispute. Some months later Anu arrives to great celebration, and he tours the gold-bearing regions in Africa. Returning, he calls an assembly of all the leaders to divvy up the tasks at hand. Enki suggests that he should have command of Eridu with the intent to build a more permanent settlement which they will call the ED.IN (yes, Eden). Enlil argues that Enki knows the land better, so he should take charge of the mining operations in Africa while he, Enlil, takes charge of the ED.IN and uses the sky chambers (planes or helicopters) to bring in more "heroes" and expand the settlements. Seeing the rivalry between his two sons as a threat to the operation, Anu suggests they all draw lots to see who should rule in the ED.IN, who will rule in Africa and who should return to Nibiru as king.

The lots are then drawn and they dictate that Anu shall return to Nibiru as king, Enlil shall be Lord of the Command over Eridu and the ED.IN, and Enki shall oversee the mines in South Africa. Although Enki is distraught by these results, Anu gives him a new title of Earth's Master in the hopes that this will soften the blow. When the results are announced, Alalu steps forward and reminds Anu that he had been promised command over the Earth, and also he still claims the throne of Nibiru. A second challenge by single combat is demanded, and Anu and Alalu once again fight for control of the throne of Nibiru. As before, Anu is triumphant, but this time he commands that Alalu must never return to Nibiru. Enraged, Alalu rises up and bites off Anu's penis and swallows it whole (I know!). Anu is medically treated by Enki and lives, but Alalu is put on trial and accused by the chief prosecutor, Enlil, of "an abominable crime." Enlil demands death for Alalu, and all are in agreement except Anu. Even though he will never again sire offspring, he believes that Alalu is poisoned by the severed member he swallowed and commands that he be taken to Mars (Lahmu) where he is to live out the rest of his life in exile. When the party taking Alalu into exile arrives at Mars, Anzu states that he wishes to accompany Alalu and see to his needs until he dies. Moved by this demonstration of loyalty, Anu agrees and instructs Anzu to prepare Mars as a way station along the path to Earth. If upon the next ship's arrival on Mars they find Anzu living, he shall be made the Lord of Mars and have command of the Anunnaki base there.

Upon returning to Nibiru, Anu announces plans for way stations on the Moon and Mars, and for orbiting platforms to be established along with a fleet of new ships to carry the gold from Earth to Nibiru. Enki busies himself on Earth with the task of designing new mining tools and devices and new planes and lifting vehicles to transport gold. Enlil goes north and begins to create a spaceport for the coming supply ships and personnel from Nibiru.

A new expedition, for the first time containing women, is readied on Nibiru. It is to be commanded by Ninmah (Exalted Lady), a daughter of Anu and half-sister of Enki and Enlil. Ninmah is a master healer and medical doctor, and she sets herself to the problems of nutrition and health that the first expeditions have encountered. "In succor and healing she was greatly learned, in the treating of ailments she excelled. To the complaints from Earth she gave much attention, a healing was she preparing!"

When the expedition arrives at Mars, Ninmah directs the landing and they home in on a signal from Anzu. Finding him recently deceased, Ninmah performs a resurrection:

Beside a lakeshore Anzu they found; from his helmet the signals were beaming. Anzu himself was without motion, prostrate, he lay dead. Ninmah touched his face, to his heart she gave attention. From her pouch she took out the Pulser; upon Anzu's heart pulsing she directed. From her pouch she took out the Emitter, its crystals' life-giving emissions on his body she directed. Sixty times did Ninmah direct the Pulser, sixty times the Emitter she directed; On the sixtieth time Anzu his eyes opened, with his lips he motioned. Gently upon his face Ninmah the Water of Life poured, his lips with it wetting. Gentle into his mouth the Food of Life she placed; Then the miracle did happen: Anzu from the dead arose!

After awakening, Anzu tells them that Alalu died with great suffering and that he buried him in a cave. Going to the cave, Ninmah and her party find nothing but bones. As a sign of respect for the only king of Nibiru ever to die and be buried somewhere other than Nibiru, Ninmah commands that a proper monument to Alalu be fashioned out of the mountain under which he was buried:

Inside what of Alalu remained they found; He who once on Nibiru a king was a pile of bones was in a cave now lying! For the First time in our annals, a king not on Nibiru has died, not on Nibiru was he buried! So did Ninmah say. Let him in peace for eternity rest! she was saying. They the cave's entrance again with stones covered; The image of Alalu upon the great rock mountain with beams they carved. They showed him wearing an Eagle's helmet; his face they made uncovered. Let the image of Alalu forever gaze toward Nibiru that he ruled, Toward the Earth whose gold he discovered!

So Ninmah, Exalted Lady, in the name of her father Anu did declare.

Today, we know this monument to a dead Anunnaki king by another name. We call it the Face on Mars.

[Chap 4-5]

The Face on Mars, tomb of the Anunnaki king Alalu.

Ninmah's ship arrives on Earth to find that a dock has been built in Eridu and she steps off along with her crew to great cheers and celebrations. The women especially are appreciated by the

110

heroes already toiling on Earth. The ship is quickly unloaded:

> Enlil and Enki their sister with embraces greeted. The heroes, male and female, by the present heroes were with shouts greeted. All that the chariot had brought was quickly unloaded: Rocketships and skyships, and the tools by Enki designed, and provisions of all kinds. Of all that on Nibiru transpired, of the death and burying of Alalu, Ninmah her brothers told.

Ninmah then proceeds to use herbs and potions she has brought to help allay the afflictions of the Anunnaki on Earth:

> For the maladies relief I have brought, Ninmah to her brothers said. From her pouch a bag of seeds she brought out, seeds in the soil to be sown; a host of bushes from the seeds shall sprout, a juicy fruit they will produce. The juice an elixir shall form, for drinking by the heroes it shall be good. Their ailments it will chase away; happier their mood it shall make!

Enlil then takes Ninmah to his abode near the new spaceport and tries to make love to her, but before he can she tells him of their son back on Nibiru, a young prince she has named Ninurta. Delighted, Enlil expresses his desire to bring Ninurta to Earth if she plans to stay there with him. She agrees. Enlil then shows her his plans for the ED.IN, including a "healing city" he will create for her. "Sixty leagues thereafter a healing city shall come into being, A city of your own it shall be, Shurubak, the Haven City, I shall name it." Enlil is ecstatically happy in this moment, and declares that the five cities he has planned shall last forever. Ninmah advises him to be honorable with his father Anu and his brother Enki. "You are wise as well as beautiful!" Enlil says to her. It is clear that at that exact moment, they are very much in love.

Enki proceeds to establish the mining base in South Africa, and Enlil succeeds in creating his cities, including Shurubak, the healing city for Ninmah to oversee. She stocks it with young, beautiful female healers who tend to the needs of the male workers as well as the new "heroes" who are now arriving from Nibiru. At this time, the number of Anunnaki on Earth numbered 600, with 300 more serving Anzu at the way station on Mars. During an address to all the workers, Anu gives all the heroes special titles to honor their exemplary place in history. Those of Earth shall be known forevermore as Anunnaki, and those of Mars shall be called the Igigi:

> Your success shall for eternity be recorded, by glorious names you shall be called. Those who on Earth are shall as Anunnaki be known, 'Those Who from Heaven to Earth Came!' Those who on Lahmu (Mars) are, Igigi shall be named, 'Those Who Observe and See' they shall be! All that is required is ready: Let the gold start coming, let Nibiru be saved!

Although everything was now ready for the large-scale mining of Earth to begin, there were many familial complications to overcome. Although Ninmah was born of a concubine, like Enki, she was Anu's firstborn daughter and was bequeathed by Anu to Enki. As we have seen though, she was enamored of her other half-brother, Enlil, who was born of Anu's legal spouse, Antu. Anu's intent was for Ninmah to bear a son to Enki; Anu would make him the legal heir to Enlil and thereby heal the breach between the two half-brothers. But when Ninmah gave birth to Ninurta, a son by Enlil, the whole plan collapsed. Anu was so angered that he declared that Ninmah would never be allowed to marry and Enki was instead married to the beautiful Damkina. Their son and the new heir was named Marduk.

They might have survived all this, but after the arrival of Ninmah and her healing maidens, things got out of hand. Enlil found himself strolling through the cedar forest near his home where he came across several of Ninmah's healing nurses bathing. He became infatuated with of one of them, named Sud, and after

112

commanding that she accompany him back to his home, he drugged and raped her. Hearing of this from Sud, Ninmah demands he be tried for his crimes and Enlil is sentenced to exile. But instead of true exile, Abgal takes Enlil to the place where Enki has hidden the Weapons of Terror from Alalu's ship. Back in the ED.IN, Sud informs Ninmah that she is pregnant as a result of Enlil's rape. As a compromise, Enki offers to commute Enlil's exile sentence if he will agree to marry Sud. Enlil agrees, and returns to marry Sud and make her his official spouse. Shortly thereafter, their first son, Nannar, "The Bright One," is born, the first Anunnaki royalty to be born on Earth.

Enki then turns his attentions to Ninmah, expressing his love for her and begging her to abandon her affections for Enlil. She complies and joins him in Africa, and is soon pregnant with a daughter. Upset that she did not bear him a son, Enki again impregnates her but she has yet another daughter. Enki becomes even more desperate, but Ninmah can't take it anymore and returns to the ED.IN, never to be married, just as Anu had decreed. Despondent, Enki calls for his son by Damkina, Marduk, to join him on Earth. Enki subsequently has five more sons by Damkina and several concubines. Enlil also sends for his son by Ninmah, Ninurta, to join him on Earth. All of these sons and daughters gave rise to the various clans on Earth as they had on Nibiru, setting the stage for war.

The Mutiny of the Igigi

As the production of gold ore began to flow from Africa, it was transported to the spaceport in the ED.IN and subsequently sent to the way station on Mars. From there, spacecraft carried it to Nibiru, where the savants processed it into a fine gold powder which was suspended in the breach in Nibiru's atmosphere. Slowly, the breach in Nibiru's atmosphere was healed by this process.

In Eridu, Enki had a towering palace built for himself and Damkina. He spent many long hours there educating his sons, especially Marduk, his chief heir. Enlil meanwhile built a towering pillar, something like the all-seeing Eye of Sauron in the Lord of the Rings movies, from which Enlil could oversee everything on Earth and communicate with Nibiru and the way station on Mars. An observatory was constructed at the top, from which Enlil could oversee "All comings and goings" and from which he first marked out the 12 houses of the zodiac.

But elsewhere on Earth and Mars, there were rumblings of discontent:

> In the Edin the Anunnaki toiled, in the Abzu (Africa) the work was more backbreaking. By teams were Anunnaki sent back to Nibiru, by teams new ones were arriving. The Igigi, on Lahmu dwelling, were the loudest in complaining: When from Lahmu to Earth they descend, a rest place on Earth they were demanding.

Enki and Enlil summon Anzu from Mars to Earth, and they take him to Africa to show him the backbreaking work being endured by the Anunnaki there. Then they take him to the capital and show him the observatory, including the Tablets of Destiny which reveal all the possible approach paths from Nibiru to Earth and the movement of the stars. Their hope is that this will show Anzu that the Igigi on Mars don't have it so bad, and they also promise relief and rest for all the Igigi who make the trip to Earth to pick up gold.

But Anzu's heart has been spoiled by greed, and he draws plans to take the kingship of Earth to add to his kingship of Mars:

> A prince among the princes was Anzu, of royal seed his ancestry he counted; Evil thoughts filled his heart when to the Bond Heaven-Earth he returned. To take away the Tablets of Destinies was he scheming, Of the decrees of heaven and Earth to take control in his heart he was planning. The removal of the Enlilship in his heart he conceived, to rule Igigi and Anunnaki was his aim! Unsuspecting Enlil at the entrance to the sanctuary Anzu let be stationed; Unsuspecting Enlil left the sanctuary, for

a cooling swim he went away. With evil purpose Anzu the Tablets of Destinies seized; In a sky chamber he flew away, to the mountain of the sky chambers he swiftly went; There, in the Landing Place, rebellious Igigi for him were waiting, To declare Anzu king of Earth and Lahmu (Mars) they were preparing!

When he discovers the theft of the Tablets of Destiny, Enlil is speechless with despair. This soon turns to anger, and he enlists Enki to help him vanquish Anzu the rebel. A conference with Anu is convened, and at Ninmah's urging, Enlil's son Ninurta steps forward and declares that he shall destroy Anzu and seize the priceless Tablets of Destiny. When Ninurta is sent against him, Anzu mocks him and declares that with the Tablets of Destiny in his possession, he is invincible. After an indecisive battle, Enki fashions a special weapon for Ninurta and tells him to use his aircraft to summon a dust storm to confuse Anzu. Ninurta follows Enki's strategy, and brings down Anzu's aircraft with the special missile Enki has designed. The Tablets of Destiny are returned to the observatory and the Igigi on Earth surrender to Ninurta. Anzu is put on trial with seven judges to decide his fate: Enlil and Sud, Enki and Damkina, and Nannar (a son of Enlil), Marduk and Ninmah. Ninurta argues there is no excuse for Anzu's rebellion, and argues strongly for the death penalty. But Marduk, Enki's son and Ninurta's rival, argues that the Igigi have valid complaints, and that they deserve a place of rest on the Earth. In the end, the judges decide that Anzu shall be executed by death ray, his body to be buried beside Alalu's on Mars, and that Marduk will be sent to Mars to address the Igigi's grievances and rule in Anzu's place. But there are more issues to be addressed!

To [Mars] Marduk was sent, the spirits of the Igigi to raise, to their well-being pay attention. On Earth changes were by Enlil and Enki discussed, to avoid unrest on Earth they were considering. The stays on Earth are too prolonged, to each other they were saying. Ninmah for

115

counsel they asked; by her changing visage they were alarmed.

Realizing that life on Earth is taking a toll, including a more rapid aging process because of the quicker day/night and orbital cycles, the two brothers build a new "Metal City" in the ED.IN to process the gold faster and to send more of it back quicker. They also decide to rotate the labor crews with new recruits from Nibiru to lessen the burden on the workers. But the new workers are young and did not live in the times when Nibiru's atmosphere was

Marduk, son of Enki.

116

deteriorating, and they quickly become dismayed by the working conditions on Earth. Enki meanwhile has become fascinated by the creatures of the Earth, and creates a "House of Life" in Africa to study them, oblivious to the unrest growing around him:

> Absorbed was Enki in those studies; what was among the Anunnaki brewing he noticed not. First to notice trouble was Ninurta: A lessening of gold ores at Bad-Tibira (the Metal City) he observed. By Enlil was Ninurta to the Abzu dispatched, what was ongoing to discover. By Ennugi, the Chief Officer, to the excavations he was accompanied, Complaints of the Anunnaki he with his own ears heard; They were backbiting and lamenting, in the excavations they were grumbling; Unbearable is the toil! to Ninurta they were saying.

Frustrated, the Anunnaki workers rebel one night and surround Enlil at his villa and demand relief. Enlil proposes that the workers be replaced, but Enki has another, fateful solution: let them create a race of primitive workers who can take over for the Anunnaki toiling in the mines.

The others are stunned, for nothing like this has ever been done before:

> They summoned Ninmah, one who of healing and succor was much knowing. Enki's words to her they repeated: Whoever of such a thing heard? they her asked, The task is unheard of! she to Enki said. All beings from a seed have descended, One being from another over aeons did develop, none from nothing ever came! How right you are my sister! Enki said, smiling. A secret of the Abzu let me to you all reveal: The Being that we need, it already exists! All that we have to do is put on it the mark of our essence, Thereby a Lulu, a Primitive Worker, shall be created! So did Enki to them say. Let us hereby a decision make, a blessing to my plan give: To create a Primitive

117

Worker, by the mark of our essence to fashion him!

What Enki said to them in essence was: "We shall create man in our own image."

The Creation of Man

Enki reveals to the astonished leadership council that a being, much like the Anunnaki themselves, already exists in the Abzu (Africa). The others are astonished, because no such creature exists in the region of the ED.IN. Enki takes them to the House of Life and shows them primitive *Homo erectus*. The others are astonished, and Ninmah declares that they are not so dissimilar to the Anunnaki's predecessors, and that they are "beings" not "creatures":

> No creature like that has ever in the Edin been seen! Enlil, disbelieving, said. Aeons ago, on Nibiru, our predecessors like that might have been! Ninmah was saying. It is a Being, not a creature! Ninmah was saying. To behold it must be a thrill! To the House of Life Enki led them; in strong cages there were some of the beings.

Enki then informs them that the beings have DNA similar to the Anunnaki themselves, and that it can be modified to create an ideal worker:

> Their Fashioning Essence has tested; Akin to ours it is, like two serpents it is entwined; When their with our life essence shall be combined, our mark upon them shall be, A Primitive Worker shall be created! Our commands will he understand, Our tools he will handle, the toil in the excavations he shall perform; To the Anunnaki in the Abzu relief shall come!

Enlil is alarmed by all of this, and speaks strongly against it primarily on moral and spiritual grounds. He points out that slavery is outlawed on Nibiru, and that it is for the "Father of All Beginning"—God alone—to create life. Ninmah argues that they are not creating life in violation of God's laws, but merely modifying existing life to suit their needs.

> Enlil at the words was hesitating: The matter is one of great importance! On our planet, slavery has long ago been abolished, tools are the slaves, not other beings! A new creature, beforehand nonexisting, you wish to bring into being; Creation in the hands of the Father of All Beginning alone is held! So was Enlil in opposing saying; stern were his words.

But Enki responds with a strongly reasoned argument:

> Enki to his brother responded: Not slaves, but helpers is my plan! The Being already exists! Ninmah was saying. To give more ability is the plan! Not a new creature, but one existing more in our image made! Enki with persuasion said, With little change it can be achieved, only a drop of our essence is needed!

Enlil still doesn't like it:

> A grave matter it is, it is not to my liking! Enlil was saying. Against the rules of from planet to planet journeying it is, By the rules of to Earth coming it was forbidden. To obtain gold was our purpose, to replace the Father of All Beginning it was not!

But Ninmah points out to her half-brother that if God has given them the ability to alter life in this way, how can it be outside of his intent?

> My brother! Ninmah to Enlil was saying, With wisdom and understanding has the Father of All Beginning us

endowed, To what purpose have we so been perfected, else of it utmost use to make? With wisdom and understanding has the Creator of All our life essence filled, To whatever using of it we capable are, is it not that for which we have been destined?

Enlil further questions whether this is by destiny, God's will, that they do this, or whether it is a fateful (free will) choice that may come back to haunt them. It is finally agreed that the matter will be presented to Anu, and he shall make the final judgment. Anu decides that the being will be created, but in the meantime the Anunnaki must return to the mines because Nibiru is still desperate for gold.

Ninmah and Enki then head for the House of Life, where in a laboratory "a clean place with brightness shining" they begin work. Their first attempts are not successful, as they take a female egg and impregnate it with male Anunnaki DNA. The creature is born by caesarian section, but it does not have the qualities they desire. A second being is fashioned, and although he looked more like an Anunnaki, he was deaf and blind. Other experiments followed, with numerous problems:

Again and again Ninmah rearranged the admixtures, of the ME formulas (Anunnaki male) she took bits and pieces; One Being had paralyzed feet, another his semen was dripping, One had trembling hands, a malfunctioning liver had another; One had hands too short to reach the mouth, one had lungs for breathing unsuited.

Enki suggests that perhaps the vessel being used for the mixing, an Anunnaki creation, is the problem, and he has Ninmah create a mixing chamber from Earthen materials. The next being is nearly perfect, but it does not possess the power of speech. Enki then makes one more radical suggestion: perhaps for proper gestation the worker being needs to be carried in an Anunnaki womb.

Ninmah is shocked by Enki's words, but recognizes the truth of them: "Wise are your words, my brother! Ninmah at long last was saying. Perchance the right admixture in the wrong womb was inserted." Now the problem was into which of the Anunnaki females shall the fertilized ovum be inserted? After some discussion, Enki suggests his wife Damkina, but Ninmah offers herself. After all, since she is the one who created the admixture, she reasons that she should be the one to bear the risk and reward:

> The admixtures by me were made, reward and endangerment should be mine! I shall be the one the Anunnaki womb to provide, for good or evil fate to face! Enki bowed his head, gently he embraced her. So be it! to her he said.

The gestation period was longer than nine Earth months but shorter than nine Nibiruan months. Finally, Ninmah gave birth to a perfect, beautiful baby boy! Enki, elated, handed her the baby to suckle and she held it triumphantly high above her head:

> He handed the newborn to Ninmah; she held him up in her hands. 'My hands have made it!' victoriously she shouted.

Enki insists that the baby be given a name: "Enki at his sister was gazing; a mother and son, not Ninmah and a Being, he was seeing. A name will you give him? Enki inquired. A Being he is, not a creature!" The baby, which they name the Adamu ("One Who Like Earth's Clay Is") is perfect in every way except for one surprise: his manhood is covered by a foreskin, unlike the penis of the Anunnaki male. This will forever mark the difference between man and the gods. In honor of her accomplishment, Enki grants Ninmah the title of "Lady of Life" and declares that the Adamu shall be spared from toil and forever remain in paradise in the ED.IN.

The time is 200,000 years ago.

Excited by their success, Enki and Ninmah ask for volunteers among the young nurses to bear more children, but after seven successful births, they realize the process will be too slow and too demanding on the Anunnaki females. They decide to fashion a female companion for the Adamu, and to do so they take DNA from Enki's rib and mix it with DNA from Damkina's rib. The baby is born blonde and beautiful, like Damkina, and they name her Ti-Amat ("The Mother of Life") after the planet that shattered the primordial Earth and mixed with it to create the modern-day Earth. Adamu and Ti-Amat are given a sanctuary in the ED.IN in which they can roam freely, and after they mature Ti-Amat creates clothing made of leaves to cover their genitals and distinguish them from the beasts. Seven females are then conceived to mate with the seven males, and after time passes they are put together and mating occurs, but no pregnancies. Confused by this, Enki realizes that they must have made a mistake in the gene splicing process, and he has Ninmah examine the male and female DNA. The "twenty-two branches on a Tree of Life" are separated, and they realize that the ability to procreate is missing. Seeing this, Ninmah adds two more chromosomes to the human Tree of Life, and the DNA of Adamu and Ti-Amat is altered. From this point forward, human DNA will have 23 chromosomes on each DNA branch, 46 chromosomes total.

One day Enlil comes across Adamu and Ti-Amat in the ED.IN and notices their loin cloths. Summoning Enki, he hears the entire story of their creation, and is infuriated. It was bad enough, he says, that they were given intelligence, and now they have the ability to procreate! Realizing that with their faster birth rate and long life, they may soon surpass the Anunnaki in numbers, Enlil once again argues against the plan; Ninmah's words telling him that they have not been granted long life cannot calm him. Enki points out that they still face mutiny among the miners unless they create the primitive workers, so Enlil's hands are tied. Still furious, Enlil, the Lord of the Earth, declares that Adamu and Ti-Amat are mere workers, and insists they be sent to Africa with the other workers, and banished from the ED.IN forever.

And so mankind is expelled from paradise, the Garden of ED.IN, for the sin of procreation.

Taking Adamu and Ti-Amat to Africa, Enki sets up a living place for them and leaves them to their own devices. Soon there is excitement all around as Ti-Amat is seen joyfully pregnant: "With child Ti-Amat was frolicking." Ti-Amat gives birth to twins, a male and female, and she and Adamu soon have other children who also mate, and in the course of one Anunnaki *shar*, the humans proliferate and begin to take over the work in the mines, which is much easier on them than it is on the Anunnaki.

At the same time, Anunnaki couples on Earth also have children, including the sons of Enlil and Enki. To their amazement, the Anunnaki children still have the long life span of their home world, but reach maturity much faster due the acceleration of life on Earth. The gold is flowing to Nibiru and the atmosphere is healing, restoring life there to something approaching normalcy.

On Earth, the Anunnaki children are given various tasks and fiefdoms, but the climate begins to change as Earth emerges from the last ice age. With growing concern, Enki sets up an observatory at the southern tip of Africa to monitor changes in Antarctica. Consulting with Enlil, he is informed that the Tablets of Destiny indicate a period of turmoil in the skies, and given "as above so below," a similar period of upheaval on Earth can be expected.

Nibiru makes an unusually close approach to the inner solar system, disrupting the asteroid belt and bombarding the worlds of the inner solar system. Mars and the Moon take massive impacts, minimizing the effects on Earth. Still, Earth takes a pounding as well, and many of the cities of the ED.IN are damaged beyond repair and the climate is disrupted with volcanic eruptions and earthquakes. Mars' atmosphere is badly damaged, and with conditions there deteriorating, Marduk requests he be permitted to return to Earth. Enki devises a plan to build a spaceport adjacent to the Metal City, and to send the gold directly to Nibiru from Earth in celestial chariots. Enlil approves of the plan but given Earth's gravity, there are likely to be problems getting significant payloads off the ground. Enki and Marduk journey to the Moon to

123

investigate it as a possible waypoint, but they find it inhospitable and unsuitable. Still, they stay there for several months to enjoy its desolate beauty and make astronomical observations. Enki, like Enlil, then marks out the 12 houses of the zodiac and gives them names. Understanding the concept of Celestial Time and surrounded by this epic beauty, Marduk laments their familial lot, forever considered inferior to Enlil's station, despite the fact that Enki has bested him in everything, as he feels he has bested Ninurta. Shaken, Enki embraces his son and declares that the supremacy which to him was denied, Marduk shall have:

> In silence did Enki embrace his son, on the desolate Moon to him a promise made: Of that of which I have been deprived your future lot shall be! Your celestial time will come, a station mine adjoining yours shall be!

Enlil is concerned with Enki's long absence, and he calls to Anu to consult and warn him of what he believes is Enki's scheming. Upon Enki's return to Earth, it is decided to phase out Mars as a way station and to build a new launch facility as had been proposed. Enki and Enlil both suggest their sons be given command of the new spaceport, but Anu thinks it is time to turn over these tasks to a new generation, and gives command of the new spaceport, named Sippar ("Bird City"), to Enlil's grandson Utu. Once the spaceport is finished, Anu visits Earth and declared that very soon enough gold will have been mined, and then all of the Anunnaki can return to their home world.

In the ED.IN, the work becomes as overwhelming as it has been eased in Africa. Without permission, Ninurta leads an armed expedition to Africa and captures and brings back many humans to be trained as workers in the ED.IN. This infuriates Enlil, but he does nothing about it. On a trip to study the humans living in the ED.IN, Enki encounters two beautiful young human girls and impregnates them. One gives birth to a girl, one to a boy. This is the first recorded mating of an Anunnaki male and a human female, something that was never planned or expected. Enki takes the children into his house and pretends they were found in reed baskets outside his palace. Damkina raises the children as her own, and they display a combination of human and Anunnaki traits. Adapa, the boy, is incredibly intelligent and becomes the first truly civilized man. Titi, the girl, is very skilled in crafts and art and is highly favored by Damkina. Adapa and Titi eventually mate, and Titi gives birth to twin sons.

Their names are Ka-in and Abael.

Adapa and Titi are the first truly modern humans, Homo sapiens sapiens. Their offspring, Ka-in and Abael and their subsequent brothers and sisters, form the first true hybrid line descended from a union of modern man and the Anunnaki. Adapa's intelligence so impresses the Anunnaki that Anu calls for him to be brought to Nibiru. This may be the source of the story of Enoch in the Old Testament, in which Enoch is taken to heaven, appointed guardian of all the celestial treasures, chief of the archangels, and the immediate attendant on God's throne.

Enki is distressed by this command from Anu, as is Enlil. Enlil laments that Adapa will learn the secrets of long life on Nibiru and become an equal to the Anunnaki:

> That by a Primitive Worker fashioning, like us the being would become, With knowledge, endowed, between Heaven and Earth will travel! On Nibiru the waters of long life he will drink, the food of long life eat, Like one of us Anunnaki shall the one of Earth become!

Enki solves this problem by lying to Adapa and telling him that the Bread of Life and Elixir of Life will kill him, and that he must refuse them if offered. He then selects two of his single sons to accompany Adapa to Nibiru in the hopes that they might find suitable wives there.

Once on Nibiru, the savants and King Anu are impressed by Adapa's depth of knowledge and intelligence, but are confused when he refuses to eat their bread or drink their elixirs. One of Enki's sons hands Anu a message crystal from Enki, and Anu retires to view it privately. In the recorded message, Enki reveals that Adapa is the result of a union between him and a human female, and suggests that if they allow Adapa to eat and drink as they do, then he will become as long lived as the Anunnaki and be essentially an equal. Anu is amused that his son's predilection for female companionship has not waned, but agrees and orders Adapa sent home to Earth. Upon Adapa's return, Enki explains to Enlil that Adapa is the result of procreation between him and a human female, and suggests that this is a good thing since it will enable them to create new humans at an even faster pace than before. Enlil, however is outraged, feeling that this is yet another affront to God which will only end badly:

> Enki his cohabitation with the Earthling females also related; 'No rules have I broken, our satiation I have ensured!' So Enki to them said. 'No rules did you break, the fates of Anunnaki and Earthlings by a rash deed you determined!' So did Enlil in anger say. 'Now the lot is cast, destiny by fate is overtaken!' With fury was Enlil seized, with anger he turned and left them standing.

Once again we see that Enlil is deeply concerned that their freewill choices (fate) will overwhelm their intended path (destiny).

Everyone is impressed by Adapa's intelligence and adaptability, and Enlil takes one of his sons, Ka-in, to be raised by his own son Ninurta, while Enki takes the other boy, Abael, to be raised by his son Marduk. Ka-in is trained as a farmer, and Abael as a shepherd. New grains and four-legged creatures (sheep) from Nibiru are imported, and the two sons of Adapa set about raising them and producing wool and meat. Ka-in is offended that Abael gets more of the credit for what has been produced, and the two brothers begin to feud. The next summer, a drought drives Abael to graze his flock in Ka-in's lands, and he is soon angrily confronted by his brother. They fight, and Ka-in kills Abael by striking him in the head with a stone over and over. Upon hearing the news, Enki

126

is enraged and after showing Adapa and Titi how to bury their son in the Anunnaki custom, Ka-in is called before a tribunal to be judged. Marduk demands Ka-in be executed, but Enki councils him "Let us not agony with agony compound!" Marduk is moved when he discovers that Abael is his half-brother, and it is agreed that instead of death, Ka-in shall be banished from the ED.IN.

Adapa grows old and dies, and even though he lived far longer than any human does today, it was still far fewer years than an Anunnaki. Climate changes begin to take a toll as Earth emerges from the last ice age, and conditions deteriorate even further on Mars, leading to unrest among the remaining Igigi. Marduk tells his father that he wishes to marry, which pleases Enki at first until he learns that Marduk wishes to espouse a human female:

> With a puzzled look, Enki was speechless; then uncontrolled words he shouted: A prince of Nibiru, a Firstborn to succession entitled, an Earthling will espouse?

Enki is calmed by Damkina, but he points out to Marduk that he will never rule on Nibiru if he takes a human wife:

> To this Marduk with a bitter laughter responded: My rights on Nibiru are nonexistent, Even on Earth my rights as Firstborn have been trampled. This indeed is my decision: From prince a king on Earth become, the master of this planet!

Recognizing that Marduk has a better chance of ruling on Earth than he ever does on Nibiru, Enki gives his consent to the union. Enlil is outraged when he hears of the marriage, and he calls to Anu to overturn it. Finding no legal means to refuse the marriage, Anu decrees that Marduk can never return to Nibiru as a prince.

The wedding takes place in Eridu, and humans as well as Anunnaki and Igigi from Mars are invited as guests. Enlil sees this as the final elevation of man to a place of equality with the

Anunnaki, and he privately fumes, but takes no action. Inspired by the Anunnaki's habit of taking human women for themselves, the Igigi see that the daughters of men are fair, and plot to take them as wives for themselves. This is identical in many ways to the story of The Watchers we learned of earlier. Like The Watchers, the rebellious Igigi numbered 200. "In a great number did the Igigi from Lahmu to Earth come, Only one third of them on Lahmu stayed, to Earth came two hundred." Frustrated with toil and loneliness, they hatch a plot to obtain Daughters of Men as wives.

What to Marduk permitted is from us too should not be deprived!' to each other they said. 'Enough of suffering and loneliness, of not offspring ever having!' was their slogan. During their comings and goings between Lahmu and Earth, the daughters of the Earthlings, the Adapite Females as them they called, they saw and after them they lusted; and to each other the plotters said: 'Come, let us choose wives from among the Adapite Females, and children beget!

The Igigi abduct human females for themselves, and Marduk appreciates their plight and argues for their demands to be met. Enki agrees, but Enlil is more furious with what he views as each new abomination against the fates and Anunnaki law.

Only Enlil was enraged without pacification: 'One evil deed by another has been followed, fornication from Enki and Marduk the Igigi have adopted, Our pride and sacred mission to the winds have been abandoned, By our own hands this planet with Earthling multitudes shall be overrun!'

Realizing they cannot return to a deteriorating Mars, the Igigi are allowed to take their spouses to two cities in Egypt that have been built my Enlil's sons.

Enlil pretends to be pacified, but in his heart he is coming to hate the humans: "In his heart things against Marduk and his Earthlings was Enlil plotting." Enlil begins to notice that, counting the humans under his command, Enki is developing quite a potential army and laments that the Earth will soon be overrun with humans. "In his eyes the Anunnaki mission to Earth had become perverted." He sends his son Ninurta to a land "over the sea" (the Americas) to find the offspring of Ka-in in exile, and establish a base there.

A series of droughts, famines and calamities dominate the next few cycles. Earth is increasingly shaken by earthquakes and bad weather, and the sun is overactive with sunspots and solar flares. Even on Nibiru, the effects are felt, and it is discovered that on its next cycle, Nibiru will disrupt the Earth to the point that a huge chunk of Antarctic ice may shear off and cause a gigantic tidal wave that would encircle the Earth. An emissary, Galzu, is sent to Earth by Anu and he reveals to Enki, Enlil and Ninmah that the longer the Anunnaki have stayed on Earth, the shorter their lives on Nibiru have lasted. He tells them that if they return to Nibiru they will surely grow sick and die quickly. They decide to ride out the coming deluge in orbiting spacecraft, and then return to Earth afterwards.

Enlil calls a council of all the Anunnaki and Igigi on Earth, and reveals to them the coming calamity. He tells all who have taken human wives that they may not take their wives to Nibiru, and that if they choose to stay they should either have places on the orbiting space platforms or journey to the highest mountaintops with their wives and hope to survive. Ninmah gives a stirring speech in which she declares "My lifework is here! The Earthlings, my created, I shall not abandon!" Unmoved, Enlil decrees that the humans must be left to die in the deluge for their perceived sins: "'Let the Earthlings for the abominations perish;' so did Enlil proclaim." Enki protests: "'A wonderous Being by us was created, by us saved it must be!', Enki to Enlil shouted." But Enlil angrily retorts to his brother that the humans must die:

From the very beginning, at every turn, the decisions

by you modified were! To Primitive Workers procreating you gave, to them Knowing you endowed! The powers of the Creator of All into your hands you have taken, Thereafter even that by abominations you fouled. With fornication Adapa you conceived, Understanding to his line you gave! His offspring to the heavens you have taken, our Wisdom with them you shared! Every rule you have broken, decisions and command you ignored, Because of you by a Civilized Earthling brother a brother murdered, Because of Marduk your son the Igigi like him with Earthlings intermarried. Who is lordly from Nibiru, to whom the Earth alone belongs, to no one is no longer known! Enough! Enough! to all that I say. The abominations cannot continue! Now that a calamity by a destiny unknown has been ordained, let what must happen, happen! So did Enlil angrily proclaim.

So here we have the root of the Genesis story of the Flood. Instead of a single, all-knowing all-seeing God that is of two minds, as he is portrayed in the Hebrew bible, we see that in fact the judgment of man is made by Enlil, an angry extraterrestrial "god" with a small "G." It is not man's wickedness that dooms him, but the misbehavior of the Anunnaki "gods" that incur Enlil's wrath. Next Enlil demands that all of the Anunnaki present take an oath to uphold his decision to let the humans perish in the Flood, and they all accede to this demand—including Enki.

Preparing to flee the Earth, Enki and Enlil agree to bury a time capsule in the ED.IN to record all that has happened during their time on Earth. Enki then goes to Ninmah, and laments that in his hatred for humanity, Enlil has lost sight of all the other living creatures of the Earth that were placed there by God (the Father of all Creation) and the Anunnaki. Secretly, he plots with Ninmah to preserve the seeds (DNA) "two by two" of all life on Earth in a special celestial chariot in orbit, the better to recreate life on Earth after the Flood.

Asleep in his chambers, Enki has a dream/vision of another

visit from the white-haired emissary Galzu. Galzu tells him that the Earthlings are destined to inherit the Earth from the Anunnaki, and that—without breaking his vow of silence—Enki must find a way to warn his son Ziusudra (Noah) of the coming Flood and how to save a portion of humanity and all the creatures of the Earth. Convinced that he has received a direct message from God, The Creator of All, Enki awakens to find a diagram of a submersible boat next to his bed. In order not to break his oath, Enki talks to a reed wall within earshot of Ziusudra, and indirectly tells him all about the Flood and the Ark he must construct. Ziusudra proceeds to construct the boat without telling the local populace what it is for, and on the anointed day Enki sends his personal navigator, Ninagal to pilot the submarine. He brings the fertilized eggs of all life on Earth with him, to rebuild the planet after the Flood.

As predicted, a huge chunk of the Antarctic ice sheet breaks away, causing a tidal wave of immense proportions that sweeps the planet. The orbiting Anunnaki are at once fascinated and terrified by the sight of it, and they watch helplessly as a storm rises and drenches the planet for 40 days and 40 nights. Ninmah and Innana weep at the sight of it all. Ninagal guides the Ark toward the twin peaks of Arrata, and Ziusudra sends out the birds as in the Biblical version. Ziusudra sets up an altar and makes a sacrifice to Enki. Enki and Enlil descend to Earth and discover Ziusudra and the Ark have survived. Furious, Enlil attacks Enki, but when Enki tells him of the dream-vision, he concedes that it must be by destiny's will that mankind has survived.

The Anunnaki descend to Earth and take stock of the situation, which is dire. Marduk and the Igigi return from Mars and inform Enki and Enlil that the planet has been devastated by Nibiru's passing and that much of the atmosphere has been lost and the waters have dried up. A call to Nibiru finds that it too was damaged by the close encounter, and the atmosphere is dwindling again and more gold is needed to replenish it. They journey to the Americas and discover that the floods have carved open the lands of North America and there are incredible amounts of gold just lying around waiting to be harvested and taken to Nibiru.

The spaceport and other facilities are quickly rebuilt, and new dominions established. Marduk is angered that he is left out of these positions of power, and to avoid a crisis or civil war, Ninmah negotiates a peace in which the spaceport is declared a neutral zone and Marduk is given the "dark lands" to oversee—Egypt.

Once in Egypt, Marduk's sons begin to feud. Asar (Osiris) and Satu (Set) find themselves attracted to two daughters of the Iggigi commander Shamgaz. Soon Osiris is married to Asta (Isis) and Set to Nebat (Nephthys). Shamgaz, concerned about the Igigis' place in the rebuilt lands of Earth, uses Nephthys to convince Set that Osiris will inherit everything from Marduk, and he and the Igigi will be left with nothing. They scheme to murder Osiris at a banquet called in his honor by poisoning his wine and shutting him in a coffin. When Isis learns of his murder at the hands of Set, she calls to Marduk for revenge and begs him to conceive an heir with her. Rebuffed, she finds the body of Osiris and uses the Anunnaki resurrection technology to extract semen from him and conceive a child that will be the rightful heir to the lands of Egypt. Although Set assumes the throne and tries to kill her, Isis gives birth to a son she names "Horon" (Horus). She raises the child to take revenge upon Set.

Meanwhile, the Igigi have begun to spread across the Middle East and are in a position to threaten the House of the Celestial Chariots itself. In secret, a new spaceport is built to ensure gold shipments to Nibiru. Horus is given the knowledge of a secret metal called "iron" by Gibil, a metal master from southern Egypt. With new special weapons, Horus defeats Set in an aerial battle lasting over two days. Horus captures Set, who was blinded in the attack, and Horus has him castrated before he is sentenced to exile with the Igigi. Placed upon the throne of Egypt, Horus is triumphant, but Marduk, having lost both his sons, is despondent and retreats from public life.

Into the void left by Marduk steps Dumuzi, Enki's youngest son and Marduk's younger brother. But he falls madly, passionately in love with Inanna, Enlil's granddaughter by Nannar:

132

The Lovers, Inanna and Dumuzi.

A love that knows no bounds engulfed them, a passion their hearts inflamed. Many of the love songs that for a long time thereafter were sung, Inanna and Dumuzi were the first to sing them, by song their love they recounted.

With Osiris gone, Enki transfers his affections to Dumuzi, and Inanna is much loved by her grandfather Enlil. Inanna is, by all accounts, a girl of exceptional beauty and accomplishment and Ninmah sees in her a chance to heal the rift between the clans of Enki and Enlil. Inanna, much like Cleopatra far later, sees that she

133

and Dumuzi have the charisma and princely power to unite the feuding nations of the world and bring a new dawn of peace and prosperity to the Earth under their rule.

But it is not to be. From afar, Marduk sees the rise of the young couple as a threat to him and when he hears of Inanna's ambitions, he hatches a plot to kidnap and murder Dumuzi. Warned of the move against him, Dumuzi escapes to the mountains, but is killed in a fall as he is being chased by Marduk's minions. Inanna demands Marduk's execution from Enki, but he argues that Marduk had no direct hand in Dumuzi's death, and refuses to take action. Inanna then goes to her grandfather, Enlil, and a council of war is decreed. Enlil demands Marduk's head, but Enki refuses and reiterates that he believes by the stars that Marduk is destined to rule on Earth. Inanna then attacks Marduk's stronghold in an aircraft, and open warfare of "a ferocity [previously] unknown" breaks out between the clans. Unlike the previous war between the human born Horus and Set, this war involves not only human soldiers, but also Anunnaki and Igigi.

Inanna chases Marduk from his domains and he takes refuge inside the Great Pyramid. Ninurta, fighting for Inanna's side, uses chemical weapons on the armies of Marduk and turns the rivers (the Nile) to blood. Horus then joins the battle against the Enlilites, but is blinded in one eye by a beam weapon. Trapped in the indestructible Great Pyramid, Marduk refuses to surrender so Ninurta and Inanna entomb him inside, leaving him to die. Ninmah negotiates a peace treaty wherein Marduk shall be allowed to live as long as he gives up his rulerships on Earth. Upon extraction from the Great Pyramid, Marduk is enraged: "'I would rather die than my birthright forfeit!' he shouted." But his wife convinces him that living in exile is preferable to dying, and he leaves for America. Ninurta enters the Great Pyramid and takes Marduk's cache of crystals which he has used for weapons, and then he destroys the crystal capstone of the pyramid to (he hopes) end Marduk's reign of power on Earth forever. The lands of the Middle East are then divided amongst the remaining princes and princesses, but the role of the ever-proliferating man has yet to be decided. Anu decides to make one more visit to Earth to sort things out.

Upon his arrival, Anu is impressed with the progress made in rebuilding the ED.IN and other facilities since the Deluge. Enki recounts the visit of Galzu and the mysterious visions he had, but Anu is confused: he tells Enki he never sent such an emissary. Stunned, Enki and Enlil tell Anu that if it wasn't for Galzu's instructions—which they assumed came from Anu himself—the humans and the creatures of the Earth would never have been saved from the Deluge! Anu further informs them that the idea that they would die if they returned to Nibiru is false; various treatments and elixirs cured the rapid aging and returned youth to those that had been on Earth for a long time. Ninmah sees that if Galzu was not an emissary of Anu, then he must be one of the Creator of All (God), and that they must heed his will. Anu agrees that it is now apparent that Earth was meant for man to inherit, not the Anunnaki:

> The will of the Creator of All is clear to see: On Earth and for Earthlings, only emissaries we are. The Earth to the Earthlings belongs, to preserve and advance them we were intended!

Based on this, it is decided that three civilized regions will created for Man, each containing a small enclave for the Anunnaki, who shall be considered gods. The Anunnaki will establish a fourth region for themselves alone in the "peninsula of the Place of the Chariots." Mankind will be ruled as the Anunnaki are, by kingship, and suitable humans will be selected to rule over the human lands as kings. The Anunnaki will also establish priesthoods, through which the secrets of science and civilization will be conveyed to the common man by Anunnaki guides.

This is the moment of the creation of the secret societies, approximately 6,000 years after the Flood.

Enlil is given lordship over the lands in the ED.IN, Enki is given the Land of the Two Narrows (Sumer, between the Tigris and Euphrates rivers), and Inanna the more distant Indus Valley.

Anu blames himself for Marduk's rebellion and journeys to

135

America where he learns that Marduk's wife has passed. He sees the cities Marduk has built and the abundant gold that is being extracted from the continents of the Americas. Anu embraces Marduk and grants him a pardon, and then leaves with one final set of instructions:

> Whatever Destiny for the Earth and the Earthlings intended, let it so be! If Man, not Anunnaki, to inherit the Earth is destined, let us destiny help. Give Mankind knowledge, up to a measure secrets of heaven and Earth them teach, Laws of justice and righteousness teach them, then depart and leave! So did Anu to his children fatherly instructions give.

Here, we catch a glimpse into the spiritual beliefs of Nibiru and see that even Anu recognizes the difference between that which is preordained by God (destiny) versus that which is the result of free will (fate). He is acknowledging in this last passage that the Anunnaki must accept the will of God and not tempt fate. This will be accomplished by giving man all that he needs to flourish and grow, including knowledge of the spirit, arts and science.

It should have ended there. But the rebellious Marduk is unhappy with the division of lands when he learns of it, and believes he should also get a piece of the action. He is especially furious that a second spaceport has been constructed in Enlil controlled lands, giving him power over who comes and goes on Earth. Ninmah is given the secret formulas for the genetic design of humans, which she keeps in a well-guarded temple.

Soon, human cities are established within the three designated regions, and kings to rule them are created by Enki using the secret genetic formulas. Impatient with the lack of progress in her region, Inanna journeys to Sumer and seduces Enki into letting her see the sacred formulas. Stealing 94 of them from Enki, she slips away while he sleeps and plans to build her own empire in the Indus Valley.

When Marduk hears of this, he becomes enraged and

demands a city of his own. Enlil ignores him so Marduk gathers his human followers and establishes a base at Babel, where he has the workers begin construction of a spaceport featuring a massive launch tower. Threatened by this development, the Enlil faction decides that if Marduk's spaceport is completed, giving humans access to space travel, they could one day stand equal to the Anunnaki. After one last entreaty to Marduk, which is rebuffed, Enlil and his followers attack the tower and the base from the air, completely obliterating it. Enlil then decides to shatter the unity of mankind by teaching them different languages:

> To scatter abroad the leader and his followers Enlil thereupon decided, Henceforth their counsels to confuse, their unity to shatter, Enlil decreed: 'Until now all the Earthlings one language had, in a single tongue they speak. Henceforth their language I shall confound, that they each other's speech will not understand!'

Thwarted in his plans, Marduk then goes to Sumer, where he expects to be named the leader of the second region. But he arrives to find his brother Ningishzidda in charge, and many of his decrees and previous judgments overturned. The brothers quarrel bitterly for over 350 Earth years, and to keep war from breaking out, Enki convinces Ningishzidda to go to the Americas and establish a new domain there. He does so, and becomes the Mayan/Aztec god Quetzalcoatl/Kukulkan, and he establishes a new count of days which eventually becomes the Mayan calendar. *"But in the new domain, where Ningishzidda the Winged Serpent was called, a new count of its own began."*

Having successfully bullied his brother out of Sumer, Marduk establishes his kingship by decreeing himself and his father Enki gods and by erasing the memory of Ningishzidda. He even has his son Osiris' face carved onto the great Sphinx in Egypt:

> Marduk as Ra, the Bright One, was worshiped; Enki as Ptah, the Developer, was venerated. Ningishzidda as

137

Tehuti, the Divine Measurer, was recalled; To erase his memory Ra on the Stone Lion his image with that of his son Asar replaced.

As Ra, Marduk then unites Upper and Lower Egypt into a single nation state. Marduk then builds a capital at Alexandria, and constructs a giant obelisk there to represent a rocket, one of the "celestial chariots" of the gods. Marduk then asks his father to be taught all the secrets of the Anunnaki, and Enki grants him each wish except for one—the knowledge of physical resurrection.

With Marduk's second region flourishing, they then turned their attention to Inanna and the Indus valley. Enki creates a new language and writing script for the region, and two cities were quickly built and inhabited. But Inanna is not as disciplined as Marduk, and her attempts to establish a viable civilization in the third region fail because of her neglect:

In the Third Region, Civilized Mankind did not fully blossom; What to Inanna was entrusted she neglected, other domains, not to her granted, in her heart she coveted.

Still mourning the loss of her beloved Dumuzi, Inanna retains her resentment for Marduk, and she establishes "a House for Nighttime Pleasure." But as she takes one human lover after another, she wakes to find each of them dead the next morning. Then one day a messenger named Banda, who was long thought dead, shows up and she believes he is the reincarnation of Dumuzi. When she takes him to her bed, she wakes to find him very much alive; the humans around her become convinced that the Anunnaki gods hold the power to resurrect the dead. Seeing that Inanna still held ideas of expanding her influence, Marduk began to study her cults and was impressed by the idea of using resurrection as a means of control. He creates a religion that promises everlasting life in the form of a resurrection on Nibiru, as a being that will live forever. He makes his son Asar/Osiris the symbolic center of this resurrection cult.

Now strengthened, Marduk's forces begin to make incursions into his brothers; neighboring lands, testing their resolve. Obsessed with ruling over all four domains, Marduk becomes even more aggressive, while in the first region, under Enlil's control, humans are living in peace and prosperity:

> In the First Region, civilization from Ki-Engi to other neighboring lands spread, In Cities of Man local rulers as Righteous Shepherds were designated; Artisans and farmers, shepherds and weavers their products far and wide exchanged, Laws of justice were decreed, contracts of trade, of espousal and divorce were honored. In schools the young ones studied, scribes hymns and proverbs and wisdom recorded. Abundance and happiness were in the lands.

But there is trouble on the horizon as Marduk continues his expansion and the restless Inanna roams from land to land, seeking but not finding an inner peace. Her father is venerated as Nannar-Sin, "Lord of the Oracles," and a city dedicated to his worship is established at Ur in what is now southern Iraq. Marduk then declares himself a god possessed of all the powers of his forebears and contemporaries, placing himself above them in his people's minds.

The other Anunnaki and demigods (half-breed offspring of Anunnaki and humans) are alarmed at the increasing fanaticism of Marduk's followers, and they confront him about his proclamations. In response, Marduk declares that by the stars, the age of his uncle Enlil (the Bull) is over and that it is now his age, the Age of the Ram, which must be recognized. Despite being shown that it was still the Age of the Bull, Marduk does not relent and continues to stir the people to his cause. Observing this from a distance, Enki laments that there are now so many humans that the tables have turned, and the once mighty Anunnaki "gods" have become dependent on the humans for their place, power and standing, not to mention their survival.

Facing the threat from Marduk and the second region, the first region decides to unite its separate city-states under a single king, and chooses Inanna to complete the task of finding the right leader. Inanna selects a military leader named Sharru-kin as the new king, and Enlil places him on the throne without hesitation. Feeling the need to move quickly, Sharru-kin sends troops to the location where Marduk had attempted to build the Tower of Babel. Considering this sacred ground, Marduk swiftly takes the area back and names it the Babili, "The Gateway of the Gods." Inanna counterattacks with beam weapons from the crystals she stole from Marduk, and many of his followers are killed:

> Babili, the Gateway of the Gods, In the heart of the Edin, in the midst of the First Region, Marduk himself established! Inanna's fury no boundary knew; with her weapons on Marduk's followers death she inflicted. The blood of people, as never before on Earth, like rivers flowed.

Marduk's brother Nergal comes to him and convinces him to wait until the signs in the heavens are correct, and that he will then peacefully establish his rulership on Earth. Marduk retreats—for the moment.

Enlil then has a vision of Galzu informing him that the age of the Bull will soon pass to the Ram, saying:

> The righteous time of benevolence and peace by evildoing and bloodshed will be followed. In three celestial portions the Ram of Marduk the Bull of Enlil will replace, One who himself as Supreme God has declared supremacy on Earth will seize. A calamity as has never before occurred, by Fate decreed, will happen!

Enlil realizes that in three periods of 72 years each (the time it takes Earth to move one degree along the 25,952-year precessionary arc) the Age of the Ram, and of Marduk, shall commence on Earth. He watches with dismay as Marduk travels the Earth, gathering more and more converts and gaining in military power. The ensuing 216 years are chaotic, with skirmishes and battles breaking out everywhere, even in the sacred fourth region of the Anunnaki. Upon his return from his voyages, Marduk is so powerful that all of the Anunnaki leaders are afraid of him and his vast armies, and when he demands their submission to his rule they quickly call an emergency war council. Enlil proposes that they scuttle the Place of the Celestial Chariots in order to keep Marduk from gaining access to space travel and even possibly invading Nibiru. The council decides that the only way to stop Marduk and destroy the spaceport is to use nuclear weapons, the forbidden Weapons of Terror taken and secreted from Alalu's skiff hundreds of thousands of years before. Enki protests vehemently, but he is overruled, and Enlil's son by Ninmah, Ninurta, and Marduk's brother Nergal are selected to retrieve them. However, Enki is able to force them to agree that the Weapons of Terror may only be used on the spaceport after all the Anunnaki have been evacuated, and that the cities—both Anunnaki and human—are to be spared. Nergal agrees, but once he gets his hands on the weapons he changes his mind.

After waiting seven days for the other Anunnaki to declare their allegiance to him, Marduk returns to Babel and declares himself the ruler of Earth. Enlil then gives the order for the attack to begin, and the nuclear weapons are used against the mission control center inside a mountain and on the spaceport itself. Not satisfied with that destruction, Nergal flies his aircraft to the Indus Valley were Marduk's son Nabu is gathering new followers, and proceeds to nuke five more cities there, wiping out Marduk's future powerbase.

The results are horrific. Nergal and the others watch helplessly as the fallout from the massive nuclear blasts spreads across the region and poisons all life in its path. The "Evil Wind" leaves virtually all of Sumer lifeless under a cloud of radioactive death. The Anunnaki flee the fallout, but almost all the humans perish in a single night:

Everything that lived, behind it was dead and dying, people and cattle, all alike perished. The waters were poisoned, in the fields all vegetation withered. From Eridu in the south to Sippar in the north did the Evil Wind the land overwhelm.

Only one city out of all that the Anunnaki had built survived— Babel.

The time was 3114 BC.

Seeing that only Babel, Marduk's seat of power, was spared from the radioactive Evil Wind, Enki persuades Enlil that it must be an omen:

Babili, where Marduk supremacy declared, by the Evil Wind was spared; All the lands south of Babili the Evil Wind devoured, the heart of the Second Region it also touched. When in the aftermath of the Great Calamity Enlil and Enki to survey the havoc met, Enki to Enlil the sparing of Babili as a divine omen considered. That Marduk to supremacy has been destined, by the sparing of Babili is confirmed! So did Enki to Enlil say. The will of the Creator of All it must have been! Enlil to Enki said.

Enlil then tells Enki of the visit from Galzu, and Enki confronts him for not stopping the use of the nuclear weapons. Enlil reminds his brother that it was *he* who broke the rules at every turn, from the creation of man to the salvaging of the genetic material in the Ark, and suggests that he could no longer tell fate from destiny. Perhaps the visit from Galzu had just been a hallucination, so he took the fateful decision to let things play out as they were intended. Seeing that Marduk's ambitions were the root of all the calamities, Enlil decides to let Marduk clean up the mess and rule as he had always wanted to.

Dejected, Enlil hugs his brother goodbye and heads for America to accomplish the mining of gold, the mission they had originally come to Earth to complete. Enki is left to ponder whether mankind is destined to repeat the mistakes of the Anunnaki, or whether a different destiny awaits them.

***

This story is alternately sad, tragic, romantic and pathetic. Yet I think it is very close to what actually happened to the Anunnaki during their time on Earth. It establishes a clear link between the Anunnaki legends of Sitchin, the dynastic Pharaohs of Egypt, and the secret societies of today. With Sumer devastated, Enki and the other Anunnaki would have naturally moved to Egypt, which was a lush paradise at the time, and established and expanded the civilization there. It is also clear from the tablets that these priesthoods and secret societies were meant to guide and civilize man, not control and dominate him. That, sadly, is what has happened and it has distorted the original intent of the Anunnaki, who are the grantors of our science and culture. Next, we will see how this usurpation of power came to distort our vision of reality, and how it ultimately led to the secrecy that has enveloped our scientific institutions, like NASA.

(Endnotes)

1 http://www.grahamhancock.com/library/uw/c27.php?p=2

2 Points 1-8 cited verbatim from Kimura, *Diving Survey Report for Submarine Ruins off Japan*, page 178

3 Points 9-12, discussions with Prof. Kimura cited in *Heaven's Mirror*, pages 216-217

4 *Der Spiegel*, 34/1999

5 Graham Hancock, *Heaven's Mirror*, pp 215-216

6 Graham Hancock *Heaven's Mirror*, pp 217

7 Schoch, *Voices of the Rocks*, pp 112

Chapter 5
The Fractures of Time

Ancient hieroglyphs depicting a helicopter, a tank and an aircraft inside the temple of Seti I in Abydos, Egypt.

As we have seen, ancient records indicate that the history of the human race, much like the 2015 film *Jupiter Ascending* asserts, is far different from the one our traditional textbooks depict. It appears that a race of beings from a planet called Nibiru visited the Earth around 400,000 years ago, looking to mine gold in an effort to rebuild the thinning atmosphere of their home planet. They also set up bases on Mars and visited the Moon, and along the way they fought wars, engaged in petty rivalries and, oh yes, crossbred themselves with primitive man to create us: Homo sapiens sapiens.

After the Deluge wiped out all they had built here, they and the few remaining human survivors rebuilt their bases and civilization in and around ancient Sumer, and the Annunaki decided to share their way of life with the humans they had genetically manipulated. After a nuclear exchange, most of Sumer was wiped out and the sole remaining Anunnaki ruler, named Marduk, went to ancient

Egypt and set up a cult around himself as the Egyptian god Ra. He also set up a special priesthood—much like The Watchers of the Bible—whose sole job it was to educate and civilize humanity.

They had one job...

This is where things started to go wrong. Instead of learning from the mistakes of their progenitors, mankind repeated them. As the few remaining Anunnaki, the "Men of renown" of the Bible, faded into history or withdrew from public life, the high civilization that they had gifted to humanity began to decay. The high priests, seeing that knowledge was power, began to hold back most of the secrets of the gods they were entrusted to inculcate in Man. They began to see themselves as being above the rest of humanity, and to withhold that which they piously deemed to be too much for the unwashed masses.

The proof of this can be found all over the ancient world in the form of megalithic temples and structures like Gobleki Tepe and the pyramids of Giza. But there is one special place, Abydos in Egypt, which carries in the stones of the temple reveal this entire hidden history. The temples are the Osirion and the Temple of Seti I.

The Osirion, a temple of homage to Asar/Osiris, the son of Marduk, was discovered in modern times by archaeologists

The watery entrance to the Osirion, Abydos, Egypt.

146

Flinders Petrie and Margaret Murray in 1902. Although attached to the temple of Pharaoh Seti I (1294 - 1279 BC) it does not appear to have been built by him. In fact, despite mainstream Egyptologists' claims, it bears little resemblance to the temple of Seti I and is most likely far, far older. It is megalithic and the jigsaw-fit stonework is the same as that seen at other places of great antiquity around the world. In short, Seti built his temple on the same site to try and grab some of Osiris power and mystique for himself.

Although a bit of an archeological mystery, Abydos remained relatively insignificant in most people's minds until the late 1990s, when a photographer named Bruce Rawles returned from a trip there and posted images of some hieroglyphs he found there on the Internet. The glyphs, spotted on an upper wall above a post in the Seti I temple, were exposed when a later clump of plastered panel, probably placed over it by Seti I's descendants, crumbled and fell to the ground. The panel behind it—which was clearly far older— showed unmistakable images of what are dead ringers for modern war machines, including a helicopter, a tank and an airplane.

The Abydos glyphs.

What, exactly, are we to make of this extraordinary find? The striking resemblance of these glyphs to modern war machines cannot be a coincidence or a mistake, in my opinion. Various Sumerian and Egyptian tablets tell of great battles fought on the land and in the sky in ancient, even prediluvial times. Logically these histories would be transferred and venerated in ancient Egypt when Marduk transferred his seat of power from Babylon to Egypt. Is it really such a surprise that we should find images of these battles and the equipment used in them in our ancient scrolls?

Comparison of an Abydos glyph with a modern M-1 Abrams tank
with side skirts.

Another tip that these depictions are exactly what they appear to be can also be found in the intensity with which they were attacked.

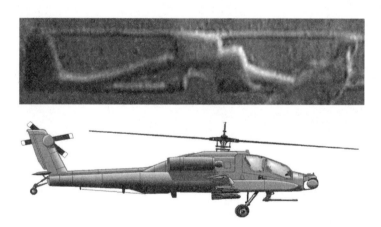

An ancient depiction of a modern vehicle, the AH-64 Apache helicopter.

Almost immediately, an altered, fake version of the glyphs appeared on the internet and was widely circulated. Obviously, this was done in an attempt to confuse the issue and convince the casual public that the real image was nothing but a fake. Even otherwise intelligent observers like Whitley Strieber were fooled by the fake and declared the Abydos glyphs a hoax. But this claim was debunked in a 1999 TV documentary, "Opening the Lost Tombs: Live from Egypt."

The show was co-hosted by my co-author on *Dark Mission— The Secret History of NASA*, Richard C. Hoagland, and in a stroke of brilliance, he put an end to the claim that the glyphs did not exist at all by convincing the producers to send a camera crew to Abydos. In one long continuous shot, they started outside the temple and then went inside and straight up to the panel in question, ending once and for all the myth that the glyphs were a fake.

Comparison of an Abydos glyph with a modern M-1 Abrams tank with side skirts. Screen capture from "Opening the Lost Tombs: Live from Egypt" showing the exact location in the Temple of Seti I of the mysterious "helicopter" glyphs.

The Egyptologists then went to Plan B and began a major offensive aimed at convincing the public that yes, the glyphs may be there, but they were anything but what they appeared to be. It was all just a Jedi Mind Trick.

"I am afraid that you have been subjected to the famous 'Abydos helicopter' mania, here," wrote Katherine Griffis-

Greenberg, a member of the American Research Center in Egypt. "There is a simple explanation to what you are seeing, at least, as we see it in Egyptology. There is no mystery here; it's just a palimpsest." A palimpsest is an academic term for a manuscript or document which has been written on more than once. The Egyptologists—none of whom had ever actually examined the panel in question up close—declared that what must have happened is that somewhere along the way Seti I's scribes had filled in older hieroglyphs with plaster and then recarved them, and that some of the fill-in plaster had fallen away when the covering panel dropped off, creating the shapes we see today.

All very plausible—but utter baloney.

For one thing, palimpsest tablets are invariably beaten up and very shoddy looking (according to the Egyptologists' own defining standards) and this particular panel is in pretty much pristine condition. At least one Egyptologist who has actually *seen* the panel up close concurs. Lumir G. Janku wrote on his website about the panel:

> There is one aspect of the inscription which is puzzling (if it is a palimpsest). The temple in Abydos (or Abdjou, as the location was called by Egyptians), is quite a remarkable edifice, especially as far as the quality of glyphs is concerned. They are all very precise and as far as I can judge, there's no trace of sloppy workmanship anywhere in the temple, bar the above inscription.

In other words, there is no sign of plastering or reworking of the panel, therefore there is no chance it is a palimpsest.

Second, what is generally ignored is what the script around these glyphs *actually says*. According to Ms. Griffis-Greenberg:

> In the photos, we clearly see '[He] Who repulses the Nine Bows,' which figures in some of the Two-Ladies names of Seti I, replaced by '[He] Who protects Egypt and overthrows the foreign countries.' The 'Nine Bows' refers

to the nine traditional enemies of Egypt, so an alternate (though not literal) translation of the phrase is: [He] Who repulses the Nine [Enemies of Egypt]."

In other words, this panel, which is in pristine condition and probably dates as far back as 5,000 years ago, just happens to depict four modern-looking war machines surrounded by hieroglyphic script describing a Pharaoh's wartime victories over the "Nine Enemies of Egypt.

But that's just a coincidence... right.

What this panel clearly establishes is that the stories of wars and conflicts among the gods are not fiction. I suspect this actually is a visual record of the wars of Horus and Set as they did battle with tanks, aircraft and attack helicopters over the throne of Osiris. And it is adjacent to the Osirion, a temple dedicated (probably by Marduk himself) to his sons memory. But there is even more.

The "corridor of the Kings" Abydos, Egypt.

In the section of the temple built later by Seti I is a passageway called the "Corridor of the Kings." It lists, in ascending order, *all* of the 76 previous rulers of ancient Egypt in a list that goes back thousands of years from Seti's time. But, largely unspoken of, is

151

the fact that it then goes on to list all of the *gods* who ruled ancient Egypt dating back *tens of thousands of years*. It is as near a complete lineal record of Pharaohic and god-like, extraterrestrial rulers as you will find anywhere in the world. The list goes all the way back to a period that the Egyptians mark and venerate as the *Zep Tepi* ("The First Time"), the time when gods and demigods like Osiris ruled over Upper and Lower Egypt. A time when technology and fearsome weapons were used to wage war amongst the gods.

All of this is of vital importance to our premise because, as we will see, NASA has an ongoing symbolic obsession with ancient Egypt, and with the story of Isis, Osiris, Horus and Set specifically. This odd obsession is due to the fact that no less than three modern secret societies, the Nazis, the "Magicians" and the Freemasons, infiltrated the space agency almost from its inception.

The traditional view of modern Freemasonry is that it was established at a meeting in a pub in London, England in 1717. But as we will see, that is not the opinion of at least two prominent Masonic scholars, Christopher Knight and Robert Lomas, who argue that Masonry's origins date all the way back to ancient Egypt—and the story of Isis and Osiris. Their book *The Hiram Key* showed that, contrary to Masonry's own lore, the Craft was not founded in London in 1717, but in fact traced its roots to ancient Egypt. They followed a trail back through time to the Knights Templars, to Jesus and the Temple of Jerusalem, then on to the architect of the first Temple of Solomon, Hiram Abiff. They concluded that the ritual of the third degree of Freemasonry was a reenactment of Abiff's murder for refusing to reveal the high secrets of the Craft, and that this same ritual was in fact derived from the ancient pharaonic rituals that paid direct homage to Isis and Osiris. They also asserted that Jesus himself was an initiate of this quasi-Masonic order, and that his real teachings had been usurped and distorted by the Catholic Church millennia before. They viewed Jesus as a martyred prophet, but not a divine being as the Church came to ultimately insist. None of this made them very popular with either the Christians or their own fellow Masons.

Over the centuries, Freemasonry has been the target of

derision, persecution and suspicion that is not generally justified. The vast majority of us know of the society through their good works, like the Shriners' hospitals we see in every major city, which usually provide medical care to the poor and the young free of charge, and by seeing our grandfathers march in Fourth of July parades along with other members of their local lodges.

However, there is a significant difference between the Masonic Craft in general, and the more specific institution which came to control key positions inside NASA—The Ancient and Accepted Scottish Rite. The Scottish Rite is an "appendant" body of Freemasonry, meaning it is not directly connected to the Grand Lodges of the Craft. The vast majority of Freemasons throughout the world are members of the Grand Lodges only. After achieving the first three degrees of the Grand Lodges (Entered Apprentice, Fellow Craft and Master Mason), the apprentice is said to have completed the so-called "blue degrees," the base knowledge required to be a Mason. Incidentally, this is where the term "getting the third degree" comes from.

If a Mason desires to continue his studies of the spiritual and ethical teachings of Freemasonry, he may elect to pursue degrees in one of several appendant bodies, of which the York Rite and Scottish Rite are the two most prominent. While the Scottish Rite is not recognized by the Grand Lodges in several countries (including England), there is no prohibition against a Master Mason joining. In the United States, the Scottish Rite is duly recognized by the Grand Lodges, and its rituals are viewed as a continuation of the base knowledge attained by the Master Mason degree. In other words, all Scottish Rite Freemasons are Master Masons, but not all Master Masons are members of the Scottish Rite.

So, when someone talks about a "33° Freemason," they are actually talking about a member of the Scottish Rite appendant body, as it is the Scottish Rite which confers the fourth through the thirty-third degrees. It is also not commonly known that while any Mason may elect to take any of the Scottish Rite degrees up to 32, he must be *invited* by the Supreme Council to attain the honorary rank of the 33°—it (like the US Senate) is a very exclusive club.

But the question we are faced with, and that we must unravel, is how did all of this culminate in 33° Scottish Rite Freemason Buzz Aldrin performing a ceremonial offering to Osiris on July 20, 1969? And how and why is that date important? To answer that, we must go back in time to the heart of ancient Egypt, and the source of our modern means of timekeeping, the Gregorian calendar.

Gaius Julius Caesar.

Our modern calendar, the "Gregorian" calendar, came into being in 1582 after Pope Gregory XIII issued a papal bull (order) to reform the calendar. The previous calendar, the "Julian," created by Julius Caesar of Rome, had been adopted by the Christian Church at the council of Nicaea in AD 325, the first of the general councils of the Church. But, it had become increasingly inaccurate and by 1582 many key religious celebrations, like Easter, had drifted far from the dates they were originally celebrated.

The reason for this is astronomical. Calendars are measurements of time, which ultimately is measured by the movements of the Earth, Moon and stars. In the Julian calendar, the average year (one Earth orbit around the sun) was measured as 365.25 days. In reality, the length of the year is significantly different. Astronomers disagree as to the correct length of the year, with some saying it is 365.2422 "mean solar days" of the "mean tropical year", and some saying it is 365.2424 days of the "vernal equinox year." The difference of the length of the Julian calendar year from the length of the real solar year is thus 0.0078 days (11.23 minutes) in the former case and 0.0076 days (10.94 minutes) in the latter case.

This error accumulates, so that after about 131 years the calendar is out of sync with the equinoxes and solstices by one whole day. Thus as the centuries passed, the Julian calendar became increasingly inaccurate with respect to the astronomical seasons. Since the sliding calendar date of Easter is determined in reference to the fixed Spring (Vernal) Equinox (a day in which the amount of daylight and darkness is very close to being equal), measured relative to the moving phases of the Moon, it was critical for the Church to have an error-free, fixed calendar reference point (the Spring Equinox) for calculating this most holy festival celebrating Christ's death and resurrection.

In order to resolve this situation, a predecessor of Gregory XIII, Pope Paul III, appointed a commission of astronomers to determine the necessary changes to the calendar. He recruited several prominent astronomers, to come up with a solution. They built upon calendar reform proposals by the astronomer

155

and physician Luigi Lilio (1510-1576) and Pitatus. When Pope Gregory XIII was elected he found various proposals for calendar reform before him, and decided in favor of that of the Jesuit Christopher Clavius (1537-1612).

The Gregorian reform consisted of the following changes.

Ten days were omitted from the calendar, and it was decreed that the day following Thursday, October 4, 1582 (which would be October 5, 1582, in the old calendar) would thenceforth be known as Friday, October 15, 1582.

The rule for leap years was also changed. In the Julian calendar a year is a leap year if it is divisible by 4. In the Gregorian calendar a year is a leap year if either (1) it is divisible by 4 but not by 100 or (2) it is divisible by 400. In other words, a year which is divisible by 4 is a leap year unless it is divisible by 100 but not by 400 (in which case it is not a leap year). Thus the years 1600 and 2000 are leap years, but 1700, 1800, 1900 and 2100 are not.

New rules for the determination of the date of Easter were adopted.

The first day of the year (New Year's Day) was set at January 1st.

The position of the extra day in a leap year was moved from the day before February 25th to the day following February 28th.

The ostensible purpose of these changes was to establish a consistent date for Easter and to bring the calendar back to the same relation with the movements of the heavens which it had at the time of Constantine's famed Nicaean Council in AD 325. In reality the reform seems to have had a very different purpose, apparently having little to do with Christ or Easter (despite the Church's public posture), and everything to do with prearranging the precise one-time placement of the complex spatial motions of Earth, the Moon and the star Sirius, which the Egyptians venerated as Osiris' wife and consort Isis.

Both Western calendars, the Julian and Gregorian, were influenced heavily by Egyptian beliefs and advocates. The Julian calendar was adopted in the (Gregorian) year 46 BC after Caesar had spent considerable time consulting with Egyptian-educated

Isis/Ninmah.

astronomer and priest Sosigenes. Caesar had arrived in Egypt in 48 BC in pursuit of his friend and rival Pompeii after defeating him in the battle of Pharsalus and ending a Roman civil war. While there, Caesar was educated in the ways of Egyptian astronomy and religion. He learned that the ancient Egyptians predicted the annual Nile flooding on the basis of the appearance of Sirius. The period between was 365.25 days, less than an hour wrong in five years. This must have seemed like a high degree of accuracy for its day. So, abandoning the Roman lunar calendar, Caesar set alternating months of 31 and 30 days with February having only

29 days except every fourth year when February 24 was repeated.

The result of this system, a 365 day year with a leap year every four, was superior to the previous Roman system and at first glance appears to be a practical and reasonably accurate calendar. But what is less clear is Caesar's motive for creating a calendrical system in the first place. Although it was inaccurate, the Roman calendar was hardly a logical concern for a warrior like Caesar. He was obsessed at this point in his life with becoming the first emperor of the Roman Empire, and creating a new calendar was hardly the type of activity which would, on the surface anyway, advance such ambitions.

What we tend to forget in our modern perspective on such things is that the men of this age were not merely politicians or soldiers or even both, but frequently priests, mystics and magicians as well. Most of them had a belief that their paths had been shaped by divine and mysterious forces, and they spent a great deal of time trying to master and understand these forces. Caesar would have been no different, and it is likely that the Egyptian queen Cleopatra introduced him to the secrets of Egyptian ritual and magic as a payment for his gift of placing her exclusively on the Egyptian throne. Her ambitions rivaled his, and showing Caesar the powers hidden in the rites and science of the world's oldest civilization would have been a tremendous bonding agent between them.

But Caesar came to the table in Egypt with an already well established understanding of the stars and ancient mysteries. He had been co-opted into the Roman college of priests and was elected Pontifex in 73 BC. He became Consul for Gaul (France) in 59 BC after submitting an extensive report on the Druid religion to the Republic. He spent several years studying them and learning their religion and astronomical sciences, which ultimately led to his authorship of a book on astronomy while stationed in Gaul.

What we can clearly see from these activities is that men of high stature in Rome, like Caesar, were trying to understand the movements of the stars and their influences over their fate in the same ways that the Anunnaki used the "Tablets of Destiny" to understand theirs. Caesar's fascination with the movements of the heavens makes no sense in any other context, nor do some of his actions.

The Druids were the guardians of most of the megalithic sites in what is now England and Ireland, including Stonehenge, Newgrange, Avebury and Silbury Hill. A recent book by Christopher Knight and Robert Lomas, *Uriel's Machine* (following on the pioneering work in the 1960s of Thom and Hawkins), makes a compelling case that these sites were astronomical and calendrical in nature, and that the knowledge of how to use them was transmitted by The Watchers, which they describe as a group of "semi-divine" beings that have counterparts in many other ancient religions, including Egypt's. The purpose of these massive instruments was to give the users a sense of where they stood in the overall time scheme relative to precession, the (roughly) 26,000-year cycle of the Earth's wobble on its rotational axis. Inherent in this apparent ancient understanding of precession is an equally unbelievable link to a prehistoric concept of "hyperdimensional physics"—a science that could conceivably impart its initiates with what must have seemed like magical powers over both nature and other human beings.

Apparently at Caesar's behest, the Roman Empire began a century-long campaign to wipe the Druids from the Earth. Caesar himself made a landing on the English coast in 55 BC, but was stymied. Eventually, the fourth Roman emperor, Claudius, succeeded in conquering Britain and decimating the Druid population.

This is all the more strange when you consider that the Druidic culture of the times was essentially a bunch of illiterate savages (because they committed all of their knowledge to memory, and did not by law write any of it down), literally running around in skins, who posed no possible military threat to Rome whatsoever. Britain possessed no great mineral wealth, and in fact was a cold, wet, and generally inhospitable place to live. So why did Rome go so far out of its way, expending significant manpower and treasure across more than a century of successive administrations

Stonehenge.

to ultimately subdue the entire population of an out-of-the-way collection of scattered northern islands and to wipe out its reigning priesthood?

The only logical answer is that the Druids possessed something of immense value or danger to Rome. If Caesar learned some valuable astrological secret in his studies with the Druids, a secret that promised unimaginable power or knowledge of the future, he would naturally want to protect this advantage for the good of Rome. His campaign against the Druids seemed calculated to eliminate the magical knowledge of the Druids and preserve the secret for the Republic (soon to be "Empire," under his command) alone. Indeed, for reasons not abundantly clear, the Julian calendar itself is ultimately anchored to Greenwich Mean Time, based in England. In this scenario, Rome's otherwise senseless campaign against the British Isles finally begins to make some sense.

Six years after his campaign in Gaul, Caesar made his way to Egypt. As we have seen previously, the Egyptians possessed high knowledge in the movements of the stars and planets, and Sosigenes was a high master of this science. In looking at the results of his wares, the Julian calendar, it becomes obvious just what he had revealed to Caesar.

The ancient Egyptian calendar centered on the annual

inundation of the Nile and the periodicity of the so-called "heliacal rising" of the star Sirius. Because of Earth's annual orbit of the Sun, Sirius "disappears" from the night sky at Giza for about 70 days each year, and has done so for hundreds of thousands of years. Its reappearance, just before sunrise in the east, is called the "heliacal rising of Sirius." "Heliacal" is taken from the Greek "Helios," the Rising Sun—which is just another form of the Egyptian term for the same phenomenon, "Horus." Even the modern word "horizon" is connected to this phenomenon, literally translating to "Horus Rising," the place where the sun/son Horus rises just after his mother Isis/Sirius during this time of the year.

Because of the ever-present effects of precession (the almost 26,000 year "wobble" of the Earth), this annual disappearance has been systematically sliding through the seasons for all of Egypt's history. In modern times this event takes place on the 5th of August. In Jesus' time, the heliacal rising was on July 20, a repetitive NASA "ritual date" which just happens to be the date of the landing of Apollo 11 on the surface of the Moon and the first moonwalk. In ancient times, circa 3300 BC, this heliacal re-emergence took place on the summer solstice (June 21st, Gregorian).

Around this same time, the melting snows of the mountains in central Africa would flood the Nile and provide much needed irrigation for the crops of this otherwise arid land. This conjunction of events led to the marking of the Egyptian New Year coincident with this magical rebirth of Sirius, the Nile and Isis. The New Year was considered to have started not at midnight, but when Sirius actually reappeared in the sky at dawn …with Horus.

In his book *Echoes of Ancient Skies*, archaeo-astronomer Dr. Ed Krupp writes about these events:

> After disappearing from the night sky (for 70 days) Sirius eventually reappears in the dawn, before the sun comes up. The first time this occurs each year is called the stars heliacal rising, and on this day Sirius remains visible for only a short time before the sky gets too bright to see it. In ancient Egypt this annual reappearance of Sirius fell

161

close to the summer solstice and coincided with the time of the Nile's inundation. Isis, as Sirius, was the 'Mistress of the Year's beginning,' for the Egyptian New Year was set by this event. New Year's ceremony texts at Dendera say Isis coaxes out the Nile and causes it to swell. The metaphor is astronomical, hydraulic, and sexual, and it parallels the function of Isis in the myth. Sirius revives the Nile just as Isis revives Osiris. Her time in hiding from Seth is when Sirius is gone (70 days) from the night sky. She (Isis) gives birth to her son Horus, as Sirius gives birth to the New Year, and in the texts Horus and the New Year are equated. She is the vehicle for renewal of life and order. Shining for a moment, one morning in summer, she stimulates the Nile and starts the year.

So the flooding period of the Nile was more than just the marker of life renewed, it marked the actual beginning of the new calendar year. Caesar would have certainly been inculcated in these ancient beliefs, as well as the many other "Sirius Mysteries" known to Sosigenes. This Sirius influence eventually made its way into the calendar we now call the Julian. From the very first instant of the Julian dating system, the influence of Egypt and Sirius could be felt.

If you roll the clock back at Giza to Julian date 0000.0000 (January 1, 4713 BC, noon GMT) you find that Sirius, this most important of celestial markers to the ancient Egyptians, is in a very significant location at the Masonic 33° below the eastern horizon. Now, the chances of rolling a calendar, any calendar, back exactly to its origin over 6,700 years ago at exactly the place we would expect to be most significant, and finding exactly the astronomical body we would expect to find in one of the few significant altitudes we would expect to find it, are, well, astronomical. Keeping in mind that the Julian calendar is timed out to the minute, and that Caesar certainly understood the significance of Sirius, I cannot fathom any other conclusion than that this is a product of intentional design. The placement of this star at 33° is a clear signal that Sosigenes and

162

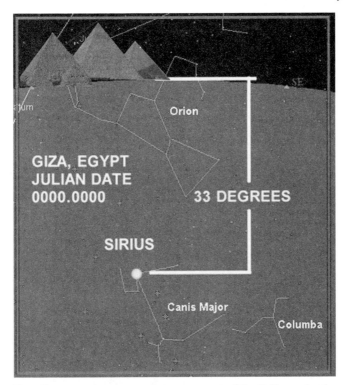

Giza, Egypt, at the exact commencement of the Julian calendar.

Caesar understood the coded basics and symbolic importance of it in astronomy and astrology. Any calendar based in the Egyptian astronomical mysteries the way this one was would almost *have* to mark its origins with respect to this most sacred star, which represented the goddess Isis.

But the question then becomes, why? Given that NASA and astronomy still uses Julian dating, the question becomes even more important in the context of this book. But the answer seems to lie in an attempt—by Caesar no less—to influence future events by creating his own "Tablet of Destiny" for the human race. The beginning of the Julian calendar set the stage for several other important alignments millennia into the future. But because of the drifting accuracy of the Julian calendar, the Gregorian adjustment was required.

The truth is that if it were not for the adjustment made in 1583, then a Masonic astronaut named Buzz Aldrin and his companion named Neil Armstrong could not have made an offering to Osiris in the Lunar Module in a specific place on the lunar surface when the stars were at a specific location above the landing site. What I plan to show you is that those events were set in motion thousands of years before the first Moon landing, and for a specific purpose.

Col. Edwin "Buzz" Aldrin as Commandant of the Air Force Test Pilot School. Note the prominent display of his Masonic signet ring.

A bit more of a history lesson is required here. In the centuries following the dawn of the Julian calendar, the powers of the Church waxed and waned, and the secular power of the once invincible Roman Empire ultimately collapsed. Islamic forces arose, and eventually took control of much of the Holy Land. Simultaneously, there were a variety of internal and external arguments over Church dogma and authority. Eventually, the Roman Catholic Church, as theological successor to the once mighty Empire of Rome, established strongholds in Spain, France, and England among other rising European nations.

In 1095, Pope Urban II declared a holy war against the Muslim invaders of the Holy Land, and launched an effort to retake the sacred city of Jerusalem, thus beginning the Crusades.

By 1099, the task had been accomplished and Jerusalem was once again in Christian hands. Then, around 1118, a new order was formed within the Catholic Church that came to be known as the "Knights Templar" (Knights of the Temple Mount in Jerusalem). An influential Cistercian monk who was probably related to some of the original nine founders of this order, St. Bernard of Clairvaux, is said to have created a monastery in Seborga in northern Italy. Documents found in this ancient monastery state that it was built to protect a "great secret."

The original nine Knights, all related through a complex series of family relationships, presented themselves to King Baldwin II of Jerusalem in 1118 and were given the duty of keeping Christian pilgrims safe on the roads and highways leading to the holy city from the port of Jaffa. Obviously, such a task was far beyond the capabilities of a mere nine men, and it was a ruse for public consumption in any event. Upon arrival in Jerusalem, the Knights, under the patronage of thde Vatican, were appointed Lords of Jerusalem and proceeded directly to the Temple Mount, the ancient site of the Temple of Solomon. They immediately began excavating the (even then) ancient ruin. It is for this work that they received their name, the "Knights of the Temple."

According to Knight and Lomas in *The Hiram Key*, the Temple of Solomon was a structure designed under the precepts of "sacred" (extraterrestrial) geometry by the earliest progenitors of Freemasonry, and was laid out in such a way as to invoke the essence of the Egyptian myths of Isis and Osiris. According to the royal (British) engineers who examined the excavations of the Templars in 1867, the Knights found a secret room beneath the Temple Mount and apparently knew exactly what they were looking for and where to find it. Just what they actually found is the subject of legend, but it has gained scholarly support recently. According to the European Templar Heritage Research Network:

> On the exterior of Chartres Cathedral, by the north door, there is a carving on a pillar, which gives us an indication of the object sought by the burrowing Templars, representing

the Ark of the Covenant, but in a rather strange context. The Ark is depicted as being transported on a wheeled vehicle. Legend recounts that the Ark of the Covenant had been secreted deep beneath the Temple in Jerusalem centuries before the fall of the city to the Romans. It had been hidden there to protect it from yet another invading army who had laid the city to waste. Hugh de Payen, one of the original nine Templar Knights, had been chosen to lead the expedition mounted to locate the Ark and bring it back to Europe. Persistent legends recount that the Ark was then hidden for a considerable time deep beneath the crypt of Chartres Cathedral. The same legends also claim that the Templars found many other sacred artifacts from the old Jewish temple in the course of their investigations and that a considerable quantity of documentation was also located during the dig. While there has been much speculation as to the exact nature of these documents, a reasonable consensus is emerging that they contained scriptural scrolls, treatises on sacred geometry, and details of certain knowledge, art and science—the hidden wisdom of the ancient initiates of the Judaic/Egyptian tradition. Until very recently these legends received short shrift from academic historians, but that situation is undergoing considerable change. One modern archeological discovery tends to support the speculative scenario that the Templars knew where to look and precisely what they were seeking. The Copper Scroll, one of the Dead Sea Scrolls discovered at Quamran, tends to confirm not only the objective of the Templar excavations but also, albeit indirectly, gives some credence to the bizarre concept of the transmission of knowledge through the generations that led to the original Templar discoveries underneath the Temple Mount in Jerusalem.

The Copper Scroll, which was unrolled and deciphered at Manchester University under the guidance of John Allegro, was a list of all the burial sites used to hide the various items both sacred and profane described as the treasure of the Temple of Jerusalem. Many of these sites have been re-excavated since the discovery of the Copper Scroll, and several of them have disclosed not Temple treasure but evidence of Templar excavation made in the twelfth century.

After their excavations were completed at the Temple Mount, the Knights returned to their homeland. Shortly afterwards the Knights were given the official seal of the Roman Catholic Church, and their numbers swelled as wealthy landowners and aristocrats joined their ranks. The Templars went on a binge of temple construction and brought back many sciences, such as astronomy, from their repeated trips to the holy land. Their order grew in stature, wealth and power quickly, and they won battle after battle against the Muslims during the various Crusades. Their secret power was supposedly that they held possession of a piece of the true cross of the crucifixion of Christ. This gave them powers over their enemies in battle, and they were said to have never lost a battle while in possession of the cross.

They eventually lost the cross in the battle of Hattin in 1187 to the Muslim Saladin. After marching on July 2nd, the Templars were surrounded and cut off from water supplies. On July 4th, they broke ranks in thirst and panic, abandoned the encampment and the cross, and were wiped out by Muslim forces. These two dates later would become crucial—not only in the Templar-inspired formation of the United States of America (as we shall see), but in the continuing hidden ritual history of NASA as well.

Ultimately, despite the loss of the cross, the Templars apparently became a threat to the Church itself. The Pope and the nearly broke King of France, Philip le Bel (1268-1314), plotted to undermine the order and seize their considerable treasures in France. On Friday, October 13, 1307, the King's men moved against the Knights and arrested and executed many of them. This is why "Friday the 13th" is now considered "unlucky."

Although the papal conspiracy with King Philip succeeded

in obtaining various confessions under torture and a considerable sum of Templar wealth, the conspirators never found the ultimate Templar treasure itself—which by then had been secreted away to Scotland. Even so, most of the Order was wiped out in the "10/13" raid (the leader, Jacques de Molay, was burned at the stake), and its members scattered across Europe and beyond. On March 22, 1312, the Church officially dissolved the order by papal bull. Surviving German members formed the Teutonic Knights, and the Scottish members went underground, only to eventually re-emerge as the Freemasons.

Whatever ancient relics and treasures the Templars held from their Jerusalem and other Holy Land excavations, they were from this moment on secreted away beneath Rosslyn Chapel in Scotland, in much the same way these same artifacts were once buried under the Temple Mount. The Chapel itself bears no resemblance to a Christian structure, as many experts who have surveyed it have verified. Remarkably, it is laid out along the same architectural lines as the Biblical dimensions given for the original "Solomon's Temple," which was apparently designed by the murdered Masonic architect, Hiram Abiff.

The key here is that the Roman Catholic Church, as the Roman Empire had done in ancient times, tried to wipe out the competition who had knowledge of the secrets they had held since at least the time of Caesar. Ultimately it backfired, as these various former members of the Knights Templar became major players in the Reformation and the establishment of the Protestant Church. It wasn't until almost three hundred years after the events of 1307, when the first openly Freemasonic king, King James VI of Scotland, took the throne in 1603 that the Templar movement began to reassert itself, culminating in the formation of modern Freemasonry in 1717.

The Germanic order, the Teutonic Knights, splintered from the Roman Catholic Church and became a powerful military order throughout Austria and the Baltic states. They eventually survived conflict after conflict throughout Europe, until Hitler's Nazi Germany made wide use of their history and heraldry in WWII.

Hitler also made it a priority to wipe out the Freemasons in Nazi Germany. Indeed, they were the first to be persecuted after the Nazis took power, not the Jews.

Eventually, the West, led by Freemasons FDR and Winston Churchill, vanquished the ancient Germanic order of the Teutonic Knights in World War II. With these ancient conflicts finally resolved and behind them, the surviving "Watchers" could then turn their sights to the next step in the grand plan to return man to the stars from which his ancestors had come.

That was when the real fun began.

Chapter 6
Into the 20th Century

"History, Sir, will tell lies as usual"
—George Bernard Shaw, *The Devil's Disciple*

The history of NASA and the influence of the Freemasons upon NASA's origins, mission objectives—and perhaps even its occult goals—cannot be understood in isolation. NASA is not a single entity, but rather a large and somewhat typical American government bureaucracy, spliced together from the remnants of many other prior organizations and institutions. Each of these groups brought a specific viewpoint and certainly specific priorities to the "American" space program in the early 1960s. Each of them had a long history and core beliefs, which they sought to both validate though the space agency's explorations, and at the same time hide from the public at large and the many foot soldiers in the agency in particular.

For most Americans, the name "NASA" brings back a rush of memories of the 1960s space race with the Soviet Union. It was a time of clean-cut, heroic astronauts, rock-jawed mission planners, can-do engineers and visionary politicians. Astronauts were hurtled into the void in primitive "capsules" mounted on rickety missiles that were barely more than contained bombs. We watched in wonder as "our" boys achieved one space miracle after another: The first American orbital flights and spacewalks, the first rendezvous and docking in space, the first manned circumnavigation of the Moon. The first manned landing and safe return. When a major catastrophe befell the men of Apollo 13, these titanic forces joined together and brought them home against

171

impossible odds. Not to be deterred, we resumed our explorations of the Moon and sent probes to Mars and the outer planets. It seemed fitting that we would describe such feats as a voyage "On the Shoulders of Titans."[1] It would be hard to imagine a more optimistic era, a time when we believed as a nation in our ability to do anything and the righteousness of our causes.

The public image presented by the agency was in every way congruent with this perspective, and more than any other part of the federal government, NASA survived the turbulent attacks of the 60s generation and maintained its squeaky-clean image of infallibility well into the 1980s. Taking on NASA is about as politically popular as criticizing Mother Teresa or Princess Diana. If ever there was a sacred cow government agency among Americans, it is the National Aeronautics and Space Administration.

A very carefully cultivated public image of honesty and openness pervades the agency, in spite of the many occasions people have had to point out its less than honest track record. What we are fighting is the public's *idealized* vision of NASA, rather than the reality that led some early beat reporters to dub the agency "Never A Straight Answer."

It is against this backdrop of true heroism and achievement that the truth stands out as nearly incomprehensible. The evidence that our friendly neighborhood space administration is something other than the benevolent civilian science agency it has always pretended to be is as overwhelming as it is disturbing, and I will document it here. The architects of these crimes against our nation are some of the same "heroes" we have been encouraged to worship as pioneers of our technological era. Their names are synonymous with America's achievements in space. Unfortunately, in many cases they are also men with secret pasts. And there are equally as many names that you have most likely never heard associated with our space program, but who had just as much influence over where we went and why we went there. They are German, Egyptian, English and American, but they are hardly representative of the best each of these nations has to offer.

What they are, in fact, are men at the very fringes of rational thought and conventional wisdom.

These fringe elements made their way into NASA in the early days like a virus spreading its tendrils secretively through a computer network. In this case, the virus consisted of three separate secret societies, all of which traced their origins back to ancient Egypt and the priesthood that the Annunaki demigod Marduk had created there to nurture and educate mankind. For purposes of clarity we shall call them the "Magicians," the "Freemasons," and the "Nazis," and deal with them separately. Each of these groups was led by prominent individuals and supported by lesser-known players. Each has stamped their own agenda on our space program in indelible—and traceable—ways. And each is dominated by a secret or "occult" doctrine that is far more closely aligned with ancient religion and mysticism than it is with the rational science and cool empiricism they promote to the general public.

The truth is, NASA was literally born in a lie and hid many unpleasant truths about itself from the beginning.

In the case of NASA and the Masons, we are fortunate that it is far easier to ascertain just what it was that the group hoped to discover (and then compartmentalize) as their members led the exploration of the solar system. But the entire picture cannot be seen without the proper historical context.

Boosted by the science of archaeo-astronomy—the practice of using computer-generated star maps to literally look back in time—I can show that NASA and the Masons appeared to be very interested in the possibility that someone (the Anunnaki) had inhabited vast tracts of real estate throughout the solar system in a far-distant epoch. They sought to discover (and then hide) not merely the existence of these ruins, but the secret of what had happened to the builders of them. Even stranger, NASA seems convinced that whatever cataclysm overtook what must have been a grand and far-reaching civilization—from which those "gods" sprang—could be about to overtake ours as well.

In their quest to uncover proof of the Anunnaki gods they heard about through myth and legend, they had the able assistance of recruits from members of the equally secretive organizations that were spread throughout the agency. In short, everybody who was anybody in NASA's early years was a member of one of these three secret societies, of which the Scottish Rite Freemasons were the dominant group.

By using these astronomy programs to an even deeper degree, we (me and my co-author on *Dark Mission*, Richard C. Hoagland) have been able to establish a pattern of behavior on NASA's part that points to an internal obsession by the agency with three gods and goddesses of ancient Egypt, specifically Isis, Osiris (Marduk's son), and Horus. It is these three gods whose story has been documented by Masonic authors Chistopher Knight and Robert Lomas as being the key to understanding the secret history of the Masonic order.

The true history of NASA cannot be understood without appreciating not just the influence that these gods of ancient Egypt had on Freemasonry, but also the corresponding influence that the Freemasons and the other groups had on NASA itself. For that, we must go back to the beginning.

The Early Years 1930-1960

NASA, as we know it today, actually evolved from several earlier organizations. One called the National Advisory Committee for Aeronautics (or NACA), was the primary source of early NASA brainpower. The NACA director, Dr. Vannevar Bush, was instrumental in launching many major aerospace projects and companies. He was co-founder of Raytheon systems, still a major defense contractor, and was director of the Office of Scientific Research and Development, which oversaw the über-secret Manhattan Project. He was also President Roosevelt's scientific advisor and played a key role in bringing many Nazi rocket scientists, like Dr. Wernher von Braun, to the USA.

He was also a 33° Scottish Rite Freemason.

That in itself is not entirely remarkable. But as we will see, Bush's fraternal association with the Masonic order ended up having a very significant impact on the American space program of the 1960s that still echoes today.

Dr. Vannevar Bush.

In many ways, Dr. Bush is the axle around which many spokes of the NASA wheel turned. With the help of Bush, the Pentagon supplied a steady stream of brainpower to NASA through its secret ballistic missile programs led by Wernher von Braun. Author Linda Hunt (*Secret Agenda*), cited Bush as having played a key role in bringing von Braun and other "ardent Nazis" to the US illegally and in violation of President Truman's executive orders, under the auspices of the now well-known Project Paperclip.

According to Hunt, when certain scientists were deemed "too unimportant" to be brought to the US by a military panel, Bush intervened with a scathing letter to the Joint Intelligence Objectives Agency (JIOA) in which he derided the military for not knowing "even elementary information on Germans whose names are as well known in scientific circles as Churchill, Stalin and Roosevelt are in political circles." He insisted that several of the scientists were "intellectual giants of Nobel Prize stature." Bush's efforts were clearly a significant factor in several of the Germans being brought to US over the JIOA's objections, and the reasons for his enthusiastic embrace of men with shady pasts are, on the face of it, not entirely clear.

Harvard's Dr. Donald Menzel, the Carl Sagan of the 1950s and 60s.

Shortly before the war, Bush was also working closely with Dr. Donald Menzel, an astronomer at Harvard University, on the development of the so-called "Differential Analyzer," the world's first analog computer. When Menzel came under fire as a potential security risk just after the war, Bush was quick and decisive in his defense of the Harvard astronomer. In Bush's testimony on behalf of Menzel in loyalty Hearings in 1950, he noted:

> I first knew DHM (Menzel) of Cambridge, MA, in either 1934 or 1935 when I was engaged in designing and building a machine known as a differential analyzer at MIT,

176

where I was then VP and Dean of Engineering. Dr. M. , who was then an Asst. or Assoc. Prof. in the Astronomy Dept. of Harvard. U, was much interested in the possibility of applying the differential analyzer to the solution of certain astronomical and astrophysical problems. This mutual interest led to a technical association of some intimacy over a period of about a year. Thereafter, until I became associated with the Carnegie Institution in 1939 we met in connection with scientific or technical matters fairly frequently, usually in connection with the development of specialized machinery for astrophysical use.

Although not overtly stated, Bush and Menzel's objective was to develop a computer that could allow them to predict the future positions of stars and planets from any point in the solar system. This would allow NASA to accurately predict the appearance of the skies above a specific landing site on a specific date and time with amazing accuracy. Why they might wish to do so will become clear shortly.

Interestingly, Dr. Bush and Menzel were also tied together in another curious twist in history, the so-called "MJ-12 documents."

In 1984, microfilm documents were anonymously mailed to the home of UFO researcher Jaime Shandera. When enlarged and printed out, the documents appeared to comprise a genuine top-secret briefing memo from 1952 to then president-elect Dwight Eisenhower. The memo described the now famous crash of a flying saucer in the New Mexico desert in 1947 near Roswell, and the recovery of bodies and a subsequent cover-up of the same events. It also listed a group of 12 members of a new organization tasked with dealing with the "alien problem." The group, called Majestic or "MJ" 12, included both Bush and Menzel as founding members. At first, debunkers asserted the presence of Menzel on the list as "proof" the documents were forgeries, since Menzel had been a frequent UFO debunker in public, having written three books on the subject. He was also the point man for the orchestrated attacks on Emmanel Velikovsky, a psychologist who had written a popular

177

book (*Worlds in Collision*) arguing for a catastrophic model of the solar system's origin. Menzel, who served as Carl Sagan's mentor at Harvard, was essentially the Carl Sagan of his day and seemed a highly unlikely member of such a super-secret organization. However, longtime UFO researcher and nuclear physicist Stanton Friedman went through Menzel's papers as part of his research for a book on the MJ-12 documents, and discovered that Menzel had led an elaborate double life. Friedman found numerous references to Menzel's participation in a variety of intelligence projects and committees, including some top-secret weapons programs that would have made him an ideal candidate for MJ-12. Friedman also makes a compelling argument for the validity of the MJ-12 documents, and the existence of MJ-12 itself. These arguments have been reinforced by the work of Dr. Bob Wood, a long time physics professor, engineer and documents expert (as well as the man who hired Friedman at the aerospace company TRW) who has found numerous confirmations that MJ-12 did indeed exist.

But, whatever the reality of MJ-12, there is no question that Vannevar Bush had a significant impact on what would eventually

Theodore von Karman (Caltech).

become known as NASA. From his position so close to so many powerful men, he was able to influence a great deal of US space science and rocket research. During the pre-war period, there were other roots of the future space agency springing up in places far distant from Washington DC.

JPL and the Magicians

At virtually the same time as the rise of NACA and the developments that led to the formation of MJ-12, a second group was vying for political power behind the scenes at what was to become NASA. Led by Theodore von Karman, a small group of maverick scientists had been heavily involved in the development of rocket fuels and engine technology for the military's early ballistic missile programs in the 1930s and 40s.

What eventually became NASA's Jet Propulsion Laboratory (JPL) started out in the 1920s as an aerodynamics testing facility under the aegis of the University of California. Called the Guggenheim Aeronautical Laboratory, California Institute of Technology, or GALCIT, it was funded by the famous Guggenheim

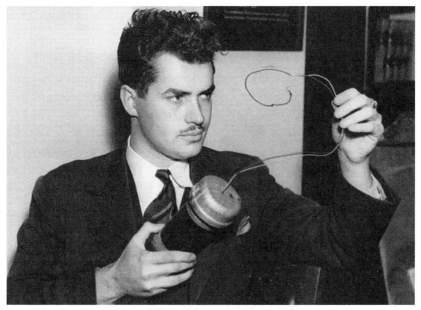

John Whiteside Parsons (Caltech).

Foundation and administered by Caltech. In 1926, the lab was put under the direction of the well-known Hungarian professor Theodore von Karman. Von Karman's chief experimental scientist was John Whiteside Parsons, a brilliant experimental field engineer who made some huge strides in the field of solid rocket propulsion under von Karman's tutelage.

Parsons however, led a double life. Killed under mysterious circumstances in his Pasadena lab in 1952, Parsons had a long fascination with black magic and the occult, and regularly practiced ritual sex orgies in his Pasadena mansion. His compatriot in many of these bizarre rites was one L. Ron Hubbard, who later went on to form the Church of Scientology, which still exerts a major influence in Hollywood today. Parsons took many of his ideas from Aleister Crowley, the self-proclaimed "wickedest man in the world," who made Parsons the head of his temple in America.

Hired by von Karmen in 1935, Parsons, perhaps not coincidentally, was born on October 2, 1914, the same day that Charles Taze Russell, the founder of the Jehovah's Witness movement, predicted the beginning of the end of the world would commence. Parsons was named for his father, a philanderer who

The JATO (Jet-Assisted Takeoff) rocket, a Jack Parsons invention (Aerojet).

was divorced by his mother soon after "Marvel" (later "John" and "Jack") was born. It is safe to assume that Parsons viewed his parent's broken marriage as a consequence of the Victorian sexual mores of the time, since he spent most of his adult life raging against those very same societal values. This probably led to Parsons' hatred of traditional marriage and religion, and his embrace of the occult.

Parsons spent the other portion of his adult life developing one breakthrough after another in rocket propulsion. He eventually founded Aerojet Corporation, which even today builds most of the solid rocket boosters for NASA and the military.

Although Parsons had no formal education, von Karman quickly came to realize he had a "rich talent for chemistry" and allowed him, his friends and associates to use the GALCIT labs. By the middle 1930s, Parsons and his pals were testing small rockets in an area of Pasadena called the Devil's Canyon. Today, the Jet Propulsion Laboratory sits on that very land. Parsons and his compatriot in chemistry and rocketry, Ed Forman, are known to have had contact during this same period with German rocket

The birth of JPL. Parsons poses with colleagues before a liquid fuel rocket test in Arroyo Seca, October 31, 1936 (yes Halloween). JPL commemorates this moment every year with a "nativity scene" laid out with mannequins on the JPL front lawn.

pioneer Herrmann Oberth and American physicist Robert Goddard (who was working alone in Roswell, New Mexico). But Parsons and his team apparently learned little of value from them since they had not achieved much themselves.

Von Karman, like Parsons, also fancied himself something of a mystic, and he was known to have claimed on many occasions that one of his ancestors had fashioned a "golem," an artificial human being in Hebrew, folklore endowed with life via magical incantations. Von Karman also loved to tell people that Parsons was "a delightful screwball" who used to recite pagan poetry before each rocket test.

Von Karman apparently shared many of Parsons' occult beliefs. He was primarily responsible for the creation of JPL (on Halloween, 1936, no less) at a rocket test in the Arroyo Seca area of the Devil's Canyon. JPL still refers to this test as the birthplace of the laboratory, and even trots out what they call a "nativity scene" every Halloween to commemorate the event. Around December 1938, Parsons, perhaps through his association with von Karman, fell in with Aleister Crowley's Ordo Templi Orientis (OTO) at their temple in Los Angeles. Initiated into the order in 1939, Parsons made a major impression on his fellow members, including Jane Wolfe, an actress who had spent some time with Crowley. She wrote of him:

> Unknown to me, John Whiteside Parsons, a newcomer, began astral travels. This knowledge decided Regina to undertake similar work. All of which I learned after making my own decision. So the time must be propitious. Incidentally, I take Jack Parsons to be the child who 'shall behold them all' (the mysteries hidden therein. AL, 54-5).
>
> 26 years of age, 6'2", vital, potentially bisexual at the very least, University of the State of California and Cal. Tech., now engaged in Cal. Tech. chemical laboratories developing 'bigger and better' explosives for Uncle Sam. Travels under sealed orders from the government. Writes

poetry– 'sensuous only', he says. Lover of music, which he seems to know thoroughly. I see him as the real successor of Therion [Crowley]. Passionate; and has made the vilest analyses result in a species of exaltation after the event. Has had mystical experiences which gave him a sense of equality all round, although he is hierarchical in feeling and in the established order.

Aleister Crowley in full 33° Masonic regalia, circa 1914

By the early 1940s, Parsons was a rising star in the OTO, and he and Crowley were exchanging letters with frequency. Crowley comes off these days as an almost buffoonish character, deeply committed to his hatred of established religions, a member of dozens of secret societies (he was a 33 degree Scottish Rite Freemason, for one), and a general rabble-rouser who wanted to overturn the religious underpinnings of Western civilization. Yet, when you read Crowley's writings, such as *The Book of the Law* (which he claimed was dictated to him by an extraterrestrial named "Lam"), they weave a complex but internally consistent tale of one man's search for intellectual freedom and spiritual knowledge. Whether Crowley truly "knew something" or not, there is no doubt that he acquired a substantive and perhaps even unique amount of knowledge about the world's ancient religions and occult beliefs.

He and Parsons set about expanding the membership of the OTO lodge in Los Angeles, and Parsons apparently was successful in getting some of his fellow GALCIT scientists to join. During this period, he was investigated frequently for reports of public nudity and bizarre rituals taking place in his Pasadena mansion. Each time, he was able to convince authorities that he was an upstanding citizen and rocket scientist and that nothing of the sort was going on. Parsons left GALCIT to start Aerojet with several of his compatriots from GALCIT, including von Karman, and they soon had a contract to produce Jet-Assisted Takeoff (JATO) devices for the military. During the war, a succession of oddballs and "bohemians" made their way through the mansion (and the OTO), until one very special man showed up in 1945.

How exactly L. Ron Hubbard came to Jack Parsons' Pasadena mansion is something of a mystery. The Church of Scientology, which he founded, claims that he was sent by the US Navy to infiltrate and break up a "black magic cult" operating in Los Angeles. Parsons' own letters (and those of other observers at the time) tell a different story. By their accounts, Hubbard found a kindred spirit in Parsons and the two quickly fell into a variety of "magical workings," mostly sexual rituals designed to achieve one short-term goal or another. By 1946, Parsons had bigger plans.

He and Hubbard decided that they would recreate a famous series of séances performed by Dr. John Dee, the Royal Astrologer to Queen Elizabeth, in the 16th century. In order to do this, Parsons decided he needed an "elemental"—a female magical partner with red hair and green eyes that could help him conjure the spirits he was looking to raise. He and Hubbard meditated intensely in the California desert for 11 days until one night Parsons declared, "it is done" to Hubbard and returned to the mansion. The next day, a red-haired, green-eyed young woman by the name of Marjorie Cameron showed up at the mansion.

Cameron herself is something of a mystery woman, having apparently made a beeline directly to Parsons' Pasadena mansion after resigning her position as a secretary to the Chairman of the Joint Chiefs of Staff in 1946. Cameron would later appear in

Marjorie Cameron in the 1940s.

Kenneth Anger's film *Inauguration of the Pleasure Dome*, and was an artist of some renown and a primary force in the New Age "Goddess" movement in the 1970s and 80s. Parsons quickly became enamored of her, and in a letter dated February 23, 1946, wrote to Crowley: "I have my elemental! She turned up one night after the conclusion of the Operation, and has been with me since."

Cameron was only too happy to participate in Parsons' ritual sex magic, and Parsons was now free to begin the major project he had in mind: the so-called "Babalon Working."

In magical circles, the Babalon Working is considered a masterpiece of the form, certainly on a par (at least in its level of ambition) with Dee and Edward Kelly's attempts to communicate with angels in the 1500s. The purpose of the Babalon Working, as Parsons and Hubbard called it, was to give birth to a "Moonchild" or homunculus, a destructive version of von Karman's golem. To do this required the magical participation of the power male Therion (Parsons) and the power female figure, Babalon (Cameron). The operation was formulated to open an interdimensional doorway, rolling out the red carpet for the appearance of the Antichrist in human form. The first step was to employ the Enochian Calls (angelic language) of Elizabethan magus John Dee while the couple had sex. The hope was that Babalon (Cameron) would become pregnant with a female child who would then at some point become the bride of Therion (her own father) and then the mother of the Antichrist.

To be sure, this was no idle exercise or an excuse for a simple orgy. As writer Paul Rydeen points out in his extended essay "Jack Parsons and the Fall of Babalon":

> The purpose of Parsons' operation has been underemphasized. He sought to produce a magickal child who would be a product of her environment rather than of her heredity. Crowley himself describes the Moonchild in just these terms. The Babalon Working itself was preparation for what was to come: a Thelemic messiah. To wit: Babalon incarnate as a living female, the Scarlet

Woman as consort to the Antichrist, bride of the Beast 666. In effect, Parsons also claimed the mantle of Antichrist for himself, as the magickal heir of Crowley prophesied in *Liber AL*: 'The child of thy bowels, he shall behold them [the mysteries of the Apocalypse]. Expect him not from the East, nor from the West, for from no expected house cometh that child.' Without the Scarlet Woman, the Antichrist cannot make his manifestation; the eschatological formula must first be complete. In whiter words, with the magickal rites of the Babalon Working, it was Parsons' goal to bring on the Apocalypse.

From the perspective of more than 50 years hence, the notion that Parsons and Cameron could give birth to a daughter whom Parsons apparently planned to eventually impregnate seems not only sick, but also absurd. But Parsons and Crowley believed that mankind was mired in the occulted "Age of Osiris"—in their view a dark time when men were ruled by arbitrary laws that denied them their proper birthright. By giving birth to the whore of Babalon, Parsons believed he was sowing the seeds of the destruction of the Western world and clearing the way for the illuminated, freer "Age of Horus."

Crowley, however, when he caught wind of what Hubbard and Parsons were attempting, became alarmed. He wrote, "Apparently Parsons and Hubbard or somebody is producing a Moonchild. I get fairly frantic when I contemplate the idiocy of these louts." Crowley evidently considered the actual raising of a Moonchild to be an incredibly risky endeavor. In his view, neither man was experienced enough in the methods (and consequences) of using Crowley's Thelemic "Sex-Magick" in this way.

After several months of trying, Parsons and Cameron apparently (and perhaps thankfully) failed in their attempts to produce Crowley's Moonchild. Eventually, they gave up, and hatched a scheme to make money buying yachts on the East Coast, sailing them to California, and selling them at a profit. The whole notion collapsed when Hubbard went to New York with

Parsons' money and Betty Northup, daughter of the founder of the aerospace company, who was the sister of Parsons' wife Helen and who had had serious relations with Parsons as well. Hubbard then ran off to Florida with the boat, the girl, and the rest of Parsons' money.

Parsons wrote Crowley and told him that when he almost caught up to Betty and Hubbard in Florida, they escaped in one of the boats. Hearing this too late to pursue them, Parsons set up a magical circle and summoned the god Bartzabel (a form of Mars) to conjure a storm. Indeed, Hubbard and Betty did encounter a fierce storm at sea, and were forced to return to Miami where Parsons had them arrested. In the end, Parsons recovered some of his money, and Hubbard went on to marry Betty and eventually form the Church of Scientology, which continues to claim to this day that Hubbard was operating on orders to break up the "black magic cult" when he got involved with the rocket scientists at JPL. In fact, I was contacted by senior members of the Church who wished to discuss these events with me in person. In October, 2008, I was invited to the visit the L. Ron Hubbard Life Exhibition in Hollywood and meet with several members of the Church. They sought to set the record straight on what they viewed as mischaracterizations in the stories about Hubbard and Jack Parsons. They were most concerned with conveying the message that none of their teachings are based in any way on the Thelemic beliefs of Aleister Crowley. My knowledge of the practices of the Church of Scientology is too limited to dispute the Church on this matter. But the remaining issues are more significant to the thesis presented here.

The Church has argued Hubbard was not so much a willing participant in Parsons' pursuits as he was an instrument of disruption inside the Ordo Templi Orientis. According to the Church, Hubbard was sent to infiltrate and disrupt the worrisome activities of Jack Parsons at 1003 Orange Grove Avenue. Documents provided to me by the Church now incline me to lean more toward this interpretation, rather than maintain the perception that Hubbard was just a con man looking to get into Parsons' pockets. What is now clear to me are the following facts:

A)   Hubbard was in fact a US Naval Intelligence Officer, as the Church has claimed, at least at some point during his service career.

B)   Hubbard was residing in the area at the time he was supposedly befriending Parsons and infiltrating the OTO, and was still an active naval officer.

C)   Hubbard would have been an ideal agent to carry out such an operation.

D)   Pasadena's OTO headquarters was indeed damaged for years by Hubbard's actions.

L. Ron Hubbard.

According to Navy documents, Lafayette Ronald Hubbard was assigned to intelligence duties in July, 1941. While it appears from his service record that he was no longer actively serving in intelligence assignments during the period he was hanging around with Parsons, he was still technically on active duty and remained in the reserves until October of 1950, well after his time in Pasadena. There is a saying in intelligence circles that goes "once an asset, always an asset," and it seems reasonable that Hubbard would have still been a candidate for just such an assignment during the period in question.

According to a handwritten memo obtained under the Freedom of Information Act, Parsons' occult activities had come under the scrutiny of the FBI and the Office of Naval Intelligence (ONI) as early as 1940. Their interest was sparked not just because Parsons was a prominent rocket scientist, but because there were a number of America's leading atomic scientists running through the OTO as well. In addition, the OTO was being run out of the New York branch by Karl Germer, a former German military officer in the First World War and a suspected Nazi agent. It was also known that Germer reported to Crowley directly, and Crowley was also considered a possible Nazi spy.

Although he was officially listed as a patient at Oak Knoll Naval hospital in San Francisco until December of 1945, a telegram from Hubbard to the Navy dated October 13, 1945 indicates he was staying in Hollywood, near Parsons and the OTO lodge in Pasadena. What he might have been doing there is speculative but the fact that the official record shows him in the hospital at that time may be an indication he was on some sort of secret assignment in Hollywood. He certainly wasn't hiding out or AWOL, as his open correspondence with the Navy proves.

The Church argues that in this postwar period the Office of Naval Intelligence was particularly worried about a group called the Federation of American Scientists. The FAS was a left-wing group of disaffected Manhattan Project veterans who were dismayed at the military uses of atomic weapons. Minutes recorded at a November 15, 1945 meeting of the FAS (again, while Hubbard was officially still in the hospital) indicate that both Hubbard and Parsons attended and participated in the meeting.

As we all know, Hubbard eventually ended up in Florida with Sara "Betty" Northrup, sister of Parsons' wife Helen (and Parsons' lover prior to Hubbard appearing on the scene), and a sailing boat named the *Harpoon*. A Bill of Sale produced by the Church shows that Parsons sold the *Harpoon* to Hubbard. The whole affair soured Crowley on Parsons, and subsequently several members of the OTO and the FAS lost their security clearances, including Parsons and Robert Cornog, one of the developers of the nuclear triggers used in the first atomic bombs. An FBI memo from the period also indicates that the Office of Naval Intelligence had "an informant" inside the group.

So, was this informant L. Ron Hubbard? Did he really go to Pasadena in order to infiltrate and destabilize both the OTO and FAS? Was his running off with Betty and the boat just a means of creating chaos in the OTO and breaking the worrisome links between Crowley and America's top rocket scientists and nuclear physicists? After seeing the documentation supplied me by the Church of Scientology, I find the premise a plausible one. Hubbard had an intelligence background, he apparently knew something of esoteric teachings and the occult from his world travels, and he did attend one of the first university courses on nuclear physics ever taught in the United States. All of these attributes would have made him an ideal candidate for such an assignment, as would his background as a relatively well-known science fiction writer, since Parsons was a huge fan of the literary form.

Honestly, based on what I know at this time, I have to say it is more likely than not that Hubbard was inside the OTO as an agent of the US government. And there is little doubt that he played a major role in the breakup of the OTO.

The whole episode, including the Babalon Working itself, soured Crowley on Parsons to the point that he wanted to remove him as the head of the OTO in America. Parsons held on to lead the OTO for a few more years, but eventually quit. After that, his life spiraled downhill (Cameron married him but left him after a few years), until he was killed in huge blast in his Pasadena lab. Ironically, this was just the fate that Hubbard had "scribed" for him in the Babalon Working.

Whatever Parsons' odd beliefs, there is no question he was massively influential in rocket technology development. He achieved in five years what Goddard and other pioneers could not in decades of work. By the time GALCIT became the Jet Propulsion Laboratory in January of 1945, Parsons' reputation had been sealed. Buildings still carry his name at Caltech, as does a crater on the back or "dark side" of the moon. both Wernher von Braun and von Karmen named him as one of the three most important pioneers of the rocket age.

It is also possible, if not likely, that Parsons, von Karman and von Braun all met at least once. Parsons was known to have corresponded with von Braun in the 1930s, and after the war, von Karman was sent to Germany to interview the German rocket scientists and tour the Nazi facilities at Pennemunde and Mittlewerk. He did meet with von Braun there, and recommended he be brought to the US, which was in violation of the directives of Project Paperclip. Von Braun and the first batch of German rocketry experts were transferred to Alabama, where von Karman and others continued to debrief them. Several letters from Parsons to Cameron during this period are postmarked in Alabama, indicating that Parsons was part of the debriefing process. What they may have discussed is perhaps more interesting than you may envision.

The German Rocket Programs

The story of Wernher von Braun, Kurt Debus, and the other German rocket scientists brought to the US after World War II

Dr. Wernher von Braun with his Nazi commander, Walter Dornberger.

may not be as strange as the story of JPL's founders, but it is, if anything, far more disturbing.

To most Americans who grew up during the 1960s, Dr. Wernher Von Braun is a "hero" of the American space program. He is largely credited as the single most important figure in the Moon rocket programs of the 1960s and 70s. Without him, there might not have been a Saturn V to carry American astronauts to the Moon. Von Braun is more rarely mentioned these days, nearly 40 years after his death, and when he is, he is usually portrayed as either a dedicated scientific visionary or a lovable buffoon, as in the film The Right Stuff.

But as Shaw says, history tells lies, and the history of von Braun and the "American" space program he pioneered is altogether different from what has been represented over the decades. As it turns out, various researchers have discovered that Von Braun was far more than just a German rocket scientist or even a mere member of the Nazi party, as some histories have freely admitted. Documents obtained from the National Archives show he was nothing less than a Major in Hitler's SS, the fearsome and fanatically loyal arm of the Nazi war machine entrusted to carry out the most inhuman acts of the regime. Writer Linda Hunt, a former CNN reporter and author of *Secret Agenda: The United States Government, Nazi Scientists, and Project Paperclip 1945 to 1990*, found survivors of the Nazi missile factories at Mittlewerk and Peenemunde who told her that von Braun not only witnessed executions and abuse of prisoners at those facilities, but on at least one occasion he ordered executions. Recently uncovered documents also show that von Braun was commissioned to come up with a plan near the end of World War II to use one of his V-2 rockets to bomb New York City with a radioactive device, a nefarious scheme which would have killed thousands, if not millions. That such a man could spend his later years standing next to presidents at medal presentations and giving speeches on the wonders of space exploration, rather than rotting in prison where he belonged, is a testament to the political realities of the Cold War.

Von Braun began his interest in rocketry at a young age. Born on March 23, 1912, in Wirsitz, Germany von Braun was the second of three children born to aristocrats Baron Magnus and Baroness Emmy von Braun. Baron von Braun served as Minister of Agriculture toward the end of the Weimar Republic, and brought his family to Berlin in the 1920s. As a child, von Braun became fascinated by the possibilities of space exploration. He received a telescope along with a copy of rocket pioneer Hermann Oberth's "A Rocket into Interplanetary Space," which influenced him to experiment with rocket motors. At the age of 16, he organized an observatory construction team, and then went on to study mechanical engineering at the Berlin Institute of Technology, where he became a member of the German Society for Space Travel. In 1932, he enrolled at Berlin University, where he assembled a team of over a hundred scientists. Von Braun's team, which included his younger brother, Magnus, performed early experiments in rocket development.

After World War I, Germany wanted to improve its defense artillery armaments and, recognizing von Braun's research and development capabilities, offered the scientist a grant to conduct various experiments on liquid-fueled rocket engines. Von Braun, who was still a student, operated at a secret laboratory on the Baltic Coast near Peenemunde, a favorite summer vacation destination of his family. Once established, the classified research he carried out there doubled as his doctoral thesis. His design was successful, and the German space program led the way in rocket development in the early 1930s.

When Hitler came to power in 1933, von Braun remained in Germany, even though he could have left and gone to France, England or America. Von Braun's team had the eyes of the Fürher on them almost from the moment he assumed power. Col. Walter Dornberger was assigned by Hitler personally to oversee the research for military applications. Evidently this ardor from the Nazi party didn't bother Von Braun all that much.

In 1939, Adolf Hitler himself visited the young scientist's labs where he was treated to an impressive demonstration of the

A young Wernher von Braun posing with the Fürher himself (inset).

capabilities of the rockets von Braun's team had been developing. The Fürher came away impressed with the demonstration, but pressed von Braun to escalate his timetable for full-scale development. Even though no new monies were immediately released to the von Braun team, a few weeks after the meeting von Braun received a letter offering a degree in the SS from Himmler personally.

The canonical NASA history is that he was "pressured" by the Third Reich to become involved in many Nazi organizations and that he agonized over the decision, but this actually seems unlikely. His aristocratic parents no doubt had many connections, even in Hitler's government, and many European aristocrats were members of secret societies like the Masons or Rosicrucians. Joining the Nazi party and even the SS might not only have seemed like a good career move, but may have come naturally to a man who was raised to consider his higher place in society as a birthright.

In fact, it is now clear that von Braun was a close personal friend of German Reichsfuhrer Heinrich Himmler, who offered him the SS degree and rank of Major. Himmler was responsible for the growth and maturation of the SS from Hitler's personal bodyguard to a massive secret organization with its own unique mission, objectives, army and internal structure.

195

It was also a secret society. Designed specifically by Himmler to be a German counterpart to the "Bolshevik, Jewish, Free Mason" influence in Europe, the SS led the persecution of Freemasons (and later Jews and other racial minorities) in Hitler's Germany. According to Dr. Nicholas Goodrick-Clarke Oxford scholar and author of *The Occult Roots of Nazism*, Hitler and Himmler considered the Nazi party to be a direct lineal descendant of the Teutonic Knights, and Hitler to be a reincarnation of Fredrick Barbarossa, the reputed founder of that offshoot of the Knights Templar. Influenced by various Aryan cults of the early 1900s, like the Thule Society, the SS created its own set of rituals and degrees much like the Masonic rites.

That von Braun (and other Nazi rocketry experts) were voluntary members of this organization is not all that far-fetched. For a man of von Braun's ambition, he might have seen his membership as not only desirable, but perhaps even a requirement considering the secrecy involved in the German rocket projects. Clearly, if he could show Hitler and Himmler he could keep a secret, they would trust him that much more with the money and resources (like the slave labor) needed in the secret rocket factories.

The only confirmed photo of SS Major Wernher von Braun in his SS uniform, standing directly behind Heinrich Himmler, Reichsführer of the Schutzstaffel (SS), at von Braun's induction ceremony (Biography Channel & National Archives).

Von Braun was certainly considered a key member of the Reich's upper echelon. A testament to this is the fact that at his induction into the SS, the only time he is known to have worn his SS uniform, Himmler himself was in attendance, and the two were photographed together. It was almost certainly a rare occasion when the Reichsführer himself attended an SS induction ceremony.

Once he had secured the money from the Nazi regime, von Braun set right to work on his task. After a number of failed attempts, von Braun perfected the A4, the world's first true ballistic missile, in the early 1940s. Shortly after, the weapon was being mass-produced at the Mittelwerk concentration camp. In compliance with Hitler's orders, the A4 flying bomb was deployed against Britain in 1944. The London town of Chiswick was devastated by the bomb, and Nazi commander Joseph Goebbels renamed the A4 the "vengeance weapon 2," or V-2.

Von Braun knew well before the end that the war was lost. As the Allies neared the capture of the V-2 rocket complex, von Braun engineered the surrender of 500 of his top rocket scientists, along with plans and test vehicles, to the Americans. Von Braun and his compatriots were brought to America under Project Paperclip, despite objections by investigators in the JIOA that considered von Braun an "ardent Nazi."

The simple fact that Von Braun, Arthur Rudolph, Kurt Debus, Hubertus Strughold, and many other German scientists with elaborate Nazi pasts were brought to the US at all is a testament to Cold War convenience. President Truman's executive order authorizing the program was very specific: no "ardent Nazis" or war criminals would be allowed into the US under Paperclip. Clearly, as a Major in the SS, von Braun at least fit the description of "ardent Nazi," if not a war criminal. Fortunately, von Braun had friends in the personages of Drs. Bush and von Karman, and apparently also Jack Parsons. Their influence was so powerful that doubts expressed by the investigators about his Nazi past were overlooked or suppressed.

Once they cleared the hurdles imposed by Paperclip, von

Braun and his team were quickly sent out to White Sands Missile Range in New Mexico. There, they conducted tests on the captured V-2s and worked on developing bigger and more powerful rockets. Von Braun quickly showed his expertise and abilities as an organizer, and was rewarded when he became technical director of the US Army ballistic weapon program. In 1950, the German scientists were transferred to the Army's Redstone Arsenal near Huntsville, Alabama, where they developed the Redstone, Jupiter, and Jupiter-C ballistic missiles. During this period, von Braun and his cohorts were so certain of their value that they made no attempt to conceal either their Nazi pasts or, apparently, their love for the Third Reich. Having beaten the system through Paperclip, they evidently didn't care who knew of their "ardent Nazi" pasts. Most, if not all, had intricate Nazi pasts and were still heavily committed to the party's ideologies, and apparently practiced its sacraments.

Wernher von Braun (third from right) in Nevada, after the war. Note the swastika on the sign. He and his friends made no attempt to hide their allegiances while working on "our" space program.

During this same period, von Braun used various avenues to sell Americans on the idea of space travel. He wrote several articles in the popular quarterly magazine Collier's, and the success of these articles attracted the notice of 33° Scottish Rite

Freemason Walt Disney. Disney hired von Braun to produce and star in three popular television films about space travel in the future. The first, *Man in Space*, aired on ABC on March 9, 1955. The second, *Man and the Moon*, aired the same year, and the final film, *Mars and Beyond*, was televised on December 4, 1957. These programs helped establish von Braun as America's most notable space expert.

They were also full of symbolic, secret messages. The kinds of messages that members of secret societies use to communicate to each other and to indoctrinate the masses.

In *Man and the Moon*, von Braun first discusses his concepts for how a manned reconnaissance of the Moon might be handled in the near future. He tells the audience in extensive detail how such a mission would be designed and carried out. Using a model of his rocket concept, von Braun sets up a dramatization of ban's first mission to the Moon. In that dramatization, von Braun's rocket takes five days to get to the Moon on a free return trajectory with a chance for one pass around the "dark side" before returning to Earth. The dramatization is like a mini-movie but clearly a mini-movie with von Braun's indelible stamp on it. As the ship reaches the Moon, the crew begins to launch flares to illuminate

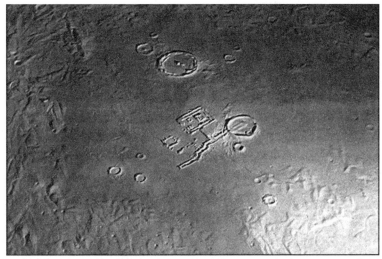

Screen capture from Disney's *Man and the Moon*, depicting an artificial base on the far side of the Moon (Mike Bara).

the darkened portions of the lunar landscape. The film does a remarkable job of accurately depicting the Moon's surface, until a dramatic event takes place. As the ship is flying along in its single pass, taking readings, a crewman suddenly announces that he has a high radiation reading at "33 degrees," a clear reference to the top rank in the Scottish Rite order. A radar operator then announces that he has an unusual formation coming up in front of them, and a flare is launched immediately.

When it detonates, the flare reveals the unmistakable, *geometric* outline of an installation, presumably an alien base, beneath them on the far side of the Moon. There is no question that this formation is completely different from anything we have seen in any of the other views of the Moon to this point, and no question that it is artificial. So what is the reaction to this sight by the astronauts? Absolutely nothing. Not a word is spoken about it in the dramatization or at any point later in the show. Von Braun simply inserted it without comment, as if it were meant to be an early cultural meme, letting the audience know what we might find on the Moon.

In 1955, von Braun became a US citizen and served as the primary Army engineer for space exploration support. In 1957, after the Soviet Union successfully launched the Sputnik satellite, the Navy was tasked with matching the Soviet accomplishment with its Vanguard rocket. Von Braun boldly predicted that Vanguard would fail. When it blew up on the launch pad, Von Braun's team was commissioned to get the US into the space race. Seizing this opportunity, the German team launched the first successful US satellite, Explorer 1, on January 31, 1958. Shortly after the mission's success, the National Aeronautics and Space Administration (NASA) was established, and von Braun had finally stamped the ticket he'd been looking to cash in for decades.

The Birth of NASA

The National Aeronautics and Space Administration was created by an Act of Congress on July 29, 1958. Its ostensible purpose was to act as a civilian science agency for the betterment of mankind and to enhance the defense of the United States of America. We have always been taught that NASA is a public agency, beholden only to the will of the people through their representatives in Congress. The Act itself however, paints a different picture. From the beginning, NASA was under the thumb of the Department of Defense, subject to the whims of the Pentagon on any issue judged to be "necessary to make effective provision for the defense of the United States." It was required under the Act to make available "to agencies directly concerned with national defense ... discoveries that have military value or significance." Such determinations were made solely by the President of the United States (obviously on the recommendation of the DOD), and were not subject to congressional oversight.

The upshot of this is that the agency was compromised from its inception. A civilian figurehead director was trotted out for the public to consume, but he was always taking orders from the Pentagon on any question it determined was in the interests of "national defense." And according to the Act, the Pentagon was accountable to no civilian branch of government on these issues. The Act establishes that contrary to its perception as a public agency, NASA is beholden to its Pentagon masters first and foremost, to its own interests second, and to the general public third, if at all. Regardless of its well-cultivated public perception as a civilian science-gathering agency, NASA has always been under the thumb of the intelligence establishment. Looking at the original management team that was placed at the agency, it's easy to see that finding men with strong Pentagon ties was a priority.

Shortly after the formation of NASA, President Eisenhower surprised many in the scientific community and passed over the respected and apolitical Hugh L. Dryden (Director of NACA since 1949, after Dr. Bush left), and named T. Keith Glennan as head instead. Glennan had been president of the Case Institute of Technology in Cleveland, was a former member of the Atomic Energy Commission, and was a staunch Republican. Glennan also had an extensive military background, having served as Director of the US Navy's Underwater Sound Laboratories during

World War II. As the first Administrator of NASA, Glennan set up a compartmentalized internal structure, far more akin to an intelligence-gathering agency than a civilian scientific program. Dryden was appointed to the post of Deputy Administrator. Under this structure, Glennan would furnish the administrative leadership for the new entity, while Dryden would function as NASA's scientific and technical overseer.

In a single day, NASA absorbed more than 8,000 employees and an appropriation of over $100 million from NACA as it was first formed. Under the terms of the Space Act, accompanying White House directives, and later agreements with the Defense Department, the fledgling agency also acquired the Vanguard project from the Naval Research Laboratory and the Explorer project and other space activities from the Army Ballistic Missile Agency (but not the von Braun rocket group). It also obtained control over the services of the Jet Propulsion Laboratory, hitherto an Army contractor. It also took over an Air Force study contract with North American for a million-pound-thrust engine, plus other Air Force rocket engine projects and instrumented satellite studies. In addition, NASA received $117 million in appropriations for space ventures from the Defense Department. Von Braun was appointed director of the new Marshall Space Flight Center in July, 1960 and given the task of developing the rockets for the new agency.

Glennan, like any good bureaucrat, moved quickly to establish the agency's monopoly over space exploration. One of NASA's first acts was to commission a report from the prestigious Brookings Institute, then the largest think tank in the world. The report was to consider the implications of discoveries that might be made during NASA's explorations. The "Brookings Report," as it came to be known, was officially called "Proposed Studies on the Implications of Peaceful Space Activities for Human Affairs." This special project was staffed by some of the greatest minds of the era, including the famous anthropologist Margaret Mead. The report makes it clear that the discovery of extraterrestrial ruins ("artifacts," the report calls them) falls under the dark blanket of

James E. Webb, NASA director and 33° Scottish Rite Freemason.

"national security" outlined in the Space Act. It goes on to state that the discovery of such ruins would be wholly destabilizing to the civilized world, and actually recommends that if such discoveries were made, they should be suppressed until such time as society could be properly "conditioned" to receive such news.

When John F. Kennedy took office in 1961, he moved swiftly to replace Glennan and restructure NASA to accomplish one of the major goals of his presidency: placing a man on the Moon by 1970. To this end, Kennedy appointed James E. Webb as the new NASA director. It is under Webb, a 33° Scottish Rite Freemason, that the influence of the various secret societies truly flourished. Within a few months, Webb had placed Kenneth S. Kleinknecht, the son of C. Fred Kleinknecht (who was the Sovereign Grand Commander of the Supreme Council, 33°, Ancient and Accepted Scottish Rite Freemasons, Southern Jurisdiction for the United States of America) as director of Project Mercury. Kleinknecht had already been selected in 1959 as one of two "single points-of-contact" between NASA and the DOD. In this dual role he was able to monitor information that traveled back and forth between Project Mercury and the Pentagon. With a lengthy history as an engineer in a variety of black programs in the 50s, he was ideally suited for this job. He went on to become a "technical assistant" to Program Mercury director Robert Gilruth in 1960, and became project manager for Mercury on January 15, 1962. Kleinknecht also became deputy project manager for the Gemini program, and was the Apollo program manager for the command and service modules. If there was a plan for the Masons to place "their" men at the highest levels of the space program, it could not have been more successful.

Von Braun and the German rocket team also made moves to establish their position within the agency. Once established as the head of the Huntsville rocket development site, von Braun moved many of his old Nazi cohorts into key positions. At von Braun's behest, Kurt Debus, a former colleague of von Braun's in the Second World War, was made the first director of the Kennedy Space Center. Debus, like von Braun, was also a Nazi party member, and he organized the space center at Cape Canaveral along the lines of the German rocket programs at Mittlewerk and Peenemunde.

Once these organizations were in place, the task of selecting the astronauts for the manned program began. Here again, a clear preference for Freemasons was expressed. Of the original "Mercury Seven" astronauts, John Glenn, Wally Schirra, Gus Grissom, and Gordon Cooper were all Scottish Rite Freemasons. Of the 12 men that walked on the surface of the moon, four were Scottish Rite Freemasons (as were several more astronauts who orbited the moon). Other astronauts may also have been members, since membership is not publicly acknowledged except by the personal choice of the member or by request of a fellow Mason. To make such a request, the requestor must have a good idea which lodge the persons they seek were members of, and the archivist must do a thorough job of checking the local lodge records. There have been persistent rumors that Neil Armstrong and Alan Shepard were also members, but it has never been confirmed, although Armstrong's father was certainly a Mason.

There could of course, be perfectly good reasons why so many of the astronauts were Masons. Many aspects of the lunar programs were secret, and the potential candidates may have seen membership in the organization as a means of demonstrating their ability to keep a secret. They may also have simply noticed that with Webb in charge of the agency, they might have a better chance

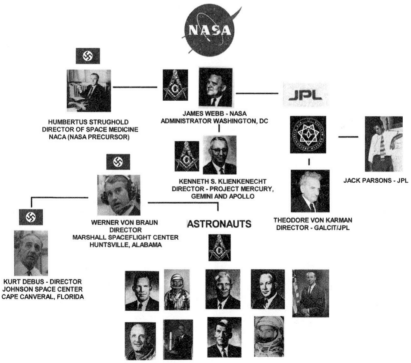

Organization chart showing Masons, SS members, and "Magicians" in key positions of power all throughout NASA in the 1960s. Everybody who was anybody at the agency was a member of one of the three secret societies.

of being selected for the choice missions if they joined as well. However, when we look at the core belief systems of not only the Masons, but of Hitler's SS and Crowley's Magicians, a picture emerges which makes a prosaic explanation for the Masonic presence at NASA seem far-fetched.

Once they had established themselves in all the key power positions at the space agency, von Braun, Webb, von Karman and the others were able to proceed with plans they had apparently been laying out for some time. With "Brookings" as a political cover, the elite members of this occult hierarchy were able to set in motion a program that appears to be no less than an attempt to confirm their shared religious belief system. As bizarre as this may sound, it appears in fact that many members of the NASA hierarchy were expecting nothing less than to find evidence of prior habitation of the solar system in their explorations. It is when you ask who, exactly, these inhabitants were that the question gets even more interesting.

While on the surface the Freemasons, the SS and the "Magicians" would appear to have little in common, the opposite is true. As I pointed out earlier, both the Freemasons and the SS shared common gods. Freemasonic historians Christopher Knight and Robert Lomas, in their two books *The Hiram Key* and *The Second Messiah*, establish with little doubt that the roots of modern Freemasonry follows a path back through history through the Knights Templar and the temple of Jerusalem in the time of Jesus, to the temple of Solomon and into ancient Egypt. They argue that at its core, Freemasonry holds the most ancient gods of Egypt—Isis, Osiris, Horus and Set—and their story as the key to their religion.

The same is true of the SS. In *The Occult Roots of Nazism*, Dr. Goodrick-Clarke shows that the early Aryan cults traced their lineage back to the Teutonic Knights (a Germanic offshoot of the Templars), at which point their ascendancy merges with the Templars and traces again to ancient Egypt. All of the Aryan cults, especially the Theosophical Society led by Madame Helena Blavatsky, had Isis worship and Osiris cults at the core of their belief systems. In *The Occult Roots of Nazism*, Dr. Goodrick-Clarke shows that Hitler and Himmler both believed that these Egyptian gods came from Atlantis, which they believed was a reference to a high civilization established on Earth by extraterrestrials. In their view, the bloodline from Horus (who was the grandson of Marduk and an Anunnaki), was the source of the Aryan race, and it was this divine right of bloodlines which gave them the right to rule over other men.

The same is true of Crowley and Parsons' JPL "Magicians." The magic being practiced by Parsons and Hubbard was a form of "Enochian Magic" which takes its roots from the Egyptian *Book of the Dead* and involves the invocation of Osiris. Without Osiris, there is no magic to behold.

What is less commonly known is that the Egyptians developed a stellar religion around the story of Isis and Osiris that retold their story in various forms. In this religion, the constellation Orion came to represent Osiris, Taurus represented Set, and Leo, Horus. The star Sirius was the living embodiment of Isis, the goddess of life and nurture. Following the edict "as above, so below," the Egyptians followed the motions of the stars for knowledge of not only the present, but for portents of the future. They, like the Anunnaki before them, had their own Tablets of Destiny in the night sky above them. By watching the stars, they knew the right time to harvest crops, make war, and marry and reproduce.

What is amazing is how this same system came to be used by NASA for an even more epic purpose—knowing the right time for the human race to return to the stars.

(Endnotes)

1 http://www.hq.nasa.gov/office/pao/History/SP-4203/cover.htm

Chapter 7
The Wink of an Eye

The very word 'secrecy' is repugnant in a free and open society; and we are as a people inherently and historically opposed to secret societies, to secret oaths and to secret proceedings. We decided long ago that the dangers of excessive and unwarranted concealment of pertinent facts far outweighed the dangers which are cited to justify it.
—*President John F. Kennedy*, April 27, 1961

Shortly after James E. Webb was put in place at NASA, John F. Kennedy made a speech in which he made the comments above that seemed to be directed right at the Freemasons. It might seem odd that he would blast secret societies, secret oaths and secret proceedings just after appointing such a prominent member of a secret society to what was the most important new agency in American history. But perhaps Kennedy was sending a signal that it was not he, after all, who had selected Webb. Maybe someone even more powerful than the president had made sure that "his" man had control of NASA in the personage of Mr. Webb.

Certainly, as America moved into the space age, the Freemasons had a lock on most of the senior positions within NASA. Even though he seemed to acquiesce to their agenda by launching the space race with Russia and pledging to send a man to the Moon within a decade, there are hints that Kennedy was at odds with NASA and Webb almost from the beginning.

On April 12, 1961, Yuri Gagarin had become the first human in space, aboard a Soviet spacecraft. The United States was shocked and six days later, NASA finally delivered a report they had commissioned on the proposed plan for space exploration—the aforementioned Brookings Report—to Congress. The delivery of the Report, which had been languishing on the desk of the previous NASA Administrator since November 30, 1960, suddenly had a new urgency.

Just about two weeks later, as if he were responding directly to the calls in the Report for NASA to consider suppression of the discovery of ET artifacts, Kennedy made a speech in which he signaled that he intended his administration to be an open one. He took the opportunity of a speech before the American Newspaper Publishers Association at the Waldorf Astoria hotel in New York City to make the comments cited above.

His speech, titled "The President and the Press,"[1] was clearly an attempt to reach out to the assembled publishers and editors in order to not only protect official secrets whose revelation might harm the national security of the United States, but also to help him in *revealing* secrets that were unnecessarily being kept. His opening comments, speaking of "secret societies" and the dangers of "excessive and unwarranted concealment" of things he felt the American people had a right to know, was an unmistakable shot across the bow of these secret societies, and I take it as a direct reference to the recommendations contained in the Brookings Report. It is also very obvious from his statement that he considered these dark forces of "concealment" to be very powerful. Why else would he ask for the press's help in fighting this battle?

A little over a month after drawing this important "line in the sand," on May 25, 1961. Kennedy addressed a Joint Session of Congress and issued his ringing call for "landing an American on the Moon" before 1970:

> First, I believe that this nation should commit itself to achieving the goal, before this decade is out, of landing a man on the Moon and returning him safely to the earth. No single space project in this period will be more impressive to mankind or more important for the long-range exploration of space; and none will be so difficult or expensive to accomplish.

This sequence of events implies that his "President and the Press" speech may have been influenced by the Brookings Report. Gagarin's flight obviously sent shockwaves through the US space and security agencies. They'd known that the Soviets were ahead in space technology, but the US wasn't even remotely close to being able to put a man in orbit. The immediate reaction was to finally send the report to Congress for review, as the game plan for the US response.

The inclusion of the key phrases about withholding any discoveries which may point to a previous and superior presence in the solar system might easily have prompted Kennedy's speech just a few days later. It was by then a foregone conclusion that the US would enter into a manned space race with the Soviets, but Kennedy was practically begging the press to help him make public the discoveries NASA might make.

Soviet premier Nikita Khrushchev's son, Sergei Khrushchev (now a senior fellow at the Watson Institute at Brown University), has stated that after the May 25th public call to "go to the Moon," Kennedy did an extraordinary thing: less than ten days later, he *secretly* proposed to Khrushchev at their Vienna summit that the United States and the Soviet Union merge their space programs to get to the Moon together.[2] Khrushchev turned Kennedy down, in part because he didn't trust the young president after the Bay of Pigs fiasco, and also because he feared that America might learn too many useful technological secrets from the Russians (who were, clearly, still ahead in "heavy lift" launch vehicles—useful in launching nuclear weapons).

Although the offer was not made public, it's easy to imagine the consternation it might have caused at the congressional level if it had leaked. Powerful congressmen, like Albert Thomas of Texas (who was Chairman of the Appropriations Committee in the House of Representatives and a close political ally of Vice President Lyndon Johnson and a staunch anti-communist), might have blown their tops if they had known about it. Thomas quite literally controlled all of the purse strings for the NASA budget and, along with LBJ, later got the Manned Spacecraft Center located in his home district in Houston. It is hard to imagine him, just a few weeks after receiving the Brookings study which called for keeping certain discoveries *from* the American people, agreeing to share these same discoveries with our Cold War enemy.

The situation was surely made worse in 1962 by the Cuban Missile Crisis, in which both nations stared down the barrel of nuclear annihilation and carefully stepped back from the brink. Far from discouraging him, these events may have emboldened Kennedy to try again. In August 1963, he met with Soviet ambassador Anatoly Dobrinyin in the Oval Office and once again (secretly) extended the offer. This time, Khrushchev considered it more seriously, but ultimately rejected it. Then in the fall of 1963 Kennedy met with Webb to discuss the proposal. This is how NASA's official history describes that meeting:

> Later on the morning of September 18, the president met briefly with James Webb. Kennedy told him that he was thinking of pursuing the topic of cooperation with the Soviets as part of a broader effort to bring the two countries closer together. [Webb would have been unaware of Kennedy's previous two offers to Khrushchev, as they were made in private talks with the Soviet premier.] He asked Webb, 'Are you sufficiently in control to prevent my being undercut in NASA if I do that?' As Webb remembered that meeting, 'So in a sense he didn't ask me *if* he should do it; he told me he thought he should do it and wanted to do it...' What he sought from Webb was the assurance that there would be no further unsolicited comments from within the space agency. Webb told the president that he could keep things under control.[3]

After receiving this assurance from Webb, Kennedy then surprised the entire world when only two days later he went before the United Nations General Assembly and startlingly repeated his offer of cooperation, for the first time in public:

Finally, in a field where the United States and the Soviet Union have a special capacity—in the field of space—there is room for new cooperation, for further joint efforts in the regulation and exploration of space. I include among these possibilities a joint expedition to the Moon. Space offers no problems of sovereignty; by resolution of this assembly, the members of the United Nations have foresworn any claim to territorial rights in outer space or on celestial bodies, and declared that international law and the United Nations Charter will apply. Why, therefore, should man's first flight to the Moon be a matter of national competition? Why should the United States and the Soviet Union, in preparing for such expeditions, become involved in immense duplications of research, construction and expenditure? Surely we should explore whether the scientists and astronauts of our two countries—indeed of all the world—cannot work together in the conquest of space, sending someday in this decade to the Moon not the representatives of a single nation, but the representatives of all of our countries.[4]

It is unclear what NASA Director Webb thought of the president's idea, but NASA insiders—as the president had feared—immediately expressed public doubts that the technical integration problems could be overcome.[5] The Western press was also very cautious. Many articles appeared resisting the idea of cooperating with a Cold War enemy that barely a year before had pointed first strike nuclear missiles at most of our major cities and sent our nation to the brink of war. The Soviet government did not make any official comment on the speech or the offer, and the Soviet press was equally silent.

But by far, the strongest objections came from within the US Congress.

As foreshadowed earlier, another, even stronger protest came from a close political *ally* of the president and vice president—Democratic Congressman Albert Thomas of Texas. Thomas made such a strong objection to the president that Kennedy personally wrote him on September 23, 1963 (just three days after his UN speech) to reassure him that a separate, American space program would continue, *regardless* of the outcome of negotiations with the Soviets:

> In my judgment, therefore, our renewed and extended purpose of cooperation, so far from offering any excuse for slackening or weakness in our space effort, is one reason the more for moving ahead with the great program to

"I WAS AFRAID SOMETHING LIKE THIS MIGHT HAPPEN IF YOU KEPT TALKING ABOUT IT."

Political cartoon mocking Kennedy's space cooperation proposal.

214

which we have been committed as a country for more than two years.[6]

Within a couple of weeks, the lack of public support, even within the US, seemed to have scuttled the idea permanently, and Kennedy began to publicly back away from his own proposal.[7] Then, strangely, the idea abruptly resurfaced.

On November 12, 1963, Kennedy was suddenly reinvigorated about it and issued National Security Action Memorandum #271. The memo, titled "Cooperation With the USSR on Outer Space Matters," directed NASA Director Webb to personally (and immediately) take the initiative to develop a program of "substantive cooperation" with his Soviet counterparts in accordance with Kennedy's September 20th UN proposal. It also called for an interim report on the progress being made by December 15, 1963, giving Webb a little over a month to get "substantive" cooperation with the Soviets going.[8]

There is a second, even stranger memo which has surfaced, dated the same day. Found by UFO document researchers Dr. Robert M. Wood and his son Ryan Wood (authors of *Majic Eyes Only: Earth's Encounters With Extraterrestrial Technology*) the document is titled "Classification Review of All UFO Intelligence Files Affecting National Security"[9] and is considered by them to have a "medium-high" (about 80%) probability of being authentic. The memo directs the director of the CIA to provide CIA files on "the high threat cases" with an eye toward identifying the differences between "bona fide" UFOs and any classified United States craft. Kennedy informs the CIA director that he has instructed Webb to begin the cooperative program with the Soviets (confirming the other, authenticated memo) and that he would then like NASA to be fully briefed on the "unknowns" so that they can presumably help with sharing this information with the Russians. The last line of the memo instructs an interim progress report to be completed no later than February 1, 1964.

This memo has been frequently misrepresented by various UFO researchers who claim that Kennedy was about to "disclose"

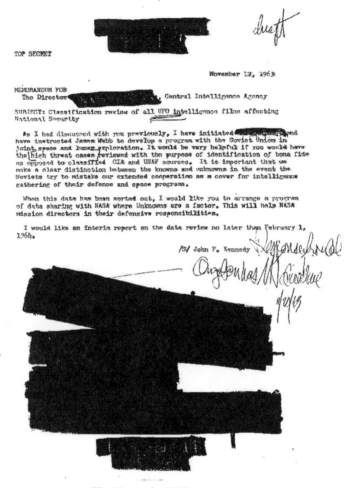

TOP SECRET

November 12, 1963

MEMORANDUM FOR
    The Director, Central Intelligence Agency

SUBJECT: Classification review of all UFO intelligence files affecting National Security

&s I had discussed with you previously, I have initiated ████████ and have instructed James Webb to develop a program with the Soviet Union in joint space and lunar exploration. It would be very helpful if you would have the high threat cases reviewed with the purpose of identification of bona fide as opposed to classified CIA and USAF sources. It is important that we make a clear distinction between the knowns and unknowns in the event the Soviets try to mistake our extended cooperation as a cover for intelligence gathering of their defence and space programs.

When this data has been sorted out, I would like you to arrange a program of data sharing with NASA where Unknowns are a factor. This will help NASA mission directors in their defensive responsibilities.

I would like an interim report on the data review no later than February 1, 1964.

/S/ John F. Kennedy

The Kennedy UFO memo.

the existence of UFOs to the American public. This is flatly not the case. The memo is about space program cooperation only, and it assumes that both countries are well aware of the existence of "bona fide" UFOs—presumably extraterrestrial spacecraft—but says nothing about releasing information on them to the public. It says only that the CIA should cooperate with NASA in starting the information transfer to *the Soviets*.

Whether this second memo is genuine or not—and it certainly is consistent with Kennedy's stated plans—what is quite clear is that something dramatic happened between late September 1963, when Kennedy's proposal seemed all but dead, and mid-November, when it suddenly sprang back to life. What could possibly have occurred to motivate Kennedy to begin an unprecedented era of cooperation with America's Cold War enemy?

To put it simply, Khrushchev happened.

Sergei Khrushchev, in an interview given in 1997 after his presentation at a NASA conference in Washington, D.C. commemorating the 40th anniversary of Sputnik, confirmed that while initially ignoring Kennedy's UN offer, his father Nikita changed his mind and decided in early November 1963 to accept it. "My father decided that maybe he should accept (Kennedy's) offer, given the state of the space programs of the two countries (in 1963)," Khrushchev said.[10] He recalled walking with his father as they discussed the matter, and went on to place the timing of his father's decision as about "a week" before Kennedy's assassination in Dallas, which would date it right around November 12-15. Later, in a 1999 PBS interview, he repeated the claim: "I walked with him, sometime in late October or November, and he told me about all these things."[11]

It is important to emphasize that Sergei Khrushchev has a unique perspective, not to mention bulletproof credibility, as a firsthand witness to this virtually unknown but solidly documented twist in space history. He is a well-respected and acknowledged scholar, serving at one of the most prestigious Ivy League universities in the United States. He has no motive to make up such history, as doing so would destroy all his credibility as a scholar he has spent a lifetime building.

So what logically happened is that, sometime in early- to mid-November, Nikita Khrushchev communicated in some way that he was willing to consider Kennedy's proposal. Kennedy responded by ramping up the bureaucracies at his end, as reflected in the two November 12 memoranda. Unfortunately, there are no declassified documents to this point which confirm that the two men had any communication during this period. Still it seems quite unlikely that Kennedy would suddenly resurrect a seemingly dead policy without some hint from Khrushchev that it would be positively received.

We do know one event that actually happened, which may have finally tipped the balance in Khruschchev's mind: another very disappointing Soviet space failure had recently occurred. A Mars-bound unmanned spacecraft code named Cosmos 21 failed in low Earth orbit exactly *one day* (November 11) before Kennedy's sudden directive to James Webb.

All we can say for certain is that as of November 12, 1963, John Kennedy's Grand Plan to use NASA and the space programs to melt the ice of the Cold War—and to *share* whatever Apollo discovered on the lunar surface with the *Russians*—was alive, vibrant and finally on its way to actual inception.

And, ten days later, Kennedy was dead.

The Third Rail of Conspiracy Theories

Whenever anyone brings up that fateful day in Dallas, November 22, 1963, and includes it in any dialog on any other subject, then that subject immediately becomes open to scorn and ridicule. If you bring the Kennedy assassination into the conversation, you'd better be ready to have half the audience throw the rest of your ideas on to the trash heap of history. The Kennedy assassination is—to use a common political axiom—the "third rail" of conspiracy theories. But, given the political necessities of the Brookings document, which insisted that any evidence of "artifacts" in the solar system should be covered up, and Kennedy's harsh criticisms of the "secret societies" which would seek to do so, I think we have to go there and take a look at just who would want Kennedy dead—and why.

By late 1963, Kennedy's personal popularity with the American people had grown stronger, and his chances of reelection in 1964 looked increasingly good. While he was generally unpopular in the South, he was actually more popular in Texas because of Lyndon Johnson, his showdown with Khrushchev over Cuba, and the dollars the space program was bringing to Texas. So here is the specter of a young, vigorous leader with rising popularity, who had openly declared his intention to reveal secrets

The Wink of an Eye

he felt the American people had a right to know (thereby ignoring the cautions embedded in the Brookings Report), and who just happened to be threatening to bring this nation's greatest enemy into the fold as an ally in our most technologically sensitive arena—the space program. Add to that the possibility that he was going to share "UFO secrets" and discoveries made on the Moon with them as well.

Probably the hidden powers behind the scenes, the "secret societies" that Kennedy spoke of in "The President and the Press," were quite willing to abide his radical ideas as long they could count on the Russians rejecting them. But, when Khrushchev abruptly changed his mind, and there was a possibility that the merged space programs might actually happen, Kennedy became far too much of a liability to tolerate. If indeed these forces of "unwarranted concealment" actually existed, they'd have had little choice but to eliminate him once he started issuing orders to begin the actual transfer of information and technology to the Soviets. Which is exactly what he was doing in the week before his assassination.

It makes little difference really whether it was a military-intelligence cabal that decided Kennedy had to go, simply because he was going to share our highly sensitive space secrets with the Russians (as the NSAM #271 makes clear) or if it was another, shadowy "secret society" that had other reasons for keeping any space discoveries from leaking out. What matters is whether or not there is any credible evidence that Kennedy was killed by anything other than a single lone nut gunman. By definition, if there was a second gunman in Dealey Plaza that sunny fall morning, then there was a conspiracy. Period.

Let me start by saying that I have little doubt that Lee Harvey Oswald was in Dallas that morning, that he was in the Texas School Book Depository sixth floor window, that he certainly fired at the President and that he may have even fired the fatal shot. That established, what evidence exists to support the idea of a second gunman, and therefore a true conspiracy?

In 1979, the House Select Committee on Assassinations

conducted an exhaustive analysis of tape recordings made around the time of the shots fired in Dealey Plaza, and concluded that they contained evidence of two overlapping shots. They determined that four shots were fired, the first, second and fourth shots by Oswald, and a third nearly simultaneous shot from another location. Experiments conducted by the Committee in Dealey Plaza concluded that the third shot came from the direction of the infamous "grassy knoll."[12] This acoustic evidence has been called into question over the years, but rebuttals and counter arguments have left the question open, despite the official findings of the Committee.

The whole issue of a second gunman on the grassy knoll could be settled if there was just one photograph or segment of film footage that showed him there. Over the years, most of us have been led to believe that no such evidence exists. As I found out, that's not necessarily true.

According to a witness who claimed to be the "babushka lady,"—so named because she wore a distinctive headscarf that day—there *was* a shot fired from the grassy knoll. In 1970, Beverly Oliver came forward to say she was the babushka lady, and that she had been filming the President when he was shot. She went

Video capture from the so-called "Marie Muchmore film" of the assassination, just a microsecond after the fatal head shot . Note the spray of blood emanating from the president's forehead. The "babushka lady" is at far right with the headscarf. Mary Moorman is standing at the far left in the black coat (A&E).

on to claim that she gave her film to FBI agent Regis Kennedy, and that it was never returned. She also claimed to have heard a shot come from the grassy knoll, and when she looked up from her camera she saw a puff of smoke in the area of the fence. There are also other films which show what may be a puff of smoke coming from the picket fence area of the grassy knoll.

In one home movie film of the assassination, known as the "Marie Muchmore film," you can certainly see both the babushka lady and Mary Moorman using their cameras at the instant the president is struck with the fatal shot. In frame by frame analysis, you can even see the first spray of blood from the president's fatal head wound. This would seem to be inconsistent with the medical evidence that dictates the head shot came from behind.

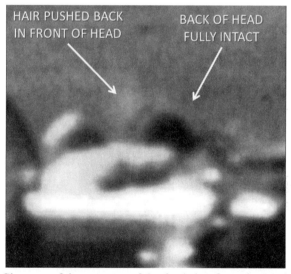

Close-up of the moment of the fatal shot from the Marie
Muchmore film of the assassination.

Indeed, screen caps taken from the Marie Muchmore film indicate that the president was hit in the head from the front, not the back as the official story claims. The image shows the president's hair sticking almost straight up, and there is a red mist (in the color frames) emanating from his forehead. The back of the president's head is smooth and undisturbed, an impossibility if he was hit from behind. What this film captured is the microsecond that the bullet entered the president's head, and it is quite obviously a hit from the front, meaning somebody besides Oswald—somebody on the grassy knoll—had to have fired the shot.

I think it's also important to note, before we go any further, that Oswald's second shot, the one that hit the president in the back and exited through his neck and into Governor Connolly, would also have been a fatal shot. This is not generally known because of the fact that the head shot was so gruesome and was captured in the famous Zapruder film, but Oswald's second shot had severed the nerve that the brain uses to tell the lungs to breathe, and even without the head shot Kennedy would have died because of this wound. The fact remains, however, that Kennedy *was* shot in the head, and the question of where the shot came from and who fired it (and for what reason) is not settled. But I think we can finally get to the bottom of some of those questions here.

The Mary Moorman Photograph

In the early 1990s, the A&E cable network showed a nine-part series called *The Men Who Killed Kennedy*. It mostly focused on a wide range of conspiracy theories and theorists, eventually concluding that Kennedy had been taken down by a French hit squad hired by Fidel Castro and endorsed by Nikita Khrushchev. Later episodes placed the focus on Vice President Johnson.

None of this was too impressive to me, especially since we now know that Khrushchev was actually hoping to work with Kennedy on the joint space effort. But there was one segment I found very interesting; it was the story of a (then) new witness, Gordon Arnold. Arnold gave the A&E show his first on-camera interview since coming forward in the late 1980s. He claimed to have just arrived in Dallas from basic training in the army, and while on leave in Dallas (on his way to his station in Alaska) had decided to go down to Dealey Plaza to film what he thought was a parade. He had no idea until he arrived that President Kennedy was in town. When he tried to get a vantage point on a freeway overpass, a man in a business suit flashed a CIA ID and ordered him out of the area. He then made his way down to the picket fence area of the so-called grassy knoll, where he stood and waited for the president's limo to come by.

According to Arnold's story, he was in full uniform, including his pointed overseas army cap, and was filming using his mother's camera, which he had borrowed for the day. As the presidential motorcade drove by, he suddenly felt a bullet zip past his ear very close, and heard a shot ring out. He hit the ground as quickly as he could. The next scene he described is completely bizarre.

According to Arnold, as he rolled back over amid the chaos, a man in a Dallas police officer's uniform confronted him, kicked him and ordered him to surrender his film. Since the officer was carrying a rifle and pointing it at him, Arnold complied. Arnold noticed three strange things about the man: even though he was wearing a uniform, he wore no policeman's hat, which would have been standard issue for a Dallas police officer. Arnold also testified that the man's hands were dirty, and that he was crying. According to Arnold, he walked away with the film behind the fence and off in the direction of the railroad yard behind Dealey Plaza. He evidently shortly met up with another man Arnold described as a "railroad worker." Arnold was so shaken by this experience that he never discussed it until the late 1980s. He figured no one would believe him anyway, since he had no proof of any of it.

But the A&E program was interested in testing Arnold's story against known photographs of the grassy knoll area. They decided to interview two researchers, Jack White and Gary Mack, who had done some work on one of the few known photographs taken of the grassy knoll area at the time of the assassination. The photograph they studied is known as the Mary Moorman photograph because it was taken by a witness named Mary Moormon, who was standing on the lawn just opposite the grassy knoll. She is visible wearing a black overcoat in the Marie Muchmore film of the assassination.

Looking at the Moorman photograph, it appears to have been taken just microseconds before the frame capture from the Marie Muchmore film. The president is not slumped over as far, and the hair at the front of his head has not been disturbed as yet. Like the Muchmore film, the Moorman photograph gives no indication of a

The Mary Moorman photograph showing the grassy knoll. This is the same area where Beverly Oliver claims she saw a puff of smoke. Gordon Arnold would have been standing inside the area marked by the white square if he was actually in Dealey Plaza where he claimed to be.

fatal head shot from behind.

The Moorman photo was a Polaroid taken with a Polaroid Highlander Model 80A, and the area of interest on the grassy knoll is about half an inch square on the photo itself. In any event, when White and Mack began to enlarge and enhance sections of the Mary Moorman photo, looking for any sign of Gordon Arnold, they got quite a surprise. An odd figure quickly stood out, right near the area Arnold said he was standing.

The figure appears to be a man in uniform, with a policeman's badge and shoulder emblem visible. His arms appear to be in a sniper's position, elbows out, as he would be if standing behind the fence and holding a rifle. Where the rifle should be is a bright flash of light, reminiscent of a muzzle flash, caught in an instant on film. In the enhancements, you can also clearly make out a receding hairline, prominent eyebrows and the fact that while the "Badgeman" appears to be wearing a Dallas policeman's uniform; he is not wearing a hat.

Just like the man Gordon Arnold had described, four years *before* this A&E program aired.

Later enhancements revealed another figure in the photo, just to the Badgeman's right. The figure is wearing an army summertime uniform, complete with the pointed overseas cap that

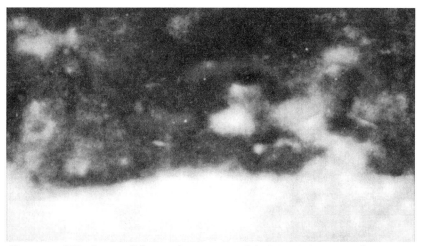

Close-up of "Badgeman" from enhancement of the Mary Moorman photo. Note position of arms, prominent eyebrows, badge reflection, lack of a policeman's hat and possible muzzle flash.

Arnold said he was wearing. There is a bright spot where the unit pin on the hat would have been placed, and the figure seems to be holding something in front of his face—perhaps the movie camera Arnold had said he was using?

Oddly, the figure is also leaning to his right, as if he is just beginning to react to the muzzle blast behind him and to his left. This is also consistent with what Arnold said he did that day. Later, yet more work revealed a third figure in the image, behind and

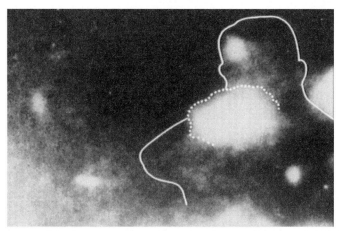

Enhancement of the Mary Moorman photo showing Gordon Arnold (left, holding film camera over his face), Badgeman (center) and the "railroad worker" (right).

225

to the right of the Badgeman, wearing a hard hat and looking off to the frame right, as if scanning for anyone who may have been looking in their direction.

So here, finally, was visual evidence confirming not only the presence of a second gunman on the infamous grassy knoll—to which so many witnesses had testified—but also the testimony of a witness who gave very specific details about both the gunman, his accomplice and his own disposition that day. There is flatly nothing in the Moorman enhancements which contradict Arnold's story, and assuming the techniques are valid, they give every reason to conclude it is a credible eyewitness account of a true event. To this day, while many have nitpicked Arnold's story (one debunker claimed it lacked credibility because on one occasion he mentioned the policeman's "dirty fingernails" as opposed to "dirty hands"), no one has yet repeated and challenged the photographic enhancements.

There are other details, too numerous to mention here, which support Arnold's story. But most compellingly, when he was shown the "Badgeman" photo for the first time (on camera) he became very upset, teared up and said he wished he'd never brought the whole thing up. Not exactly the reaction of a publicity seeker, in my opinion.

Arnold's account and presence on the grassy knoll was confirmed by then Senator Ralph Yarborough, who was in the motorcade in a car behind Kennedy's. Yarborough stated that he looked to his right (toward the grassy knoll) and saw a man "jump about 10 feet... and land against a wall." Some critics of Arnold's story have claimed that Yarborough was actually referring to Bill and Gayle Newman, a couple with two small children who hit the ground to protect their children when they heard shots coming from behind them, but they were standing on the grass at the edge of the sidewalk and were nowhere near the wall Yarborough describes.

There have been "analyses" by critics who have claimed that the Badgeman can't possibly have actually been there because (according to their calculations) he'd have to have been 40 feet

Google Earth street view showing a woman standing at the exact location of the Badgeman figure in the Mary Moorman photograph.

tall to be seen in the photo, or that the picket fence is too tall for anyone to have stood behind it and gotten off a clear shot. A quick perusal of Google Earth puts those absurd notions to rest. The street view shows a woman, probably well under six feet tall, standing in the exact location of the Badgeman figure. Obviously, an average-sized man could easily have stood behind the fence and fired the fatal shot from that location.

But the question still hangs in the air: who was the Badgeman? There are some that have pointed out a striking resemblance between the visible facial features of the Badgeman and slain Dallas police officer J. D. Tippit. Tippit had a very unique receding hairline pattern, and the Badgeman figure has that exact same pattern. He also shares the Badgeman's long, heavy eyebrows, and the size, position and proportion of the ears also appears to be exactly the same.

Tippit, according to the official canon, was killed in the line of duty by Lee Harvey Oswald a short time after the assassination, and it is for that crime that Oswald was originally arrested in a nearby movie theater. What I find interesting is whether somehow Tippet, by all accounts a loyal police officer and an admirer of Kennedy, was convinced to participate in the assassination out of some sense of higher duty to his country. This might explain why

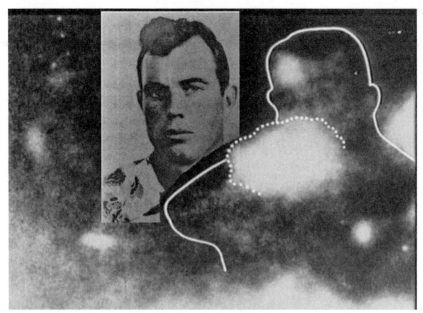

Slain Dallas police officer J. D. Tippit alongside the Badegman figure. Notice the exact match of hairline, eye spacing, eyebrows and ears.

the Badgeman was crying when he confronted Gordon Arnold. As an admirer of Kennedy, it would have been a difficult task indeed to end his life, even in the service of what he considered to be a higher motive. But to my mind, there is little doubt as to the authenticity of the Badegman figure and Gordon Arnold's story, or the fact that in my opinion, J. D. Tippit is a dead ringer for the Badgeman figure in the Moorman photo. And the figure's lack of a policeman's hat is very consistent with Gordon Arnold's account of his experience.

So what we now have is two shooters, four shots, and a dead president. Oswald was in the sixth floor window of the Texas School Book Depository, and Tippit was on the grassy knoll. Very conveniently, both shooters, Oswald and Tippet, were dead within twenty-four hours of the assassination, Tippit at the hands of Oswald and Oswald at the hands of Jack Ruby.

A photograph shown on *The Merv Griffin Show* in 1966 shows Ruby standing in front of the depository less than 5 minutes after Kennedy was killed. According to official timelines, Oswald was still in the building at this point, slipping out a few minutes

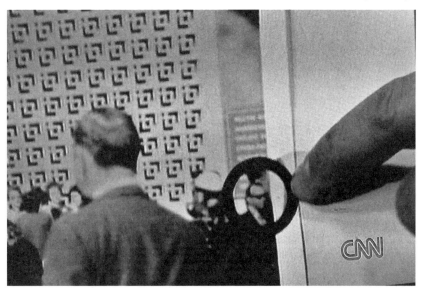

Broadcast image from *The Merv Griffin Show* in 1966 showing Jack Ruby in Dealey Plaza less than five minutes after the assassination.

later. If anyone doubts that this was Ruby, researcher Mark Lane later showed the official Warren Commission version of the photograph in which Ruby was deliberately cropped out, as if he was not there. Since the Warren Commission took the official position that Ruby was not there that day, why would they bother to crop him out if not to cover up his suspicious presence?

If Ruby knew Oswald and Tippit, what was he doing there? Perhaps it was his job to make sure Oswald killed Tippit before he himself killed Oswald. There certainly are still so many unanswered questions that no one can be sure of exactly what happened, except that something doesn't add up, and something was very, very wrong in Dallas that day, and in the days that followed.

It isn't difficult to figure out how it all went down. Ruby was probably involved with both Tippit and Oswald in various nefarious schemes, and the two men were recruited by him for the job. Oswald was set up in the sixth-floor window of the Texas School Book Depository, and Tippit on the grassy knoll. When the presidential motorcade went by, Oswald began firing and hit Kennedy in the back. Moments later, Tippit, the "Badgeman"

229

Jack Ruby shooting Lee Harvey Oswald in the basement of the Dallas Police headquarters. No one knows to this day how Ruby got into the basement with a loaded gun.

that Gordon Arnold described, fired from the grassy knoll and hit Kennedy in the head, killing him instantly. Ruby was in Dealey Plaza to make sure the job got done, and Oswald slipped out to meet Tippit at a predetermined location. Instead of joining Tippit, Oswald had orders to kill him, and that's exactly what he did. The next day, someone let Ruby slip into the basement of the Dallas police headquarters and he took out Oswald, making Jack Ruby the only remaining witness who knew the details of the plot.

And he wasn't talking.

The Wink of an Eye

How this all connects to NASA, beyond the memo from Kennedy instructing NASA to begin sharing highly classified information with the Soviets 10 days before his murder, is through all of the Masonic symbolism surrounding the event. As we already know, NASA at this time was replete with high-ranking Freemasons, from James Webb to Kenneth Kleinknecht to many of the astronauts. As we also know, the number "33" has great significance, especially for the Scottish Rite. It retrospect, NASA and the Freemasons had their bloody hands all over the assassination.

You can start with the fact that Dealey Plaza itself is very near the 33rd parallel (32° 46' to be exact) and that the 33rd parallel runs through the north end of the city. In that respect, the only better place for a Masonic "take out" of the president would be Phoenix, Arizona, which sits squarely on the 33rd parallel and was set up that way by 33° Freemasonic president Ulysses S. Grant. In addition, Dealey Plaza is the birthplace of the city of Dallas, and the location of the first Masonic lodge in the state of Texas. An Egyptian obelisk, a common symbol of Freemasonry, stands in the Plaza along with a plaque commemorating the event and acknowledging the lodge. Oh, and the exact location of this now razed lodge? You guessed it, the Texas School Book Depository building. And many people have noticed over the years that the date of the assassination, 11/22, adds up to 11+22 = 33.

Since I'm now satisfied that I have presented strong evidence of a conspiracy in Dallas, the next question becomes, beyond "the Masons," who was behind it.

The plan for Kennedy to go to Texas had been introduced the previous spring, when Vice President Lyndon Johnson (a 33° Freemason) stated that Kennedy might visit Dallas in the summertime. It wasn't until September that a letter from Johnson aide Jack Valenti officially announced the Texas campaign swing. The trip centered around a special testimonial dinner in Dallas for none other than Congressman Albert Thomas, the man who held the NASA purse strings and who Kennedy, by all accounts, adored. Thomas was dying from terminal cancer, and Kennedy was greatly relieved that he had decided to run for reelection and had avoided having an open seat in Congress to contest. Originally proposed as a one-day trip for November 21, by October Lyndon Johnson had become involved in the planning and a second day was added, November 22.

Less commonly known, or even spoken of, is the fact that as soon as Kennedy left for Texas, workers began tearing up the Oval Office for a complete remodel that neither the president nor Mrs. Kennedy appear to have been aware of. The tasteful blue-grey carpet that Kennedy had preferred was to be replaced with a garish, blood red atrocity that Johnson kept during his entire stay in the presidency. Symbolically, it is very Masonic in the sense that it could have represented Johnson literally swimming in the blood of his predecessor, John F. Kennedy. And curiously, the remodel was planned, organized and overseen by Johnson's wife, Ladybird Johnson. Mrs. Kennedy appears to have had little to no involvement.

It's almost as if "they" knew Kennedy wasn't coming back...

President Kennedy with Congressman Albert Thomas in Houston the night before the assassination

Kennedy was in a festive mood the evening of November 21, pointing out Thomas' many contributions to the space program (which he was now about to hand over to the Russians!) and declaring him to be a good friend. His speech at the dinner in Houston was well received. "Next month, when the U.S. fires the world's biggest booster, lifting the heaviest payroll into—that is, payload," here the president paused a second and grinned. "It will be the heaviest payroll, too," he quipped as the crowd roared. The

President resumed in a serious vein:

> The firing of that shot will give us the lead in space. And our leadership in space could not have been achieved without Congressman Albert Thomas. 'Your old men shall dream dreams, your young men will see visions,' the Bible tells us. Where there is no vision, the people perish. Albert Thomas is old enough to dream dreams and young enough to see visions…[13]

Kennedy departed after his speech, followed soon by Thomas and Vice President Johnson. They both accompanied him to Dallas the next morning on Air Force One. Upon arrival in Dallas, another extremely strange event occurred at Dallas' Love Field. On all the previous stops, Mrs. Kennedy had been given a bouquet of a dozen yellow roses, symbolic of the famous "Yellow Rose of Texas" folk song. In Dallas, on November 22, 1963, just an hour or so before her husband would be killed, Jacqueline Kennedy received a bouquet of a dozen red roses—which are

Johnson takes the oath of office. Note Jacqueline Kennedy, right, Ladybird Johnson (to Johnson's left) and Vice Presidential Aide Jack Valenti, kneeling next to flowers. Between Valenti and Ladybird is Congressman Albert Thomas of Texas (wearing a bow tie).

symbolic of death. Even she was heard to remark on it as the first couple entered the limousine.

After the shooting, Kennedy was rushed to Parkland Memorial Hospital, but was obviously already dead. Doctors tried in vain to revive him, and the *Houston Chronicle* noted that Congressman Thomas waited outside the emergency ward until word came that Kennedy was dead. Vice President Johnson was then whisked away to an undisclosed location. Later that evening, once Kennedy's body was aboard Air Force One, Johnson took the oath of office.

We've all seen the iconic photo, with a somber Johnson, his hand on the Bible (actually a Catholic missal—a liturgical guide to celebrating mass—which was found aboard Air Force One), standing next to a dazed Jacqueline Kennedy as various aides looked on. One of the most prominent men in the background is a distinguished, bow-tied gentleman who is watching the proceedings very closely. Of course, it is Congressman Albert Thomas. What most of us have never seen is the next photo, taken immediately after the oath was completed. In it, LBJ has turned immediately to his right. His facial muscles appear to be contorted into a broad smile as he makes eye contact with Congressman Thomas. Thomas, also smiling, returns the gesture with—of all

The "wink" photo, as Congressman Thomas and President Johnson
celebrate the death of John F. Kennedy.

things—a *wink*. While everyone else remains somber, Thomas and Johnson are the only two people in the picture who are smiling. The unspoken message between the two men could not be more clear: "We got him!"

Over the next few weeks, Johnson made a show of arguing to continue Kennedy's plans for Soviet cooperation in space. But in December, Congress, led by Representative Thomas, passed a new NASA funding bill expressly forbidding the use of NASA funds for cooperation with Russia, or any other nation:

> No part of any appropriation made available to the National Aeronautics and Space Administration by this act shall be used for expenses of participating in a manned lunar landing to be carried out jointly by the United States and any other country without consent of the Congress.[14]

The same provision was repeated in subsequent NASA appropriations, continuing until the death of Congressman Thomas in 1966.

Keep in mind that Johnson had enormous political capital to continue any initiative of the martyred Kennedy that he so chose in those days and weeks following the assassination. He used much of that to slam through many legislative priorities, including various big government boondoggles like Medicare, Medicaid and Welfare programs, and other wildly expensive programs, which today threaten to force our country into bankruptcy. Obviously, continuing the space cooperation initiative wasn't much of a priority, or he could have easily had it passed.

There are a couple of curious postscripts to this story.

By most accounts, Johnson should have still been president by 1969 when Neil Armstrong and Buzz Aldrin first walked on the Moon. He was constitutionally able to stand for reelection in 1968, but his great unpopularity because of his mishandling of the Vietnam convinced him to forsake a second elected term and retire from public life. You would have thought, after being the head of the space program for so many years as Vice President and then continuing part of Kennedy's vision after his death, that Johnson would have been keenly interested in the events of July 20, 1969. But, as reported by presidential historian Doris Kearns Goodwin, Johnson not only didn't watch the lunar landing himself, he refused to let anyone at his Texas ranch watch it either, and ordered all the TVs to be turned off.

Perhaps, in the twilight of his life, having had ample time to reflect on his own actions, the space program was no longer a source of pride for him, but of shame.

Recently, Saint John Hunt, the surviving eldest son of E. Howard Hunt—an infamous CIA operative actively involved with Watergate and long rumored to have also been a key player in the Kennedy assassination—released a "deathbed confession tape" from his father. In a story published in *Rolling Stone* magazine, Saint John Hunt stated his father admitted to being one of the famous "three tramps" in photos of Dealey Plaza taken after the assassination and detailed specific players involved in the Kennedy assassination. The tape contains an admission by Hunt that, above the CIA operatives and contractors who actually planned and carried out the plot to kill Kennedy (including E. Howard Hunt himself) was one "top man" who orchestrated the whole thing.

Lyndon Baines Johnson.

All of this leads to an even bigger question. What was so important that compelled Johnson and various other NASA-affiliated individuals to kill Kennedy? What could they have known about the Moon and what we might find there that would push them to take such an incredible risk and in such a public way?

Perhaps, nothing less than the true history of the human race itself.

(Endnotes)

1 http://www.jfklibrary.org/Historical+Resources/Archives/Reference+Desk/Speeches/JFK/003POF03NewspaperPublishers04271961.htm

2 http://www.pbs.org/redfiles/moon/deep/interv/m_int_sergei_khrushchev.htm

3 SP-4209 The Partnership: A History of the Apollo-Soyuz Test Project http://history.nasa.gov/SP-4209/ch2-4.htm

4 http://www.jfklibrary.org/Historical+Resources/Archives/Reference+Desk/Speeches/JFK/003POF03_18thGeneralAssembly09201963.htm

5 http://history.nasa.gov/SP-4209/ch2-4.htm#source72

6 *Public Papers of the Presidents of the United States*, Lyndon B. Johnson, 1963-1964 I (Washington, 1964), pp. 72-73

7 SP-4209 "The Partnership: A History of the Apollo-Soyuz Test Project" http://history.nasa.gov/SP-4209/ch2-4.htm

8 http://www.jfklibrary.org/Asset+Tree/Asset+Viewers/Image+Asset+Viewer.htm?guid=%7BBFF5BEE4-D3FC-422D-9D39-946104F2B845%7D&type=lgmpd&num=1

9 http://209.132.68.98/pdf/kennedy_cia.pdf

10 http://www.spacewar.com/news/russia-97h.html

11 http://www.pbs.org/redfiles/moon/deep/interv/m_int_sergei_khrushchev.htm

12 http://mcadams.posc.mu.edu/russ/jfkinfo/jfk8/sound1.htm

13 *Houston Chronicle* coverage, Nov. 22, 1963 Edition: Blue Streak, by Stan Redding and Walter Mansell, Chronicle Reporters

14 Public Law 88-215, An act making appropriations... for the fiscal year ending June 30, 1964, 88th Cong., 1st sess., 1963, p. 16

Chapter 8
The Occult Space Program

The original Apollo program patch from the 1960s. Why is the constellation of Orion so prominent?

With Kennedy done away with in a ritualistic murder full of Masonic symbolism, the true powers that be within NASA were now free to proceed with their secret agenda for America's space program. As we have seen, there were at least three factions at work there, the Masons, the Nazis and the Magicians. They all traced their origins back to ancient Egypt and the story of Isis, Osiris and Horus, and they were all working toward the common goal of getting to the Moon. What was not revealed to the American public was just what these quiet operators were hoping to find there, how they intended to get there, and what they planned to reveal about what they found. But the trail they left is both symbolic and familiar, and traces all the way back to Zep Tepi, the Egyptian "first time" when the Anunnaki walked the Earth.

The first hint of this larger Ancient Alien agenda in our space program was laid out in the Apollo program patch itself. On the patch, the Earth and Moon are depicted with a loop circumnavigating from the Kennedy Space Center in Florida to the Moon and back. On the lunar disk is the face of Apollo in profile, and a large "A" adorns the center of the patch, presumably a reference to Apollo. But what makes little sense in the context of Apollo, a Greek deity, was that overlaying the patch was the constellation Orion, which had no link to Apollo in the mythology, with the three prominent belt stars making up the cross in the A.

So the obvious question is, what is a mythological Egyptian stellar deity doing on a patch representing an official US governmental exploration of the Moon? This is especially vexing considering the program was known under the name of the Greek sun god, Apollo, rather than the Greek goddess of the Moon, Diana, for example. The entire motif makes no real sense. Unless the "A" means something else entirely. Something directly related to Orion...

Like "Asar."

As we discussed in our book *Dark Mission*, Richard Hoagland and I concluded the "A" actually stood for Asar, the Greek derivation of the Egyptian "Osiris." As we have already learned, Osiris was the first son of the Anunnaki god Marduk /Ra (Mars), and was killed by his jealous brother Set. Isis, his wife, half-sister and consort, "resurrected" him sufficiently to conceive Horon/Horus, his avenging son who defeated Set and ruled over Egypt in his father's stead. This story is at the root of not only the mythologies of the three secret societies, but also of the ancient Egyptian stellar religion. The Egyptians held to the axiom "as above, so below," and, having been taught the stories of the gods by Marduk/Ra, they watched the sky incessantly for signs and portents of the future. In fact, one researcher, Graham Hancock, has actually declared the pyramids at Giza to be giant "meridian machines," designed to track the movements of the night sky across that crucial north/south marker.

In that ancient and venerable religion, a few stars and constellations held special meaning. Orion was the stellar representation of Asar/Osiris, rising and falling and marking the Earth's precessional cycles over the eons. Sirius, the brightest star in the night sky, represented Isis, the mother goddess of life and Osiris' wife and consort. Leo the Lion, with its bright "heart of the lion" star Regulus, represented Horus. Later, Horus was depicted as a Falcon God as well.

So what the patch really represented was not the publicly presented Greek mythology of Apollo, but rather the occulted, behind-the-scenes mythology of the secret societies—the story of Isis and Osiris. And it was the movement of the three key gods of the Zep Tepi across the skies that the Egyptians read to decide when to go to war, when to harvest crops and when to expect major events to occur.

You have to research the ancient mythical texts of Egypt extensively to understand the symbolism at work here. Certain positions in the sky had great significance, with the horizon and the meridian easily the most significant. To the Egyptians, the horizon represented a sort of netherworld between dimensions. By "dimensions" the Egyptians meant life and death. To them, death was simply the next step on a lifelong quest to be reunited with the god Osiris (Orion). When a stellar object, like the star Sirius, was on the horizon it meant that the goddess Isis herself was moving from the world of men to the world of the gods. The meridian marked an object's traverse from east to west in a nocturnal rising and setting that symbolized the daily birth and death of the sun. When a nighttime object crosses the north/south meridian, it attains its highest point in the night sky. It was at this moment that the object (be it Sirius, Orion's belt, or Regulus, the heart of Leo the Lion) was most alive. From that brief moment, and for the rest of the evening, it would descend to the west, slowly decaying toward death. Once you understand this religion and the various characters in it, then certain naming conventions and symbols of the Apollo program become very interesting to say the least.

It is notable, for instance, that the Apollo 15 lunar module was named Falcon, publically declared to be a reference to the Air Force Academy mascot. Since mission commander David Scott was a graduate of the Academy, the name made sense. But, in Egyptian stellar religion, the Falcon is also associated with Horus, the avenging son of Osiris.

The Lunar Module Horus?

As you go down the list of names of the Apollo spacecraft, there are many more such double meanings. The Apollo 16 LEM had been named Orion, an obvious reference to Osiris, and the Apollo 11 Command Module, Columbia, drew its name from Columba, a 6th century monk who (in Masonic lore) brought a "sacred stone" to Scotland from Egypt. English monarchs are still crowned while sitting on a throne over this Stone of Destiny today. Also, Apollo 13's Lunar Module, which served as a lifeboat saving the lives of Jim Lovell, Jack Swigert and Fred Haise, was named Aquarius, after the Egyptian keeper of the Nile.

According to the mission commander, Jim Lovell:

> Contrary to popular belief, it was not named after the song in the play, *Hair,* but after the Egyptian God, Aquarius. She was symbolized as a water carrier who brought fertility, and therefore, life and knowledge to the Nile Valley, and we hoped our Lunar Module, Aquarius, would bring life back from the Moon.[1]

But the most significant clue was found by Hoagland in the autobiography of Edwin "Buzz" Aldrin, the second man to walk the surface of the moon. In *Return to Earth*, Aldrin describes a bizarre "communion ceremony" that took place on the surface of the Moon:

> During the first idle moment in the LM before eating

our snack, I reached into my personal preference kit and pulled out two small packages which had been specially prepared at my request. One contained a small amount of wine, the other a small wafer. With them and a small chalice from the kit, I took communion on the moon, reading to myself from a small card I carried on which

Aldrin's official Apollo 11 crew portrait. Most sources crop this image to disguise Aldrin's prominent display of his Masonic membership ring (NASA).

243

I had written the portion of the Book of John used in the traditional communion ceremony.[2]

Aldrin also made it clear that Armstrong did not share his enthusiasm for the ceremony. According to *Return to Earth*, he looked on with an "expression of faint disdain (as if to say, 'what's he up to now?')." This little-discussed event more recently was dramatized in the HBO miniseries *From the Earth to the Moon*, and was basically portrayed as Aldrin describes it.

Aldrin made no real secret of his Masonic associations, but neither did he overtly comment on them (nowhere in *Men from Earth* did he mention his Masonic ties, for instance). Yet he did, on occasion, engage in specific acts to indicate his support for the Craft. When he posed for the official Apollo 11 crew portrait, he made sure that his Masonic signet ring was prominently visible, an act he repeated when Armstrong took his photo in the lunar

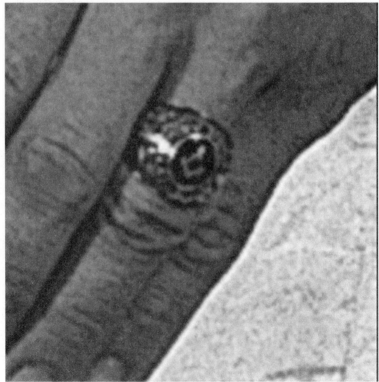

Close-up of Aldrin's ring.

module shortly after landing. One wonders how Mrs. Aldrin felt about it when she discovered that her husband chose to wear his Masonic signet ring, rather than his wedding ring, in these two instances.

My friend Ken Johnston (32°), who has been a great help in these matters, also found that Aldrin had carried a Masonic apron with him to the moon, and upon returning, delivered it personally to Sovereign Grand Commander Smith and C. Fred Kleinknecht (father of Kenneth, who was the Apollo CSM program manager) at the House of the Temple in Washington D.C., in a very solemn ceremony.

Aldrin presenting the 33° Masonic apron he took to the Moon on Apollo 11 to Grand Commander Smith in the House of the Temple in Washington D.C.

The question that is unanswered in all of this is what exactly Aldrin *did* with the ceremonial Masonic apron on the Moon. After all, there's no point in bringing a ceremonial apron 239,000 miles to the Moon with you if you're not going to perform a ceremony of some kind, is there? After all, we did have an admission by Aldrin that he had performed some kind of "communion ceremony" in the Lunar Module before the first Moon walk. What if there was more to it?

We quickly found out there was. Not only is the Catholic

245

communion ceremony a recreation of a much earlier Egyptian rite, it just happens to be connected to the main player in all of these machinations—the Egyptian god Osiris. A eucharist was commonly performed in ancient Egypt as part of the offerings celebrating Osiris.

So given all this, the next logical step was to see if we could pinpoint the exact time of Aldrin's eucharist ceremony. After that, it seemed that a look at the sky over the Lunar Module at the time of the ceremony might also prove interesting, since the ancient Egyptian religion was, as I've established, a stellar one. After reviewing the transcripts of the communications between Houston and the LM, the likely time of the ceremony Aldrin performed was quickly established: it was 33 minutes after the landing.

It didn't take Hoagland long to plug the date, time and location of the first lunar landing at Tranquility Base into his astronomical software. Along the way, he did some research into the significance of the date of the landing, July 20, 1969, in Egyptian history. He soon discovered that July 20 was an extremely significant date in Egyptian lore, linking back to the heliacal rising of Sirius (Isis) in the pyramid era. So on this sacred day, at this anointed time, what did the skies over Tranquility base have to say to the ancient gods of Egypt?

Sirius, the stellar equivalent of the goddess Isis herself, the same goddess whose story forms the basis of the Masonic religion, was precisely 19.5 degrees above the Tranquility Base horizon.

This was a surprise. We had expected to find Sirius at 33 degrees, or perhaps on the horizon or the meridian (both very significant "power positions" in the Egyptian stellar religion). But 19.5 degrees was only important in the context of Hoagland and Erol Torun's work on Cydonia, the Face on Mars and their Geometric Alignment Model. It was a key figure in understanding the Hyperdimensional Physics model that fell out of those observations, but it wasn't, as far as we knew, significant in Freemasonry. Was it possible that there was a bigger connection between the ruins of Cydonia and the rituals of ancient Egypt? And did NASA, through the knowledge of its Masonic members,

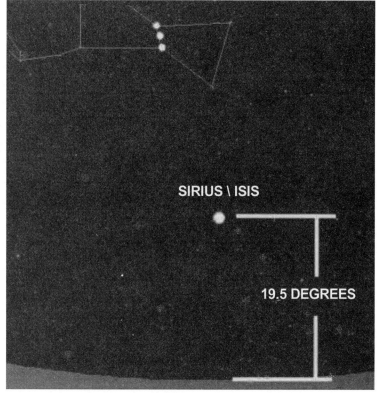

SIRIUS \ ISIS

19.5 DEGREES

Sky above the Apollo 11 Tranquility Base landing site 33 minutes after
the landing of the Lunar Module Eagle.

somehow know and understand this link?

The first thing to try and determine was if this was all just a
lucky coincidence. What were the odds that Sirius would be in this
"power position" merely by chance?

Perhaps there were numerous places where such a coincidental
alignment could have taken place that day. A discussion with
former NASA mission planner Marv Czarnik quickly put that
notion to rest.

Let's begin with the basics: Going to the Moon (or any other
planet) with current propulsion technology (such as Apollo's
Saturn V), requires a tremendous amount of careful prior mission
planning. This is because fuel and rocket thrust are very limited.
Leaving for a specific planetary destination with a precisely timed,
pre-planned arrival time and specific landing site in mind, requires

an immense amount of detailed knowledge of key celestial mechanics. Simply put, in order to get from here to there a mission planner (like Czarnik was) had to have a detailed knowledge of all relative planetary and spacecraft motions ranging from precise planetary orbits to planned spacecraft departure and arrival times, to the individual planetary rotation rates themselves. The latter critically impact mission departure and arrival times, if not landing site geometry itself.

It is important to remember that everything in space is constantly in motion. Everything is spinning on its own axis, orbiting the center of the solar system, or orbiting another object as it's moving around the Sun (like another planet). With current rocket technology, if you wish to arrive and land at a specific place, at a specific time, on a specific object, that priority—and that priority alone—determines everything else about that specific planetary mission. This includes any and all secondary considerations such as science experiments to be done, or operational planning. Decisions related to landing site geology, angle of sunlight at the time of landing, communications geometry to Earth, etc., are all subservient to this consideration as well.

And, if you want to land on another planet so that the stars above that planetary landing site (which have zero scientific relevance, if you take the non-conspiratorial perspective) conform to some kind of specific celestial pattern—say, the configuration of Orion and its associated constellations over the pyramids at Giza as they would have appeared several thousand years ago—that decision, and that decision *alone*, will determine every other aspect of that extremely complex mission.

Period.

Faced with this, we quickly discovered that Apollo 11's landing site in the Sea of Tranquility was the one and only place on the entire lunar surface where this specific alignment (Sirius/Isis at 19.5 degrees above the horizon) could take place precisely 33 minutes after the Eagle (remember, the Anunnaki called their "celestial chariots" eagles) touched down.

The next thing to look at was the (then) future Apollo 12

landing site at time Aldrin "took his communion." Hoagland considered this a good candidate location because NASA had landed there previously, with the unmanned Surveyor 3 probe several years earlier. When he looked at that landing site, he discovered Orion, with the center belt star Alnilam, on the horizon. So, at the moment of Aldrin's offering to Isis, Isis/Sirius herself was at the "tetrahedral altitude" of 19.5 degrees above the horizon at Tranquility Base, while Orion/Osiris was dead *on the horizon* (again, a very significant position in the ancient Egyptian stellar religion) at the future Apollo 12 landing site. It was almost as if these two places had been set up as temples in some kind of crazy, occult ritual system. As we looked deeper into this pattern, it became obvious that that was exactly what we were dealing with.

Surveyor 3 had touched down in Oceanus Procellarum just a few hundred yards from where Apollo 12 would land 33 months later, on April 20, 1967. What struck us immediately about that date was not that it had some significance in ancient Egyptian lore (it didn't seem to), or even that it there was another suspicious "stellar event" related to the landing (the Moon itself was exactly 33° above JPL as the engineers there guided her to a safe landing). The thing that struck us most about the date and time was that it just happened to be Adolf Hitler's birthday. If that wasn't enough, we soon discovered that NASA—remember, an agency dominated by German rocket scientists, former Nazis, and SS members like von

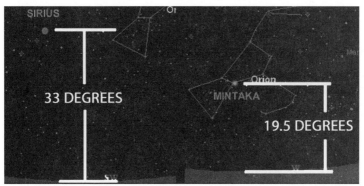

Alignment of Sirius/Isis at 33° above the landing site of the Apollo 16 Lunar Module Orion (Osiris), and Orion's belt 19.5° over mission control in Houston at touchdown, April 20, 1972 (Hitler's Birthday).

Braun at all levels—had also landed on the Moon on Der Furher's birthday a second time, with Apollo 16 in 1972. Not only that, but that particular Lunar Module had a very interesting name—Orion. The literal "stellar embodiment" of Osiris.

Of course, if you look at the skies above the Apollo 16 landing site, and over mission control in Houston, you'll find the Star Gods of ancient Egypt once again in rapt attendance…

To sum it up, NASA had landed a lunar module named Osiris on the Moon on Hitler's birthday, with Sirius at 33 degrees above the horizon and Orion's belt star Mintaka at 19.5° above mission control in Houston, a "stellar coincidence" which would not have been possible even two or three minutes later. This single landing, with its magical alignments in two places in the solar system, on Hitler's birthday, cannot have been a coincidence or accident of mission planning. It had to be planned that way. But beyond the obvious ritual associations, the question was why?

To answer that question, there were many others to consider. For one, how could we know that Aldrin was performing his ritual according to stellar observations? It was possible that the Eagle wasn't even facing toward Sirius when he performed his communion ceremony, so how could he know the right time to drink his wine and eat his bread? And how could we determine exactly how NASA's Ritual Alignment System worked?

The second question was actually easier answered than the first. Once Hoagland and I began simply looking, all kinds of "19.5s" and "33s" simply fell out of the pattern. For instance:

•The first (and at the time only) launch pad at the White Sands Missile Range where Wernher von Braun did his postwar V-2 rocket tests was (you guessed it) not Launch Pad 1, but Launch Pad 33.

•The one and only runway at Kennedy Space Center at Cape Canaveral was Runway 33.

•"Canaveral" itself is a Spanish word that translates as "reeds," so the name translates as "Cape of Reeds." Osiris was frequently associated with reeds. They may just as well have called it the "Cape of Osiris."

•The two major launch complexes for the Apollo and shuttle missions were Launch Complexes 39A and 39B. Not 39 and 40, but 39A and 39B. 39 divided by two is 19.5.

•If you stood at the base of the Great Pyramid of Giza and set your compass to "333" (a derivation of "33") and followed that compass heading, you would end up on the doorstep of JPL.

•The landing site of Apollo 17 at the base of a hexagonal "mountain" named the South Massif was at precisely 19.5° north (see my book *Ancient Aliens on the Moon*).

•The landing site of the Mars Pathfinder probe in 1997 was 19.5° latitude by 33° longitude (see my book *Ancient Aliens on Mars*).

And so on…

I could go on, but what's the point? After dozens of such coincidences, it was clear NASA was following some kind of stellar ritual pattern that involved power numbers, stellar alignments and ancient Egyptian gods. Figuring it out was the next step.

The first place we turned was back to the original Aldrin communion ceremony. Sirius had not been on the meridian or horizon, but rather at the "tetrahedral" altitude of 19.5 degrees. What was the possible connection between this number, significant only in the context of possible ruins at Cydonia on Mars (see *Ancient Aliens on Mars*), and the 33 degrees of Masonry? What if there was another, secret code of sacred "power positions" known only to a select elite of the Egyptian priesthood, that was preserved down through the ages by first the Templars, then the Masons, and all the way to NASA? The implications of such an idea were staggering. In order for this premise to be correct, then NASA must have known about the concepts of tetrahedral physics that Hoagland and Torun had deduced at Cydonia almost from the beginning of the agency, and certainly by the time of Apollo.

One of the mysteries of Scottish Rite Freemasonry is just what the true meaning of the "33rd degree" is. Some argue that the number 33 has no significance whatever, that it is just the next level after the 32nd degree, after which the founders of the Craft just didn't have anything more to teach their initiates. However, given the crucial importance of each and every symbol (recall how Aldrin took the apron to the Moon and back) in the day-to-day activities of the Craft, it seems preposterous that Albert Pike simply pulled "33 degrees" out of a hat.

Clearly, the authors of the Old Testament understood that the number itself was the key to many things, that it somehow held tremendous power. Some Biblical scholars have referred to Jeremiah 33:3 as "God's phone number." It marks the moment of darkness for Jeremiah where God shows him how he can be reached, and how the powers he possesses can be accessed. "Call on me in prayer and I will answer you. I will show you great and mysterious things which you still do not know." —Jeremiah 33:3

So if "33" is a key code to figuring out how to access the power of the gods, why do we see Sirius at 19.5 degrees above the Apollo 11 landing site, instead of 33 degrees? How do the two numbers connect, if at all?

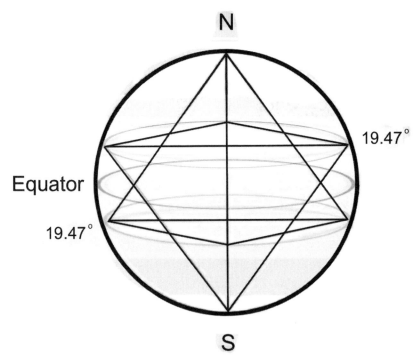

Double star tetrahedron embedded in a sphere, a key aspect of understanding hyperdimensional physics.

It turns out the number 33 *is* significant in the underlying mathematics of Cydonia, and therefore Hoagland and Torun's tetrahedral, or "hyperdimensional" physics. Engineer and probabilities expert Mary Anne Weaver has pointed out that one of the basic trigonometric functions of a circumscribed tetrahedron, the sine of 19.471—the key "circumscribed tetrahedral angle" at Cydonia—is .3333. That in of itself would be merely "interesting" if it were the only mathematical link between 19.5 and 33, but there is another, more significant link.

A tetrahedron is one of the so-called "Platonic solids," so named because the Greek mathematician Plato was one of the first to popularize them (although, like some modern science popularizers, he actually "borrowed" them from the earlier insights of another Greek genius, Pythagoras). Each of the Platonic solids (there are only five) is characterized by the fact that they are all "regular" polyhedra, i.e., polyhedrons that have regular polygonal faces, or faces with a straight-sided figure with equal sides and equal angles. In other words, they will all fit neatly in a sphere, with no edges or angles protruding through the surface. Of these, the simplest, and therefore the first among them, is our old friend the tetrahedron. Each of these Platonic solids is commonly identified among mathematicians with the notation {p, q}, where p is the number of sides in each face and q is the number faces that meet at each vertex. This number is called the "Schläfli symbol" in this nodal system. The tetrahedron has three sides on each face and has three faces that meet at each vertex. As a result, its nodal designation in the Schläfli system would be {3,3}.

Or, obviously, "33."

By simply taking out the comma we can see that, every bit as much as the ubiquitous 19.5, the number 33 says, "look to your tetrahedrons." It is just a little less obvious, a little harder to figure out, a little more *coded*.

So it makes complete sense that a secret society, perhaps with an ancient knowledge of Anunnaki hyperdimensional physics at the core of its high mysteries, would choose the 33rd level as its symbolic highest level of enlightenment. Most observers would never figure it out. At least, not before we got a good look at Cydonia. Certainly, the hyperdimensional aspects of 33:3 could unlock these "great and mysterious things" that the Lord is alluding to (see my second book, *The Choice*).

And the Cydonia connections go even a bit further.

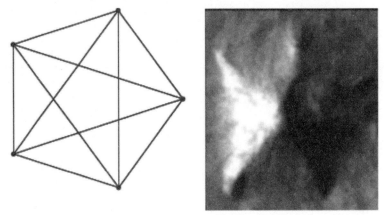

A pentatope, a fourth dimensional form, and the D&M pyramid of Mars.

There is yet another mathematical form, called a pentatope, which fits into this numeric system. The Schläfli symbol for this object is 3,3,3, or 333, obviously. The pentatope is the simplest regular figure in four dimensions, representing the four-dimensional analog of the solid tetrahedron. As such, it would hold the key to accessing spatial dimensions higher than our traditional three, and is essentially a three-dimensional tetrahedron as it would be seen in four dimensions. The two-dimensional form of this four dimensional object is a pentagon with the vertices connected by lines. And which just happens to bear a striking resemblance to the so-called "D&M pyramid," Torun's "Rosetta Stone" at Cydonia.

So, either I had to conclude that there was some sort of ritual game going on at NASA, perpetrated by a select few in a position to set landing sites and times, pick vehicle names, and manipulate events around the positions of key Egyptian stellar deities, or I was just seeing a pattern where none really existed. Given all the 19.5s and 33s Hoagland and I had already found, I completely discounted the latter possibility. Especially after I discovered just who selected the Apollo landing site days and times.

Dr. Farouk El-Baz during his time at NASA (on left).

Dr. Farouk El-Baz is an Egyptian geologist whom the Apollo astronauts dubbed "the King," or Pharaoh. He was the man most responsible for selecting the Apollo landing sites and as cited in no less an authority than Wikipedia, was secretary of the Landing Site Selection Committee for the Apollo lunar landing missions, Principal Investigator of Visual Observations and Photography, and chairman of the Astronaut Training Group. He also was "The key scientist who helped NASA plan and identify the Moon landing location for [the] Apollo 11 historic moon landing on [sic] 1969."[3] He is also a man whose family had many extensive connections to the Egyptian government. But more interesting than that, his father was a religious scholar who taught at the Al-Azhar religious schools. His specialty? Studying the ancient stellar religions of Egypt.

In other words, the man who picked the landing site for Apollo 11 and the other Apollo missions was an Egyptian "geologist" and academic whose father was one of the world's foremost experts on the ancient Egyptian stellar religion as expressed in the ritual stellar alignments during Aldrin's admitted "communion ceremony." So proving that Aldrin did indeed perform the ceremony under a ritual alignment of the heavens became the key to validating the model.

According to Aldrin's original account in his autobiography *Men from Earth*, the communion ceremony took place "during the first idle moment in the LM before eating our snack." In *Dark Mission*, Hoagland and I had presumed that this ceremony took place exactly 33 minutes after the landing of Eagle on the lunar surface, during an odd one-minute long comm break at that point in the mission. (The significance of the 33 minute timing should be obvious by now.) *First Man*, Neil Armstrong's 2005 authorized biography, also discusses the communion ceremony but places it at a different time.

In Armstrong's version, the ceremony actually took place several hours after the comm break at the 33 minute mark. By that time, Armstrong and Aldrin were getting ready to suit up and head out of the LM for the historic first moonwalk. *First Man* actually quotes from the com transcript from the precise moment that Armstrong says it happened. Taking this information, I went to the Apollo Lunar Surface Journal web site and tried to find the exact corresponding dialog. Unfortunately, the LSJ gave the Mission Elapsed Time (MET) of the dialog in total mission hours, and Armstrong's book gives it in days and hours. After some cross-checking I was able to correlate the two times exactly. At MET 105:25:38, or 3 hours and 41 minutes after landing (approx. 23:59 UTC on July 20, 1969), the following dialog took place:

> Aldrin: Roger. This is the LM pilot. I'd like to take this opportunity to ask every person listening in, whoever and wherever they may be, to pause for a moment and contemplate the events of the past few hours and to give thanks in his or her own way. Over.

A roughly nine-minute -ong comm break follows this statement by Aldrin. Presumably, during that time he performed his communion ceremony and then the astronauts ate their pre-EVA meal during this silence, as Aldrin had described.

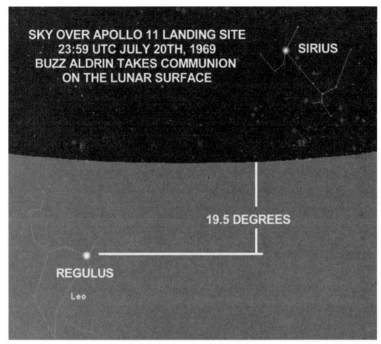

Sky over Apollo 11 landing site, Tranquility Base, July 20, 1969 during Aldrin's communion ceremony.

The next question was obvious. Were there any symbolically significant stellar alignments occurring at that precise moment, as there was during the earlier com break at the 33-minute-after-landing mark? The answer was yes.

By 23:59 UTC, Sirius had drifted beyond the significant 19.5° altitude over the landing site that it occupied during the initial ceremonial window. But at the same moment—and for a period of only a few seconds—Regulus, the "heart of the lion" in the constellation Leo (and one of only a handful of stellar objects we regard as significant for our Ritual Alignment Model) was rising at precisely 19.5° below the landing site.

The importance of this really can't be overstated. Had there been no such alignment, the entire Ritual Alignment Model could have been falsified. Instead, we once again find one of the very few significant objects in our model exactly where the model would predict it to be.

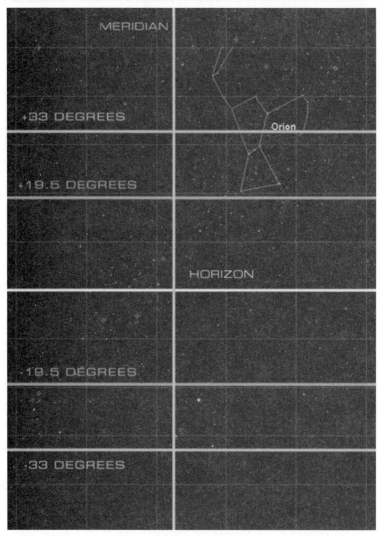

Graph of the locations that qualify as a "hit" in the Ritual Alignment Model. Only five degrees of stellar latitude and one degree of stellar longitude are included in the model. Fully 96% of the sky is off limits to qualify as a hit.

Leo, as we covered in Chapter Five, represented Horus, the son of Isis and Osiris in the ancient Egyptian stellar religion. As his father's avenging son, Horus was equal in stature to his parents and was, along with them, one of the gods of ancient Egypt who appears time and time again in the mythology of NASA. Furthermore, Regulus is the only star in the constellation of Leo which we recognize as significant in the Alignment Model. The notion that such an alignment could be simply coincidental stretches credulity to the breaking point, especially in the context of all the other similar alignments I've cited previously and in *Dark Mission*. Only five stellar objects in the entire sky have any significance in our version of the ancient Egyptian cosmology: the three belt stars of Orion, representing Osiris; Sirius, representing Isis; and Regulus in Leo, representing Horus. And only five narrow bands of stellar altitude (19.5° above and below the horizon, 33° above and below the horizon, and the horizon itself) have any significance. The chances of a second hit around the same ceremonial event are miniscule.

Whether there were two different ceremonies, one secret (and probably Masonic) ceremony at 33 minutes after landing, and one public ceremony three hours and 41 minutes after that, or whether there was only the one ceremony, as Armstrong and Aldrin both admit now, it makes no difference. At the 33 minute window, Sirius (Isis) was 19.5° above the landing site, and at the latter occurrence Regulus (Horus) was at 19.5° below the horizon. Either way, they both fit the model perfectly.

And Aldrin did take the Scottish Rite 33° apron with him to the Moon. Such a garment serves only one purpose—to be worn during a solemn Masonic ceremony. It seems unlikely that such a dedicated servant of the Craft would take the apron on the 239,000 mile voyage to the Moon unless he was going to use it for some ceremonial purpose. The least likely scenario is that he took it all the way to the Moon and then never took it out of his Personal Preference Kit.

Prior to making this new discovery, it seemed to me that something symbolically significant took place in the LM 33 minutes after landing. One unanswered question was vexing: had Aldrin and Armstrong actually *seen* Sirius from inside the Lunar Module that day? Without knowing which direction the LM was facing on the lunar surface, it wasn't possible to know with certainty that Aldrin could have taken the measurements necessary to determine when it was time to pay homage to Isis, Osiris and Horus in a communion ceremony. Even though it would have been part of the mission plan, it would still require a set of readings from the lunar surface to nail down their absolute location. Theoretically, they could have taken alignment measurements of other stars besides Sirius, but that would have made the process much more complicated and uncertain given the primitive state of navigation computers at that time. In the course of going over the transcripts, I was pleased to find this little exchange, which took place literally when we suspected Aldrin was performing his Masonic ceremony, 33 minutes after the Eagle first touched the lunar surface:

> 103:22:30 Armstrong: "From the surface, we could not see any stars out the window; but out my overhead hatch (the overhead rendezvous window), I'm looking at the Earth. It's big and bright and beautiful. Buzz is going to give a try at seeing some stars through the optics."
> 103:22:54 Duke: "Roger, Tranquility. We understand. Must be a beautiful sight. Over. "

The "optics" that Armstrong refers to in this exchange is the Alignment Optical Telescope (AOT), a device that was used to determine the Lunar Module's orientation relative to two specific stars. By plugging the relative positions of several stars into the Apollo Guidance Computer, the precise axial orientation of the LM could be determined. Further in the transcript, Aldrin leaves a hint as to the real use of the AOT:

> 103:15:01 Aldrin: "Houston, Tranquility standing by for Go on AGS to PGNS align and a lunar align. Over."
> 103:15:09 Duke: "Stand by. (Pause) Tranquility,

Houston. You are Go for the AGS to PGNS align, and then the lunar align. Over."
103:15:26 Aldrin: "Roger."

The PGNS, or "pings" as it was commonly called, stands for Primary Guidance Navigation and Control System. "AGS" is a reference to the Abort Guidance System, a backup system that could be used to rendezvous with the Command Module in the event that the main navigational computer failed. The checklist for Apollo 11 called for frequent alignment of the AGS over the course of the mission, allowing mission control guidance engineers to get better and better fixes on the spacecraft's exact location and orientation as the mission wore on.

The official NASA position is that this device wasn't used to determine the actual position of the spacecraft, only its orientation. But Aldrin himself disputes this in his 1969 NASA technical debrief:

Aldrin: "The idea was to get a gravity direction and then to do a two-star alignment and look at the torquing angles after the two-star check which would then give an indication as to what the drift had been since the last alignment. The initial gravity alignment, combined with the two-star alignment, would produce a new location of the landing site."

In other words, what Aldrin was attempting to do was to align the guidance system to get the orientation and position of the Eagle on the surface of the Moon, something that would be absolutely critical if his real task was to determine the precise time for his Masonic ceremony. This would apply whether we are discussing the hypothetical 33-minute-after-landing event or the acknowledged public communion ceremony almost four hours later. Aldrin then goes on in the technical debrief to explain exactly how he did the alignment:

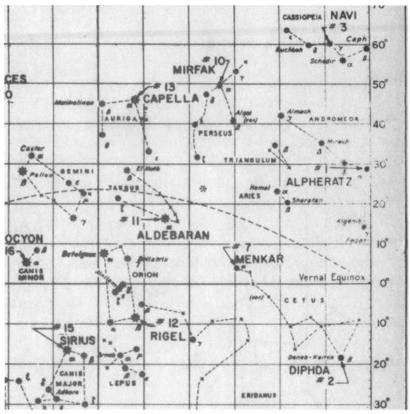

Image of Apollo 11 star chart taken to the Moon in the Lunar Module Eagle and actually used by Buzz Aldrin to triangulate the position of the Eagle on the lunar surface.

Aldrin: "Had we landed straight ahead (instead of being yawed left 13 degrees), my intent was to use Rigel in the left detent number 6 and Capella in the right detent. The 13-degree yaw moved Capella out of the right-rear detent, but Rigel was in good shape there. That's the one I used first. I then selected Navi in number 4 detent, the right rear, and that wasn't particularly satisfactory. It was quite dim and it took a good bit longer than I had hoped to get the marks on that."

Here are the actual star charts that Aldrin used to take his measurements and align the Inertial Measurement Unit:

If, as Aldrin states, Rigel was "in good shape" in one of the detents, it would have been easier for him to use Sirius for that alignment instead. Rigel is the brightest star in the constellation of Orion (Osiris) and is only a degree or so in right ascension from Sirius. But Sirius is a much brighter star (the brightest in the night sky) at a visual magnitude of -1.60 versus 0.30 for Rigel. This means that if Aldrin could see Rigel, he could absolutely have seen Sirius. In fact, it would have been much easier to see Sirius, since it is on the order of six times brighter than Rigel, and relative brightness was an issue trying to sight stars from the lunar surface, as Aldrin states.

So the fact remains that there is no doubt, at least in the authors mind, that NASA absolutely launches, lands and performs key events in the space program not based on scientific or academic reasons, but to serve some bizarre and ancient occult belief system. This system, containing the secrets that must have been passed down to them by the gods themselves, like Marduk and Asar and Enki and Ninmah, is nothing less than NASA's own version of the Anunnaki Tablets of Destiny. I don't know if NASA does this because they believe that if the stars are not right, the missions will fail, or if they do it simply to follow the traditions passed down from the gods and cared for by the secret societies over the millennia. What I do know is that NASA continues to follow these rituals to this day, on virtually every mission they undertake.

It is unclear whether the Masons, the Nazis and the Magicians were rivals or allies behind the scenes at NASA. What is clear is that they shared many philosophical and religious beliefs, expressed in the many ritualistic homages to shared gods and in the now universal appreciation of tetrahedral or "hyperdimensional" physics. What they each hoped to achieve by following these practices is less clear, but what they did is indisputable, if a little improbable.

But it is only improbable on the surface. Once you penetrate the belief systems of the Nazis, Masons, and the Crowley-esque Magicians, as we have done in this book, it becomes far less of a reach. All of these groups have their roots in ideologies and religions based on the myths of Isis and Osiris, and each also practiced the exact type of rite I am alleging took place with the ritual alignment pattern. Once you are armed with this information, then understanding why von Braun would choose to land a spacecraft named Orion on the Moon on Hitler's birthday becomes a far less mind-bending proposition.

What we have done here is to essentially reverse engineer somebody else's religion without access to any of the documentation needed to unlock the code. It is akin to writing about the beliefs of the Christian Church without the benefit of a copy of the New Testament.

But perhaps we don't need it. As we piece together the remnants of our shattered history, rebuilt from the ruins of Sumer and Egypt and Gobekli Tepe and Babylon and the ED.IN, maybe NASA, in the personage of the late Neil Armstrong, has already given us our answer.

Neil Armstrong on the surface of the Moon.

Maybe, when he stepped on the lunar surface and spoke the words, "That's one small step for man, one giant leap for mankind," he didn't make a grammatical error. Maybe he meant *exactly* what he said. Maybe the "man" he spoke of was us, Homo sapiens sapiens. Maybe the "mankind" he spoke of was the larger human family, including the Anunnaki, the Igigi, Marduk and Ninmah, Enki and Enlil. Maybe he was telling mankind that their children were returning to the stars, from whence they came.

And maybe when we meet them again for the first time, we can carry this bigger message to those that came before us:

There is no "them" anymore. There's only "us."

(Endnotes)

1   Jim Lovell, *All We Did...* p.77
2   Edwin Aldrin, *Return to Earth, p233.*
3   http://en.wikipedia.org/wiki/Farouk_El-Baz

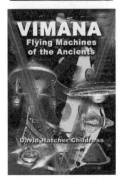

ANCIENT ALIENS ON THE MOON
By Mike Bara
What did NASA find in their explorations of the solar system that they may have kept from the general public? How ancient really are these ruins on the Moon? Using official NASA and Russian photos of the Moon, Bara looks at vast cityscapes and domes in the Sinus Medii region as well as glass domes in the Crisium region. Bara also takes a detailed look at the mission of Apollo 17 and the case that this was a salvage mission, primarily concerned with investigating an opening into a massive hexagonal ruin near the landing site. Chapters include: The History of Lunar Anomalies; The Early 20th Century; Sinus Medii; To the Moon Alice!; Mare Crisium; Yes, Virginia, We Really Went to the Moon; Apollo 17; more. Tons of photos of the Moon examined for possible structures and other anomalies.
248 Pages. 6x9 Paperback. Illustrated.. $19.95. Code: AAOM

ANCIENT ALIENS ON MARS
By Mike Bara
Bara brings us this lavishly illustrated volume on alien structures on Mars. Was there once a vast, technologically advanced civilization on Mars, and did it leave evidence of its existence behind for humans to find eons later? Did these advanced extraterrestrial visitors vanish in a solar system wide cataclysm of their own making, only to make their way to Earth and start anew? Was Mars once as lush and green as the Earth, and teeming with life? Chapters include: War of the Worlds; The Mars Tidal Model; The Death of Mars; Cydonia and the Face on Mars; The Monuments of Mars; The Search for Life on Mars; The True Colors of Mars and The Pathfinder Sphinx; more. Color section.
252 Pages. 6x9 Paperback. Illustrated. $19.95. Code: AMAR

ANCIENT ALIENS ON MARS II
By Mike Bara
Using data acquired from sophisticated new scientific instruments like the Mars Odyssey THEMIS infrared imager, Bara shows that the region of Cydonia overlays a vast underground city full of enormous structures and devices that may still be operating. He peels back the layers of mystery to show images of tunnel systems, temples and ruins, and exposes the sophisticated NASA conspiracy designed to hide them. Bara also tackles the enigma of Mars' hollowed out moon Phobos, and exposes evidence that it is artificial. Long-held myths about Mars, including claims that it is protected by a sophisticated UFO defense system, are examined. Data from the Mars rovers Spirit, Opportunity and Curiosity are examined; everything from fossilized plants to mechanical debris is exposed in images taken directly from NASA's own archives.
294 Pages. 6x9 Paperback. Illustrated. $19.95. Code: AAM2

ANCIENT TECHNOLOGY IN PERU & BOLIVIA
By David Hatcher Childress
Childress speculates on the existence of a sunken city in Lake Titicaca and reveals new evidence that the Sumerians may have arrived in South America 4,000 years ago. He demonstrates that the use of "keystone cuts" with metal clamps poured into them to secure megalithic construction was an advanced technology used all over the world, from the Andes to Egypt, Greece and Southeast Asia. He maintains that only power tools could have made the intricate articulation and drill holes found in extremely hard granite and basalt blocks in Bolivia and Peru, and that the megalith builders had to have had advanced methods for moving and stacking gigantic blocks of stone, some weighing over 100 tons.
340 Pages. 6x9 Paperback. Illustrated.. $19.95 Code: ATP

LOST CITIES & ANCIENT MYSTERIES OF THE SOUTHWEST
By David Hatcher Childress

Join David as he starts in northern Mexico and searches for the lost mines of the Aztecs. He continues north to west Texas, delving into the mysteries of Big Bend, including mysterious Phoenician tablets discovered there and the strange lights of Marfa. Then into New Mexico where he stumbles upon a hollow mountain with a billion dollars of gold bars hidden deep inside it! In Arizona he investigates tales of Egyptian catacombs in the Grand Canyon, cruises along the Devil's Highway, and tackles the century-old mystery of the Lost Dutchman mine. In Nevada and California Childress checks out the rumors of mummified giants and weird tunnels in Death Valley, plus he searches the Mohave Desert for the mysterious remains of ancient dwellers alongside lakes that dried up tens of thousands of years ago. It's a full-tilt blast down the back roads of the Southwest in search of the weird and wondrous mysteries of the past!

486 Pages. 6x9 Paperback. Illustrated. $19.95. Code: LCSW

TECHNOLOGY OF THE GODS
The Incredible Sciences of the Ancients
by David Hatcher Childress

Childress looks at the technology that was allegedly used in Atlantis and the theory that the Great Pyramid of Egypt was originally a gigantic power station. He examines tales of ancient flight and the technology that it involved; how the ancients used electricity; megalithic building techniques; the use of crystal lenses and the fire from the gods; evidence of various high tech weapons in the past, including atomic weapons; ancient metallurgy and heavy machinery; the role of modern inventors such as Nikola Tesla in bringing ancient technology back into modern use; impossible artifacts; and more.

356 PAGES. 6x9 PAPERBACK. ILLUSTRATED. $16.95. CODE: TGOD

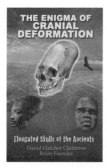

THE ENIGMA OF CRANIAL DEFORMATION
Elongated Skulls of the Ancients
By David Hatcher Childress and Brien Foerster

In a book filled with over a hundred astonishing photos and a color photo section, Childress and Foerster take us to Peru, Bolivia, Egypt, Malta, China, Mexico and other places in search of strange elongated skulls and other cranial deformation. The puzzle of why diverse ancient people—even on remote Pacific Islands—would use head-binding to create elongated heads is mystifying. Where did they even get this idea? Did some people naturally look this way—with long narrow heads? Were they some alien race? Were they an elite race that roamed the entire planet? Why do anthropologists rarely talk about cranial deformation and know so little about it?

250 Pages. 6x9 Paperback. Illustrated. $19.95. Code: ECD

LOST CONTINENTS & THE HOLLOW EARTH
I Remember Lemuria and the Shaver Mystery
by David Hatcher Childress & Richard Shaver

Shaver's rare 1948 book *I Remember Lemuria* is reprinted in its entirety, and the book is packed with illustrations from Ray Palmer's *Amazing Stories* magazine of the 1940s. Palmer and Shaver told of tunnels running through the earth—tunnels inhabited by the Deros and Teros, humanoids from an ancient spacefaring race that had inhabited the earth, eventually going underground, hundreds of thousands of years ago. Childress discusses the famous hollow earth books and delves deep into whatever reality may be behind the stories of tunnels in the earth. Operation High Jump to Antarctica in 1947 and Admiral Byrd's bizarre statements, tunnel systems in South America and Tibet, the underground world of Agartha, the belief of UFOs coming from the South Pole, more.

344 PAGES. 6x9 PAPERBACK. ILLUSTRATED. $16.95. CODE: LCHE

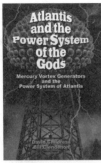

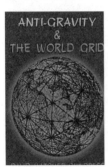

COVERT WARS AND BREAKAWAY CIVILIZATIONS
By Joseph P. Farrell
Farrell delves into the creation of breakaway civilizations by the Nazis in South America and other parts of the world. He discusses the advanced technology that they took with them at the end of the war and the psychological war that they waged for decades on America and NATO. He investigates the secret space programs currently sponsored by the breakaway civilizations and the current militaries in control of planet Earth. Plenty of astounding accounts, documents and speculation on the incredible alternative history of hidden conflicts and secret space programs that began when World War II officially "ended."
292 Pages. 6x9 Paperback. Illustrated. $19.95. Code: BCCW

PRODIGAL GENIUS
The Life of Nikola Tesla
by John J. O'Neill
This special edition of O'Neill's book has many rare photographs of Tesla and his most advanced inventions. Tesla's eccentric personality gives his life story a strange romantic quality. He made his first million before he was forty, yet gave up his royalties in a gesture of friendship, and died almost in poverty. Tesla could see an invention in 3-D, from every angle, within his mind, before it was built; how he refused to accept the Nobel Prize; his friendships with Mark Twain, George Westinghouse and competition with Thomas Edison. Tesla is revealed as a figure of genius whose influence on the world reaches into the far future. Deluxe, illustrated edition.
408 pages. 6x9 Paperback. Illustrated. Bibliography. $18.95. Code: PRG

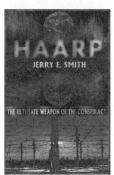

HAARP
The Ultimate Weapon of the Conspiracy
by Jerry Smith
The HAARP project in Alaska is one of the most controversial projects ever undertaken by the U.S. Government. At at worst, HAARP could be the most dangerous device ever created, a futuristic technology that is everything from super-beam weapon to world-wide mind control device. Topics include Over-the-Horizon Radar and HAARP, Mind Control, ELF and HAARP, The Telsa Connection, The Russian Woodpecker, GWEN & HAARP, Earth Penetrating Tomography, Weather Modification, Secret Science of the Conspiracy, more. Includes the complete 1987 Eastlund patent for his pulsed super-weapon that he claims was stolen by the HAARP Project.
256 pages. 6x9 Paperback. Illustrated. Bib. $14.95. Code: HARP

WEATHER WARFARE
The Military's Plan to Draft Mother Nature
by Jerry E. Smith
Weather modification in the form of cloud seeding to increase snow packs in the Sierras or suppress hail over Kansas is now an everyday affair. Underground nuclear tests in Nevada have set off earthquakes. A Russian company has been offering to sell typhoons (hurricanes) on demand since the 1990s. Scientists have been searching for ways to move hurricanes for over fifty years. In the same amount of time we went from the Wright Brothers to Neil Armstrong. Hundreds of environmental and weather modifying technologies have been patented in the United States alone – and hundreds more are being developed in civilian, academic, military and quasi-military laboratories around the world *at this moment!* Numerous ongoing military programs do inject aerosols at high altitude for communications and surveillance operations.
304 Pages. 6x9 Paperback. Illustrated. Bib. $18.95. Code: WWAR

ORDER FORM

**10% Discount
When You Order
3 or More Items!**

One Adventure Place
P.O. Box 74
Kempton, Illinois 60946
United States of America
Tel.: 815-253-6390 • Fax: 815-253-6300
Email: auphq@frontiernet.net
http://www.adventuresunlimitedpress.com

ORDERING INSTRUCTIONS

✓ Remit by USD$ Check, Money Order or Credit Card
✓ Visa, Master Card, Discover & AmEx Accepted
✓ Paypal Payments Can Be Made To:
  info@wexclub.com
✓ Prices May Change Without Notice
✓ 10% Discount for 3 or More Items

SHIPPING CHARGES

United States

✓ Postal Book Rate { $4.50 First Item / 50¢ Each Additional Item
✓ POSTAL BOOK RATE Cannot Be Tracked!
  Not responsible for non-delivery.
✓ Priority Mail { $6.00 First Item / $2.00 Each Additional Item
✓ UPS { $7.00 First Item / $1.50 Each Additional Item
  NOTE: UPS Delivery Available to Mainland USA Only

Canada

✓ Postal Air Mail { $15.00 First Item / $3.00 Each Additional Item
✓ Personal Checks or Bank Drafts MUST BE
  US$ and Drawn on a US Bank
✓ Canadian Postal Money Orders OK
✓ Payment MUST BE US$

All Other Countries

✓ Sorry, No Surface Delivery!
✓ Postal Air Mail { $19.00 First Item / $7.00 Each Additional Item
✓ Checks and Money Orders MUST BE US$
  and Drawn on a US Bank or branch.
✓ Paypal Payments Can Be Made in US$ To:
  info@wexclub.com

SPECIAL NOTES

✓ RETAILERS: Standard Discounts Available
✓ BACKORDERS: We Backorder all Out-of-
  Stock Items Unless Otherwise Requested
✓ PRO FORMA INVOICES: Available on Request
✓ DVD Return Policy: Replace defective DVDs only
ORDER ONLINE AT: www.adventuresunlimitedpress.com

**10% Discount When You Order
3 or More Items!**

Please check: ✓

☐ This is my first order   ☐ I have ordered before

Name			
Address			
City			
State/Province		Postal Code	
Country			
Phone: Day		Evening	
Fax	Email		

Item Code	Item Description	Qty	Total

Please check: ✓

	Subtotal ▶	
	Less Discount-10% for 3 or more items ▶	
☐ Postal-Surface	Balance ▶	
☐ Postal-Air Mail (Priority in USA)	Illinois Residents 6.25% Sales Tax ▶	
	Previous Credit ▶	
☐ UPS	Shipping ▶	
(Mainland USA only)	Total (check/MO in USD$ only) ▶	

☐ Visa/MasterCard/Discover/American Express

Card Number:

Expiration Date: Security Code:

✓ SEND A CATALOG TO A FRIEND: